Strategy and Structure

Strategy and Structure

SHORT READINGS FOR COMPOSITION

Fourth Edition

William J. Kelly

Bristol Community College

PEARSON
Longman

New York San Francisco Boston
London Toronto Sydney Tokyo Singapore Madrid
Mexico City Munich Paris Cape Town Hong Kong Montreal

Publisher: Joe Opiela
Senior Marketing Manager: Sandra McGuire
Production Manager: Stacey Kulig
Project Coordination, Text Design, and Electronic Page Makeup: Electronic Publishing Services Inc., NYC
Cover Design Manager: John Callahan
Cover Image courtesy of iStock
Photo Researcher: Rona Tuccillo
Senior Manufacturing Buyer: Dennis Para

Library of Congress Cataloging-in-Publication Data

Strategy and structure : short readings for composition / [edited by] William J. Kelly. — 4th ed.
p. cm.
Includes bibliographical references and index.
ISBN 0-205-56558-1 (pbk.)
1. College readers. 2. English language—Rhetoric—Problems, exercises, etc. 3. Report writing—Problems, exercises, etc. I. Kelly, William J. (William Jude), 1953–

PE1417.S7685 2007
808'.0427—dc22

2007007919

Please visit us at www.ablongman.com

ISBN 13: 978-0-205-56558-0
ISBN 10: 0-205-56558-1

To Timothy Matos and Jeremy Wright,
the humanist and the scientist,
my sons-in-law extraordinaire.

Contents

10 Comparison and Contrast 211

Thematic Contents

Biography and Autobiography

Education and Religion

Ethics

Human Behavior

Humor

Language, Communication, History, and the Arts

Lifestyle, Media, and Business

Racial, Ethnic, Gender, and Cultural Concerns

Social Problems

Sports, Leisure, and Specialized Skills

Preface

To become a better writer, read more.

This idea is certainly not original. American statesman Benjamin Franklin, among others, acknowledged that what he had read in his youth influenced the style of his own writing. In fact, if people did nothing more then derive pleasure from an essay and imitate the writer in their own writings, their writing would be better.

But mere appreciation of the quality of the writing and imitation of the writer's mastery in expressing the message aren't enough. Improving writing through reading involves recognizing the significance of a piece of writing and then responding in some way to it. *Strategy and Structure* is designed to help develop the skills necessary to do so. It presents a wide range of outstanding writing to be enjoyed, discussed, and analyzed. At the same time, it provides guidelines that will help achieve genuine mastery of writing.

The Arrangement of Text

Strategy and Structure is arranged to make it easier to master writing. The first two chapters focus on critical reading and the writing process. Chapter 1, "Writer as Reader," shows students how to recognize the strategies and techniques a writer has used so that they will be prepared to use these strategies and techniques themselves. It also features an annotated essay, "The Reading Disorder," by student writer Lyn Metivier, that demonstrates the process that should be followed. Chapter 2, "Prewriting: Generating Ideas," Chapter 3, "Composing: Developing an Effective Draft Essay," and Chapter 4, "Revising: Refining Your Writing," walk students through the various stages of the writing process. These chapters also introduce the concept of meeting the needs of the reader by recognizing the important relationships between aim (the purpose) and form (the rhetorical modes) in an essay.

The remaining 9 chapters contain 36 writings, arranged on the basis of the modes and covering a wide variety of subjects, many embodying multicultural experiences. The collection contains works by such outstanding writers as Anna Quindlen, Langston Hughes, Stephen King, Diane Ackerman, and Frank McCourt, among others. Chapter after chapter, this collection provides challenging, stimulating readings, plus a challenging variety of assignments, some drawing from personal experience and others calling for consideration of the world beyond the personal.

An important feature of *Strategy and Structure* is that Chapter 13, "Argument," presents argument not as a mode but as an aim. This focus on argument as an intent or purpose makes perfect sense because it reflects the actual process involved: a writer naturally uses whatever combination of modes that will convince a reader of the validity of a particular stand on an issue.

The Presentation of the Readings

Chapters 5 through 13 all follow the same pattern. First, the mode is briefly discussed and explained, and then four essays dominated by that mode are presented. The first essay in each chapter is annotated to show how the writer has taken advantage of the mode.

The remaining three essays in each chapter are followed by four sets of questions, each focusing on a different aspect of the piece of writing. The questions are generally open-ended to allow a range of answers, always a great lead-in to spirited class discussions. "Understanding the Significance" deals with basic comprehension of the selection. "Discovering the Writer's Purpose" concentrates on the writer's message. "Examining the Writer's Method" covers matters of structure and arrangement. And "Considering Style and Language" emphasizes particular stylistic devices used and examines the meanings of key words from the selections.

Each essay is also followed by a section titled "Your Turn: Responding to the Subject," consisting of two writing assignments stemming from or reacting to the essay. Fifteen additional topics for development are also provided at the end of each chapter. This arrangement ensures that a broad, stimulating range of possibilities to analyze and create successful writing appears chapter after chapter.

Writing Tasks Beyond the Classroom

In addition to the 36 readings and surrounding instructional apparatus, Chapters 5 through 13 of *Strategy and Structure* conclude with a feature called "Writing at Work," brief innovative sections that offer opportunities for types of writing done beyond the classroom. Each "Writing at Work" section presents a piece of real-world writing that relies on a particular mode, including a fundraising letter from Oxfam America; a section from the *Massachusetts Driver's Manual*; a portion of the web page for the Earth & Sky broadcast; and a page from the program for the avant-garde theater company Blue Man Group.

Each of these readings is followed by discussion questions and then by an entertaining and engaging writing assignment called "Practical Application." It offers an opportunity to apply the principles presented in the chapter to a real-world writing situation. Each assignment consists of a scenario calling for the use of a mode in a specific type of document—for example, a memorandum, an op-ed piece, a short report, and a position paper. In addition, each assignment includes guidelines about approach and format, as well as a model prepared by a student writer in response to a similar scenario. These "Writing at Work" sections therefore serve as a genuine bridge between the classroom and the workplace.

New in this Edition

The fourth edition of *Strategy and Structure* features a number of significant changes. New instructional material appears in each chapter, including many new and highly relevant examples and passages to illustrate aspects of the writing process and the different modes. In addition, 19 readings—more than half—are new to this volume, some never before anthologized. These new selections include

- an essay by jazz superstar Wynton Marsalis about the grave implications of the New Orleans disaster caused by Hurricane Katrina
- a piece by advertising and business writer Bernice Kanner on the creative use of aromas and scents by some companies and institutions
- a recollection by writer and memoirist Frank McCourt about a college essay that caused him great embarrassment
- an excerpt from novelist Jamaica Kincaid explaining the enormous love she has for her house
- an essay by columnist and political commentator Charles Krauthammer on the matter of steroids and baseball superstar Barry Bonds

Like the other readings in the text, these new readings are intriguing and challenging, sure to inspire thought and spur class discussion.

Several of the "Writing at Work" sections have also been revised to include new readings and new student models. In addition, all chapters now include helpful checklists that offer guidance for essay development and assess mastery of the material discussed.

An Instructor's Manual to accompany this edition of *Strategy and Structure* is available from the publisher. This manual contains teaching suggestions and answers to the questions. To order the Instructor's Manual, use ISBN 0-205-57666-4.

Acknowledgments

I want to thank a number of people for their support as I revised Strategy and Structure. First, thanks once again to John M. Lannon, University of Massachusetts, Dartmouth (retired), and Robert A. Schwegler, University of Rhode Island, for their invaluable guidance and friendship. Thanks also to Paul Arakelian, University of Rhode Island, Paul F. Fletcher, Professor Emeritus, Bristol Community College, and Jack W. Warner, Commissioner of Higher Education for Rhode Island, for their steadfast support and interest.

A number of my colleagues at Bristol Community College deserve special thanks, as well, for their continued encouragement and support, especially Debbie Anderson, Gabriela Adler, David Feeney, Elizabeth Kemper French, J. Thomas Grady, Cynthia Hahn, Deborah Lawton, and Arthur Lothrop. Once again, I offer thanks to the following student writers whose work appears in the text: Ian Alamilla, Christine Baker, Jessica A. Fletcher, Steven M. Haugh, Alline Lelis, Lyn Metivier, and Therese MacKinnon.

In particular, I want to thank Nicole C. Matos, College of DuPage, whose influence looms large in this edition. She suggested many of the new example passages throughout the text and offered guidance relative to a number of the essays included in this essay. I am deeply grateful for her help. That she is also my older daughter makes her assistance all the more significant.

Several people at Longman deserve my thanks, too. Jessica Riu, Editorial Assistant in the Humanities section, ably moved the manuscript through the initial stages of production before placing it in the capable hands of Lake Lloyd, who made the finished product look so good. Most of all, I offer thanks to Joseph Opiela, whose support and enthusiasm for *Strategy and Structure* remains an important motivation for me. I am delighted to have the chance to work under his guidance again.

As always, I owe the most to my family. The lessons that my late parents, Mary R. and Edward F. Kelly, taught my brothers and me still loom large. My parents-in-law, Flo and Leo Nadeau, continue to offer their unflagging support of me and of my work, and I remain deeply grateful. I also want to thank my daughters, Nicole C. Matos and Jacqueline M. Wright, and their husbands, Timothy Matos and Jeremy Wright. No parent could be luckier—or prouder—than I am.

But most of all, I offer thanks to my wife, Michelle Nadeau Kelly. More than 35 years after we first met, Michelle continues to amaze me with her beauty, her intelligence, her dedication to her family and her profession, her compassion, and her insight. Because of her, my life remains rich and my work possible.

William J. Kelly

1

Writer as Reader

Developing Your Abilities

The best way to improve your writing is to write. There is no substitute for sitting down and developing, shaping, and refining an idea. To master writing, you have to write. It's that simple.

A number of strategies can help you to hone your writing skills, however. Taking a writing class, during which you'll be immersed in writing, is certainly one of them. Another is examining how other writers have successfully developed essays. The rationale behind this method is simple: by analyzing how other writers have handled a topic, you will be prepared to follow similar approaches when the situation arises. The more writing techniques you become familiar with, the better prepared you'll be to approach a topic in a variety of ways.

In short, an important step in developing your writing skills is to develop your critical reading skills, that is, your ability to note not just what the writers say but what they mean and how they've expressed it. Critical reading skills enable you to uncover the architecture of a piece of writing. You accomplish all of this by

- identifying *the writer's purpose;*
- involving yourself in *active reading;* and
- focusing on *the writer's approach.*

THE WRITER'S PURPOSE

What's the point here? That's the implied question that all readers have. In general terms, the answer is that every piece of writing fulfills some *purpose* or aim: to *inform, entertain,* or *persuade.* Although a piece of writing may fulfill more than one of these purposes, chances are that one aim will dominate.

For example, consider an essay maintaining that the ever-increasing number of patients seeking cosmetic surgery is proof that American society is too concerned with personal appearance. The primary purpose would be to persuade. If the paper focused on another aspect of the same subject, such as describing one of these surgical procedures, the primary intent would be to inform. If the essay discussed the dramatic improvement in self-esteem enjoyed by one of the patients, the primary intent would be to entertain.

Generally speaking, the writer's purpose appears in the first few paragraphs. The title often gives a hint, too. Therefore, as you begin reading, pay close attention to the opening. After reading through the first few paragraphs, stop and annotate: write a brief note to yourself in the margin or on a separate sheet of paper identifying the main idea. If, as you continue to read, you come across examples or details that show that your original interpretation was incorrect, simply go back to the beginning and reread so that you can gain a full and accurate sense of the writer's purpose.

ACTIVE READING

What's going on between the lines? When you read strictly for pleasure, you generally move quickly, focusing on the overall effect of the piece. You don't necessarily consider the writer's motives, choice of language, construction, and so forth. Your goal is to take pleasure from the writing without investigating it.

Active reading is different. *Active reading,* as the name suggests, means reacting to and interacting with the writing; it means reading the piece several times, examining it in detail each time. As a result, you will still derive pleasure from it, but you will also understand why the essay has the overall effect that it does.

Active reading involves establishing a context, identifying the structure, focusing on key ideas, and responding to the material.

Establishing a context. *What's* going on? *Who* is involved? *When* did it happen? *Where? How? Why?* These are the questions that a news story generally answers in its opening sentence to establish a *context,* a setting or grounding, for the reader. It's important to recognize the context because this information represents the foundation and focus of the document. Therefore, as you read, answer these questions.

Identifying the structure. How is the writing set up? In most cases, the essays you examine consist of three parts: introduction, body, and conclusion. The *introduction,* often a single paragraph, sets forth the main idea and provides direction for the reader. The *body,* a series of paragraphs, supports or illustrates the main idea. The *conclusion,* generally a single paragraph, restates the importance of the main idea and supporting paragraphs and brings the paper to a logical close.

As you read, note where one section begins and the next ends. Then look at each part separately. In the introduction, identify the *thesis,* the writer's main idea. In the body, highlight the examples or details that best support or explain that idea. And, in the conclusion, note any restatement of the main point or emphasis of some other point of view expressed in the body.

Focusing on key ideas. What support does the writer offer? To understand a writer's point fully, you need to focus on the key ideas used to make that point. Therefore, as you read, look for cue words, such as *important, vital, crucial,* and so forth, as well as specific names, dates, distances, amounts, conditions, statistics, and concrete details. Also try to identify the main or topic sentences of the various paragraphs in the essay. Generally speaking, a *topic sentence* represents the primary or dominant idea of the paragraph. The other sentences provide details and examples intended to illustrate or support this idea.

Responding to the material. What do you think of the piece? Why? Your answer to these two questions will help you greatly in understanding the writing you are evaluating. Writing is an extension of thinking. As you articulate your reaction to the piece, you will also be making sense of it. You might even write two reactions, one after you complete your first reading and the other after your more thorough readings. You'll no doubt discover some elements or aspects in the second critique that you missed in the first. As a result of this process, you will gain a greater understanding of the writing.

THE WRITER'S APPROACH

How did the writer do that? How has the writer begun the paper? Developed it? Brought it to a close? In addition to figuring out what the writer means, it's also important to figure out what techniques and strategies the writer has used to make that point.

For example, recognizing the writer's purpose can help you discover the overall meaning of a piece of writing. What is the writer's primary purpose? Is it to persuade, to inform, or to entertain? In addition, does the piece fulfill a secondary purpose?

As the Preface and Table of Contents illustrate, this book focuses on writing from the standpoint of the *rhetorical modes,* that is, organizing strategies or patterns of writing. As Chapter 4 explains, the modes include *narration, description, example, process, definition, comparison and contrast, cause and effect,* and *division and classification.* When you examine a piece of writing, note how the writer has combined these organizing strategies in the essay.

But more than anything else, ask yourself this question: What stands out—what element or aspect catches your eye, causes you to stop, makes you connect with the point being made? Perhaps it's the way the writer opens the essay—or closes it. Perhaps it's the writer's humor or reverence or passion. Perhaps it's a striking image or a poignant scene. Regardless of what it is, that particular element or aspect helps make that writing successful, so it is worth your effort to figure out what it is; that way you will be able to use a similar approach in your own writing.

Remember as you read that a good piece of writing touches the reader or engages the reader in some way, inspiring responses like "Me, too" or "Yeah, I know what that feels like"—and, maybe just as often, "That's not the way it happened to me" or "I don't agree at all!" When you read, identify what the writer has done to make this happen. The better able you are to find out how a writer has reached or connected with you, the better prepared you'll be to reach or connect with your own reader.

The Process Illustrated

In the following essay, "The Reading Disorder," student Lyn Metivier discusses how her love of reading has affected her life. The selection has been annotated to show you how to make the critical reading process work for you.

The Reading Disorder

Purpose: She explains, in a lighthearted way, her reading "problem"—her great love of reading—so her main purpose is to entertain, with persuasion and informing secondary.
Introduction: Her use of personal anecdote draws the reader in, setting her reader up for the discussion to follow.
Thesis: She lets her reader know her secret, that reading creates problems in her life.

As I turn the last few pages of *Memnoch the Devil,* the final book in Anne Rice's *Vampire Chronicles,* I am both saddened and relieved. I know that when I finish this book, all the characters I have thought about constantly over the last few weeks will be dead to me. Lestat, with whom I have fallen in love, will no longer exist, and that familiar feeling of melancholy will come over me once again, another of the many disruptions in my life caused by my reading disorder. 1

At the same time, however, I am also relieved. The constant haze I have been in since first starting these books will lift, and I can get back to my daily routine and real life. After the mild depression passes, I will have a surge of energy as I emerge back into reality. I will wait several months before attempting another book. 2

Key ideas: These are emotions she associates with reading.

I am an obsessive, compulsive reader. I don't know that there has ever been any documentation of such a disorder, nor have I looked. I have simply given myself this name because of the irrational way I behave when I am involved in a book. 3

She adapts the name of an actual psychological disorder to specify the nature of her disorder.

For days *Memnoch the Devil,* the hardcover because I could not wait for the paperback, had been sitting on the nightstand next to my bed. It taunted me like an unopened bottle of vodka within the grasp of a wavering alcoholic. I dared not open it yet; preparations had to be made. 4

Key detail: This backs up her point about her "obsession."

Note tone: She pokes fun at herself.

Understand that when I read a book, I read it cover to cover in as few sittings as are physically possible. This is not a conscious decision. Once I open a book and begin reading, my disorder takes over, and I become so involved in the story that everything else around me ceases to exist. The laundry piles up, the beds don't get made, and the dirty dishes are left to 5

Body: These episodes all illustrate or support her main idea, that she has a "disorder" that affects her life.

Context: The details demonstrate how her "disorder" affects her life—good use of cause and effect.

Great details, key ideas: All are showing the effects of her "illness."

pile up in the sink. Suppers usually consist of something delivered from a local fast food or Chinese restaurant. Finishing the book is my only priority.

Her tone here is nice!

She uses narration and cause and effect to explain the origin of disorder.

6 I didn't know it then, but this disruptive way of reading started with the very first novel I ever picked up. I was eleven years old and complaining to my mother that I was "booored." She suggested, as she always did, that I go read a book. For some reason, after giving her the usual "Yeah, right, Ma" face, I took her advice and went upstairs. Then I began looking through her collection of best sellers and hardcover classics. My mother's taste in books always amazed me; she could go from a Stephen King novel to *The History of England,* without missing a beat. Every other week, something new was arriving from the Doubleday book club.

The specific book titles are good details.

7 Then I found it. *Rich Man, Poor Man* was wedged between *Lady Chatterly's Lover* and a well-worn copy of *The Exorcist*. After standing there for a few minutes skimming the first chapter, I shut myself in the room I shared with two of my sisters and started to read.

The body continues.

Key ideas: Her details emphasize how affected she is by her disorder—good use of cause and effect.

8 I emerged two days later, unshowered, tired, and completely oblivious to anything that may have occurred that weekend. I had only stopped reading to eat, sleep, and perform bodily functions; I slept only because my eyes refused to stay open. I was beaming with excitement at my discovery. So this is what my mother was talking about. I couldn't wait to open my next book.

She uses narration effectively to show the extent of her "disability."

Key ideas: She shows the effect of the disability by using specific titles.

9 When I was a teenager, this method of reading was far from a problem. Spending an entire weekend in my room, with a book, I was a teenager's parent's dream. I had no desire to go to the mall or the movies, and even a phone call from my best friend was an unwelcome

interruption. I was deep in the world of *Little Women* and *The Diary of Anne Frank.* At this point, only my already weak social life was suffering.

She uses narration effectively to show how her "problem" resurfaces. She provides great transition here.

However, after I got married and started 10
my family, this was no longer the case. Forgetting the ramifications of my little habit, I would often pick up a book whenever I had a free hour in the morning. Lying across my bed or curled up on the couch, I would tell myself that I had only one hour.

She uses good description here, with great specific details!

This is a wonderful phrasing!

The next thing I knew, it was supper- 11
time and I was still in the clothes I had worn to bed the night before. Swollen remnants of Lucky Charms would be stuck to the morning's cereal bowls, and the shopping list was untouched and still stuck to the refrigerator door, under the rubber chocolate chip cookie magnet. A beautiful day would have flown by, and I hadn't even noticed. My mind was inside that book.

Key ideas: She uses cause and effect to show the results when she didn't "feed her habit"—same playful tone, comparing her love of reading to a real addiction.

Because of my habit, the times when I 12
did have to stop reading, either to pick the kids up from school, to get ready for work, or to just be a mom, I was almost always cranky and intolerant. I would sometimes snap at the kids if they took too long eating their dinner or taking a bath, and I would often skip pages when reading them a bedtime story. I rushed impatiently through tasks with an irrational feeling that I was missing something while the book was closed.

The body continues.

This is an excellent specific example!

Key idea: She is "powerless."

Once I even went so far as to call in sick 13
to work because I was so close to finishing the book I was reading that I couldn't bear to work for the next eight hours not knowing how it was going to end. I was out of control. It had never occurred to me that this innocent passion of mine would turn out to disrupt my life so much.

Key idea: Desperation leads her to avoid her "drug" completely.

At first, realizing that I could no longer 14
function this way, I just decided to stop reading altogether. The daily newspaper

was the only thing I allowed myself. I avoided the library, the bookstores, and the paperback section of the supermarket, hoping this would curb my cravings for a new book. I wouldn't discuss the latest books with my mother or brother, and I asked them to stop giving me the ones they had just finished. This method worked a little. I didn't pick up any new books. Instead, I just reread everything I already had at home.

The body continues.

Key idea: Like an addict, she finds a way to get a "fix"—repeats main idea.

Finally, I decided to come up with some kind of compromise. I loved reading and didn't want to give it up, but I hated myself and the way I behaved as a result. I needed to figure out a way to balance my everyday life with my favorite pastime. 15

She uses good technique to connect with her reader.

Good: She reiterates her main idea.

Unfortunately, as every obsessed person would admit, this was easier said than done. As soon as I picked up the next book, the compulsion started again. I read it completely, with little regard for any of my other responsibilities. My recognition of my problem hadn't done anything to eliminate it. 16

Key idea: She recognizes the root cause and the solution.

Then one day an answer dawned on me. I was finishing Stephen King's *The Stand* for the third time when I realized something: the only time I do have control is when I'm not actually in the middle of reading something. Once I finish a book, I can take as much time as I want before picking up another one. With this in mind, I was ready for "recovery." 17 18

The body continues.

Now I no longer just pick up a book and begin reading. I have some specific guidelines set for when I find something that beckons me. I found that summertime works the best. My schedule is less demanding then, and the longer days give me more time to work with. 19

She uses process well to explain how she now deals with her "disability."

My routine usually starts with getting up early in the morning, immediately

She makes good use of specific details concerning the "management" of her "problem."

doing the dishes and laundry, and quickly cleaning the house. I go to the grocery store to make sure there is enough food for the next few days and I'll often make dinners in the crock-pot, because the average meal cooked this way takes eight hours and requires no supervision. Then I find something to keep the kids busy for a while. I'll either pick up a movie or video game or plan a project they can do without my help. I am not a beach person, but because it means being able to read without feeling guilty, I'm out the door with sunscreen in hand at the mere mention of the word.

Conclusion: She restates her main point.

Good tone: She ends on a light note.

Now, I realize I'm not completely cured and probably never will be, but at least I'm no longer dysfunctionally literate. And, although my "to read" list grows daily, the temptation to relinquish all my friends, family, and worldly goods in exchange for residence in a well-lit, book-lined cave no longer tortures me—not much, anyway.

Response: I like this essay! She does a wonderful job explaining how reading makes her feel. Her tone is great—she is "addicted" to reading; I like how she calls herself an "obsessive, compulsive reader." I also like how she talks about what happens when she reads (laundry and dishes pile up, take-out food instead of the supper she had planned, calling in sick to work) and how she feels when she doesn't read ("cranky and intolerant," "snap at the kids," etc.). I love to read, so I know exactly what she means!

Exercises

1. Clearly, Lyn Metivier's primary purpose in "The Reading Disorder" is to entertain. The annotation accompanying the first paragraph indicates that the essay also informs and persuades. In a paragraph of 50 to 100 words, explain how her essay fulfills these additional purposes.
2. What is your overall impression of this essay? Briefly spell out what you think of the piece and why.

3. In your judgment, what feature or element in Metivier's essay stands out above everything else? In a paragraph of 50 to 100 words, identify this feature or element and explain why it stands out for you.
4. Now it's your turn to put the critical reading process to work. Choose one of the essays from Chapter 13 and answer the following questions:
   a. The primary purpose of this essay is to persuade, but what specific point is the writer advocating?
   b. What is the context of the essay?
   c. What is your reaction to it?
   d. What specific writing techniques or patterns of writing has the writer used?
   e. What specific feature or element stands out above other aspects of the essay? Why?

2

Prewriting: Generating Ideas

Examining the First Stage of the Writing Process

You've probably heard it said, and you might even have thought it yourself: "Good writers are born, not made. It's as simple as that." Don't believe it, however. If you can think and you can speak, you can write. Of course, as with anything in life—music, mathematics, athletics, drawing, and so on—some people have more natural talent than others, and for these individuals success comes more easily.

But success in writing is indeed attainable for the rest of us. What's required is a willingness to work at it, to take the time to master the writing process. Understanding the first stage of this process, called *prewriting,* is your first step toward success. Prewriting involves identifying a focus and developing supporting ideas through the use of proven prewriting strategies, which include

- freewriting;
- brainstorming;
- clustering;
- branching; and
- maintaining a journal.

The Principles and Approaches of Prewriting

It's the rare athlete who can achieve the big shot or execute the record-setting leap without warming up. The same is true for a writer. Many people find writing initially difficult because they don't devote enough time to warming up, or prewriting. In prewriting, you develop a focus and discover the seeds of information that you'll cultivate into a full essay.

Basically, prewriting includes all the work you do prior to putting ideas in the more complete form that they will take in the various drafts you produce. Any technique you use to slow yourself down and force yourself to examine a topic can be a good prewriting technique. If you haven't yet developed a prewriting system that works for you, however, there are a number of methods other writers have found effective that you should consider.

FREEWRITING

Perhaps the best known prewriting technique is *freewriting,* through which you identify a subject and for a specific period of time—usually ten minutes or so—write down everything that comes into your head about that topic. Your goal is to overcome the inhibitions that most of us have about making mistakes; you want to unleash creativity and generate as many details and examples as possible. As you freewrite, don't worry about drifting away from your subject or about correct sentence structure, and don't worry about making errors, repeating ideas, or making sense to anyone else. Nobody but you will ever see these preliminary ideas. Sorting through the material and expressing them in a form that someone else can understand comes later.

A brief piece of freewriting about the Internet might look like this:

Using the Internet—I can't believe all the stuff I am able to do—click on Netscape and I can go anywhere—I like Google the best of all the search engines they have at school—just type in a name and click on and you're there. I had to make a five-minute presentation for my intro to marketing course about stereotypes in advertising—in fifteen minutes visited fifteen different sites about this subject and printed up a bunch of information that I was able to base my presentation on. My professor said I was lucky because not all the material out there on the Internet is reliable—have to check all sources carefully. Can get right into the collections in the library right from the college's site—so easy. You can read so many newspapers and magazines right on-line—just type in the address and up the stuff pops on the screen. Web logs—Blogs—too, some of them by ordinary people and some by professional writers—shopping, people can order just about everything right over the Internet, airline tickets, clothes, you name it. One of the guys I work with went on vacation last year, he did the whole thing, picking the place to stay, setting up airline tickets, renting a car, all on the Internet and all for less money than it would have cost him to go through a travel agent. You can also search the Internet to try and find someone you've lost contact with.

As you can see, while there is some occasional drifting away from the subject, this freewriting does contain a number of possibilities for development: the power and influence of the Internet, for example. In addition, there are several details here that could be developed to support the idea that the Internet has greatly influenced our world.

BRAINSTORMING

Another effective freewriting method is *brainstorming.* When you brainstorm, instead of listing everything that you think of, you list only those bits of information that are directly connected to your subject in a kind of rough outline. A brainstorming piece about the Internet would look like this:

Power of the Internet
Get information from all over the world in a second
    Research for school projects—easier and faster than a traditional library
    Needed information for my aunt on diabetes because she's just been diagnosed—got it all in about 12 minutes
Communications
    You can use the Internet to make phone calls for free
    Search for people you've lost track of or for family genealogies
    Easily stay in touch with anybody with email—instant messaging, too
Consumer Stuff
    Shopping on-line, get prices, actually purchase items—clothing, computers, vacation packages
Changing the way businesses operate?
    Most major companies plus a lot of small ones have web pages.
    Cheap advertising?
Potential Problems
    Anyone can publish anything on the Internet, not like traditional publishing—is information reliable? verifiable?
    How about scams—can your credit card numbers be stolen more easily?
    Perfect way for someone to distribute a computer virus?

With brainstorming, as this example shows, you are deliberately choosing which details to include, so this activity produces fewer pieces of information. The advantage with brainstorming, however, is that you don't tend to drift from your subject. As a result, all of the material you end up with is more closely connected to your topic.

CLUSTERING

Clustering is a prewriting technique that visually emphasizes connections among the ideas you develop. To create a clustering, write your topic in the middle of the page and circle it. As you think of related ideas or details, write them down and circle each one. Then draw lines to connect the new ideas to the ideas from which they developed. Continue this process until you have thoroughly examined the subject. The result is a series of ideas and examples, with lines showing how they relate to each other. A clustering on the impact of the Internet would look like this:

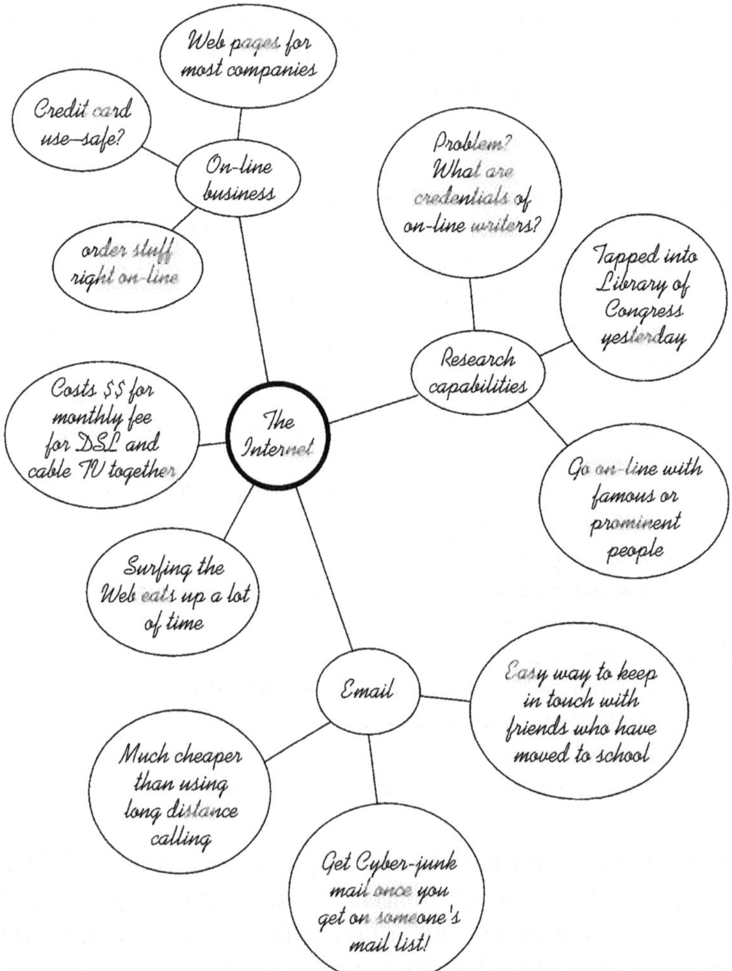

Clustering, like brainstorming, results in fewer ideas, but the material you develop is all directly connected, as this model demonstrates. If you are the type of person who reacts best when the connections between ideas are actually drawn out, clustering may well be the solution for you.

BRANCHING

Another prewriting technique with a visual twist is *branching*. To create a branching, first list the topic on the left side of a piece of paper. Then when related ideas come to mind, list these points to the right of the original idea, using lines to connect them. Continue this process as one idea suggests another, listing the resulting ideas from left to right across the page, as this illustration shows:

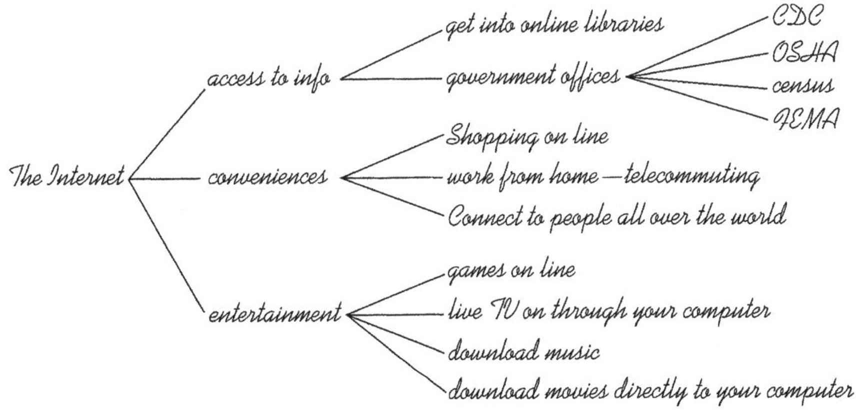

As this example shows, branching leads you from one aspect of a topic to other, more specific aspects. As an added advantage, each branch holds an arrangement of related ideas. This focused organization allows you to concentrate on one area of your topic now and save the other areas for development later on.

The Proper Fit for You

Freewriting, brainstorming, clustering, and branching have all proved to be effective prewriting techniques. To find out which approach is right for you, try them all and choose the one that suits your own style of working. You can also use a combination of methods or adapt one in a way that makes you feel comfortable.

Remember—prewriting lays the foundation for a successful paper. Therefore, whatever method makes planning your paper easier for you is the proper choice.

MAINTAINING A JOURNAL

Another way to develop ideas from which essays grow is to maintain a journal, a notebook that you devote to writing. Think of it as an idea book where you can list your thoughts, incidents that interest or disturb you, or questions about the world that have troubled you. You can also use it as a way to respond to a classroom lecture, a performance of some kind, and so on. Good writing develops from good ideas, and writing in a journal on a regular basis—at least two or three times a week in addition to the other writing you are working on—is a great way to develop good ideas. The practice alone is worthwhile, but an added advantage to maintaining a journal is that some of those great ideas may actually lead you to great papers.

Exercises

1. As this chapter indicates, the work you do before you begin to write your ideas in an organized fashion is all-important to your success. This chapter also contains explanations and examples of freewriting, brainstorming, clustering, and branching. In order to decide which technique—or combination of techniques—works best for you, try each of them, choosing from among the following subjects. Keep the practice sessions for each technique to ten or fifteen minutes.

Your first date	A person's right to privacy
Required college courses	Inappropriate public behavior
True justice	Stress in your life
Adult responsibilities	Sexism in society
Legalized gambling	Reincarnation

2. Which technique did you like best? Which technique did you like least? In a brief paragraph, explain your choices.
3. Examine the material you produced for all the techniques. Circle or underline ideas that seem the most promising.
4. Select the prewriting practice material that you would be most interested in developing into an essay and, in a brief paragraph, indicate a focus you might follow in writing about this subject and why you feel this way.

3

Composing: Developing an Effective Draft Essay

Moving from Ideas to Essay

Once you have worked through the prewriting stage, generating good ideas on a particular subject and identifying a possible focus, you are ready to move to the second stage of the writing process: composing. In prewriting, you pour out your ideas with little conscious attention to structure. When you move to composing, though, you make a conscious effort to:

- arrange your ideas in the correct essay structure, emphasizing the focus or thesis;
- amplify your ideas so that they communicate your ideas to your reader; and
- ensure that your writing is unified, organized, coherent, effectively worded, and, when appropriate, properly documented.

Recognizing the Structure of an Essay

From a structural standpoint, an effective essay can be divided roughly into three parts: the introduction, the body, and the conclusion.

THE INTRODUCTION

The *introduction* of your essay is usually a single paragraph that contains the *thesis.* This part of the essay plays an important role in your paper. An effective introduction not only provides a clear direction for the reader, but it also makes the reader want to continue reading. As the readings in this book show, writers employ a number of devices or techniques to achieve these ends. Sometimes the introduction includes an *anecdote,* a brief, entertaining story that emphasizes the overall point of the essay. At other times, an introduction includes relevant statistics or facts, famous sayings or quotations, leading questions, and so on. No single technique is always appropriate; the requirements of a particular essay will help shape your introduction. Remember: whatever enables you to fulfill your reader's needs to be directed and to be encouraged to read more is the proper choice.

THE BODY

The *body* of an essay is the series of paragraphs through which you develop the thesis and provide support for it. There is no set number of paragraphs that make up an effective body; the length will differ, depending on the subject and focus of your paper. Keep in mind, however, that the paragraphs of the body must be *amplified*—that is, fully detailed and specific, unified, and organized. (See "Amplifying to Meet the Needs of Your Reader," pages 24–25.

THE CONCLUSION

The *conclusion* is the part of your paper—usually a paragraph—that brings it to a logical, pleasing, or appropriate end. Often the conclusion is a restatement of the *significance* of your essay, that is, the overall message expressed by the thesis and the supporting information. In most cases, you don't introduce any completely new ideas in a conclusion. As with an introduction, however, you may occasionally bring your paper to a close by using a relevant quotation, raising a question, telling an anecdote, and so on. Whatever technique helps you bring your paper to an effective close is the right choice for that particular essay.

This figure illustrates the structure of an essay:

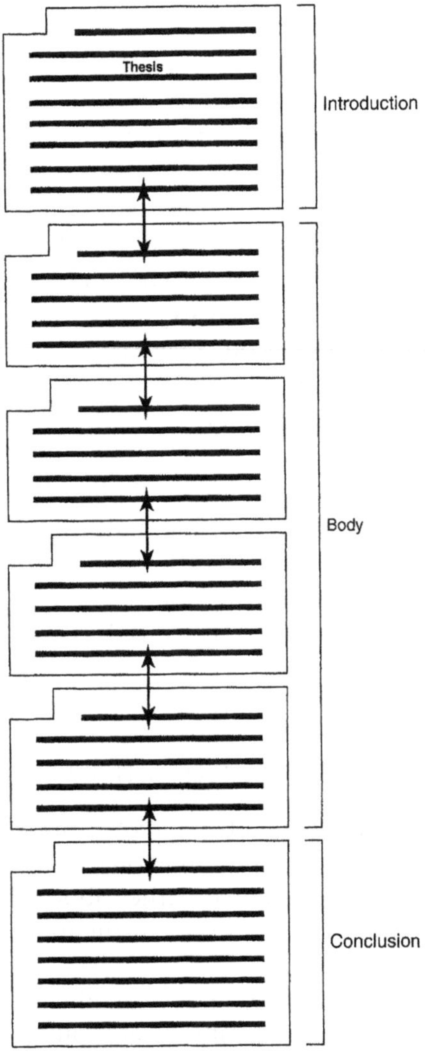

The Structure of an Essay

Notice that the introduction and conclusion appear larger than the other paragraphs. That's because the introduction contains the thesis—the main point—and the conclusion restates or reemphasizes it. Notice also that the arrows between paragraphs point in both directions. The arrows signify that the paragraphs relate to one another as well as to the thesis expressed in the introduction and reemphasized in the conclusion.

Understanding the Thesis: The Bridge from Prewriting to Composing

With prewriting, your goal is to develop a specific focus on a subject and to provide information to support that focus. Once you have prepared this preliminary work, your next step is to create the bridge between prewriting and composing: the *thesis,* the encapsulation in sentence form of the focus you've selected. In other words, the thesis is the part of your paper that provides a clear direction for your reader, setting up your reader's expectation of the paper that follows. Although sometimes the thesis is expressed in a single sentence, at other times it will be spread out over several sentences. As long as your thesis gives your reader insight into what is to come in the rest of your essay, it makes no difference whether that thesis is one sentence or more than one.

Of course, as with other aspects of the preliminary stages of writing, the thesis you create for your first draft is tentative. Writing is an act of discovery, and as you complete that first draft, you may find that your original focus is shifting a bit. There's no problem with this. If your focus has shifted and the paper itself is good, simply adjust the thesis in a later draft.

DEVELOPING AN EFFECTIVE THESIS

An effective thesis is generally composed of two parts: a topic and the writer's attitude toward, opinion about, or reaction to that topic. The prewriting material presented earlier about the Internet and its influence might generate a thesis such as the following:

> In the last few years, no technological advance has had more impact on the way people communicate, pursue information, and conduct business than the Internet.

In this example, the topic is the Internet, and the opinion is that it has been a major influence on various aspects of people's lives.

As long as the material that follows the thesis in the draft provides plenty of support and illustration for this idea, your paper will be a success.

Another way to recognize an effective thesis is to note what it is not. For example, an effective thesis is not an announcement:

I plan to show that over the last 10 years the Internet has greatly influenced our world.

In most cases, restating the thesis so that you eliminate such expressions as "I plan," "I intend," and "This paper concerns" will help you change an announcement into a thesis, as long as the remaining sentence provides a clear direction for your reader.

A thesis is also not a statement of fact:

The Internet is under no government control or censorship.

Because a fact is merely a verifiable truth, it doesn't by itself present much room for discussion. Effective writing develops from your opinion, your reasoning based on facts. To turn a fact into an effective thesis, you need to take that fact and add your reaction or attitude.

Nor is a thesis a title:

The Internet: The Doorway to the Entire World

For one thing, often a title is not a complete sentence. Also, a title is designed to provide a broad hint of your paper's subject matter and to encourage your reader to begin reading. It ususally doesn't specify your focus on that subject, however. A good title can be a valuable addition to a completed paper, but you must not depend on the title to direct your reader. That's the job of your thesis. If the title is good, keep it, but provide an effective thesis too.

PLACING THE THESIS EFFECTIVELY

Because your reader depends on the thesis to provide direction, where you place it is important. If you are responding to a statement or an essay question or taking a specific stand on an issue, making the thesis the first sentence of the introduction (shown here underlined) is obviously the most direct way to bring your idea across to the reader:

<u>In the last few years, no technological advance has had more impact on the way people communicate, pursue information, and conduct business than the Internet</u>. With a few clicks of the computer mouse, people can contact anyone from a friend in the next

> house to a perfect stranger on the other side of the globe. They can search for information in major on-line libraries and from a wide variety of other sources. They also have the opportunity to communicate with nationally and internationally recognized experts, just by hitting a few keys on the keyboard. For both corporation and consumer, the Internet has forever changed the way business is conducted. Today everything from clothing to computers to vacation packages is available on-line, making the shopping experience simpler and cheaper for the companies and the customers.

Sometimes, depending on the subject you are writing about, you might find it more effective to place the thesis (shown here underlined, with the transitional word *however* added) later in the introduction so that you can ease your reader into your stance:

> As the twenty-first century begins, people enjoy lives made increasingly better by advances in technology. <u>In the last few years, however, no technological advance has had more impact on the way people communicate, pursue information, and conduct business than the Internet</u>. For those on-line, conferring with people anywhere in the world starts with a few simple clicks of a computer mouse. The availability of the Internet also means that both beginning students and serious scholars now have at their fingertips vast repositories of information. Thanks to the Internet, businesses can set up virtual retail centers, and consumers can do their shopping in front of their glowing computer screens rather than in some crowded mall.

Often you may feel that the thesis would make a fine bridge between the introduction and the body of your paper. In such cases, you would place your thesis (shown here underlined, with the transitional phrase *In fact* added) at the end of the introduction:

> The number of technological changes witnessed at the end of the twentieth century is amazing. For example, in the 1980s most people had never heard of the Internet. Personal computers had become commonplace by the early 1980s, enabling people to perform a variety of tasks more quickly and effectively, but for the average PC user that was the end of the computer's use. By the early 1990s, however, all of this changed with the advent of the Internet. Once their computers were on-line, people were suddenly able to do things that before they could only

dream of. In fact, in the last few years, no technological advance has had greater impact on the way people communicate, pursue information, and conduct business than the Internet.

The final decision about where to place your thesis should be based on the location that best serves your reader. The secret to writing a successful paper is to be flexible as you work through the process. Therefore, try the thesis in more than one location in the introduction, and then choose the spot that best communicates your ideas to your reader.

CREATING EFFECTIVE CONTENT AND CORRECT FORM

The composing stage marks the point at which you begin to focus more attention on the development of effective content—the information you choose to include in your paper. When you prewrite, you don't need to worry if your initial material makes sense to anyone else. Nobody but you will see this material. Prewriting material is writer-centered; it makes sense to you as the writer but not necessarily to anyone else. But in composing, your goal is to produce a writing that is reader-centered. In other words, you must create a paper that makes sense to somebody else.

Whenever you compose, your goal is the same: to communicate your ideas on a subject to someone else. This figure, called the communications or rhetorical triangle, shows this relationship:

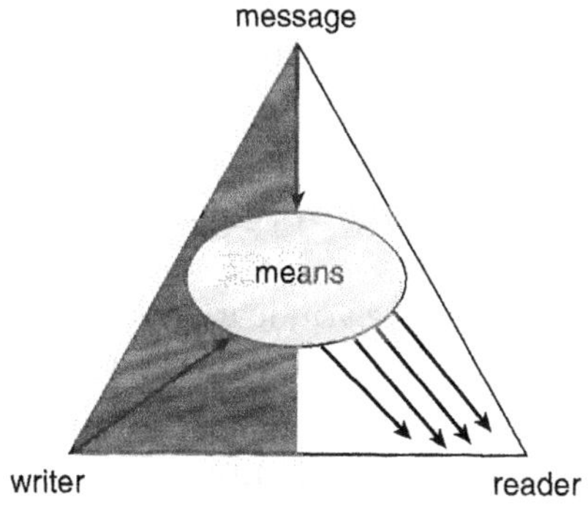

When you compose, you as the *writer* use the written word—the *means*—to communicate your ideas about your *subject* to your *reader.* In this figure, the shaded portion to the left represents what you know or want to communicate about the message. As the figure shows, a gap always exists between the writer and the most important person involved in the process: the reader receiving the message. To overcome this gap—to meet the needs of your reader—you must provide information that is unified, organized, and coherent, with plenty of transition.

The composing stage also marks the point at which you begin to focus on matters of *form*—spelling, grammar, usage, punctuation, and so on. When you prewrite, you don't need to worry about mistakes in form because only you will see this material. In the composing stage, you take the ideas you've generated and develop a competent first draft, a paper that must communicate your ideas simply, directly, and correctly to your reader.

FOCUSING ON YOUR READER

In prewriting, your goal is to generate the rough material from which you will develop your essay, so it isn't especially important that this initial material make sense to anyone but you. With *composing,* however, you must make sure that the information you write communicates your ideas to someone else who may lack your overall background and knowledge. In other words, you must make sure that your writing meets your reader's needs.

Sometimes you will know exactly who your reader is. For example, if you are writing a follow-up letter after a job interview, you know that the reader will be the person who interviewed you.

However, for much of the writing you'll do, your reader won't be so clearly identified. In these cases, you must imagine a reader. It may help to think of a specific person, someone you know slightly but not well. The danger in relying on someone close to you is that the two of you share too much common knowledge. Unless you assume that you are writing to a stranger, you may omit information necessary to communicate with your actual reader.

Sometimes you may find it easier to focus on the *average reader.* Think of how you were *before* you learned detailed information about your subject. The average reader is just the way you were then. What kinds and degrees of information did you need to know? The average reader needs the same types of examples and details.

Amplifying to Meet the Needs of Your Reader

To fill the gap of knowledge separating you and your reader, you must *amplify.* In other words, you must supply the kinds of specific details and examples that enabled you to understand the subject. When you amplify, you create a more complete picture for your reader, and as a result, you meet your reader's needs.

Imagine, for instance, that you have just signed up for high-speed broadband Internet service. Before you signed up, you didn't really understand the difference between high-speed service and dial-up Internet service. After doing a little research, you discovered that unlike dial-up service, high-speed Internet service doesn't rely on a personal telephone line. This difference means that a high-speed user won't face the kinds of interruptions from phone use and disconnections that frequently occur with dial-up service. In addition, high-speed service means instant access to the Internet and much faster download speeds. Of course, you also discovered that high-speed service costs more—in some cases, more than twice as much per month.

These details are the kinds of facts you need in order to know which type of Internet service is the better choice. Such details will therefore help the average reader, someone who lacks this specific information, make the right choice of Internet service.

It's especially important to keep the needs of the average reader in mind when your subject is personal, unusual, or complex. These topics may seem easy or ordinary to you, but that's because of the background knowledge you've already developed. Personal, unusual, or complex subjects won't be so familiar for most readers. To help reduce this unfamiliarity, provide the kinds of details and examples that enabled you to understand the subject in the first place.

Maintaining Unity

In addition to amplifying so that your reader gains a full understanding of what you have to say, you must also ensure that you express those ideas in such a way that they are directly connected to your subject. In other words, you need to make sure to maintain *unity*.

When a paper is unified, all the information you provide directly supports or illustrates your main idea. When details or examples don't specifically relate to the main idea, they disrupt unity and must be eliminated from the writing.

Consider the following brief paragraphs from an essay about the current popularity of tattooing:

> The history of decorating the body goes back thousands of years. For example, natives of some islands in the South Pacific tattoo

their faces with intricate designs. The markings are cultural and indicate matter of rank, family, and community. Among the most recognizable are the swirling shapes making up what is called the *moko* of the Maori people of Polynesia.

Some of these islands in the South Pacific are still experiencing volcanic eruptions. For instance, the Kilauea volcano on the big island of Hawaii is extremely active. Residents often joke that Hawaii is the fastest growing state in the union because the lava from the volcano flows down to the Pacific, gradually enlarging the area of the island.

The first paragraph provides some relevant historical background about tattooing, so it preserves the unity of the essay. But the second paragraph has no direct connection to tattooing. As a result, it disrupts the unity of the essay and needs to be edited out of the paper.

Establishing Organization

In the composing stage of writing, you also focus your attention on how to *organize* the material in the most effective way possible. The most common methods for arranging an essay are *chronological order, linear order, spatial order,* and *emphatic order.*

Chronological order is the arrangement in which the various episodes making up the situation or occurrence take place in time. Whenever you recall a series of events in order, as you would, for example, if you were writing about the time you received a ticket for speeding and not having your license in possession, chronological order is a natural choice.

With chronological order, you would first talk about seeing the blue flashing lights in your rear-view mirror and pulling over, and then facing the state trooper who asked for your license and registration. Next you would tell about discovering that you didn't have your license with you, and finally about being told that your fine would double if you didn't show up at the police barracks with your license within an hour. Chronological order makes the story easier to understand because the sequence is clear.

Sometimes, you deliberately break up chronological order by using a *flashback,* an episode presented out of sequence to help emphasize or explain some point. In the essay about receiving a ticket, for example, your reader might wonder why you would leave home without your license. To answer that question, you might include a flashback explaining that earlier in the day you took your credit card out of your wallet to make an on-line purchase; then you drove away from home with your wallet, with your license in it, still on the kitchen table.

Linear order is a variation of chronological order. You use linear order when you list steps or procedures that must be presented in a specific order. A recipe, for instance, and a set of instructions for assembling a toy wagon use linear order.

Spatial order is the arrangement you use whenever you need to explain where one thing exists in relation to other objects. If you were describing an accident scene involving several cars and a school bus, spatial order would make it easier for your reader to visualize where the cars were in relation to one another. For example, a small sports car was traveling *in front of* the school bus and was *behind* a car that suddenly stopped, causing the bus to crash *on top of* the sports car and the three cars *following* the bus to slam into one another. As the italicized words show, spatial order enables the reader to make sense of the chaotic accident scene.

Emphatic order involves arranging your details and examples in such a way that each point builds in order of greater importance. Presented this way, the reasons compel your reader to continue on. Your initial point should be lively enough to spark and hold your reader's interest and to begin cultivating acceptance of your point of view. Each of the following points should grow increasingly stronger so that your argument builds to a forceful, convincing conclusion.

For a paper asserting that animals should not be forced to perform for our pleasure in circuses, zoos, or aquatic parks, you might begin with the convincing point that the environments in zoos, circuses, and aquatic parks are considerably different from and significantly smaller than the ones in the wild. You might follow this up with the stronger point that these animals, accustomed to living in social groups in the wild, are frequently kept in isolation in captivity. You could then conclude with the most compelling point of all, that forcing animals to perform tricks and behave in ways that they don't in nature is simply cruel. As you can see, with emphatic order, each point draws and feeds the reader's interest.

Preserving Coherence

In addition to keeping your essay unified and arranging it effectively, you must also make sure that the resulting paper is *coherent,* that all the elements are clearly connected. To maintain coherence in your writing, you need to provide that connection, which in writing is called *transition.* One way that writers provide transition is to repeat key words (or their synonyms), phrases, and ideas. In addition, writers often use these common transitional expressions:

To Add or Restate

again	in conclusion
also	in other words
and	moreover
besides	next
finally	too
further	to sum up
in addition	

To Compare or Contrast

although	in spite of
and	likewise
as	nevertheless
at the same time	on the other hand
but	regardless
despite	still
even though	though
however	yet
in contrast	

To Illustrate or Specify

accordingly	indeed
after all	in fact
as a result	of course
because	particularly
consequently	specifically
for example	therefore
for instance	thus

To Show Time or Place

after	once
as soon as	presently
below	since
currently	soon
earlier	then
here	there
immediately	until
lately	when
later	where
now	

Using transition ensures that each idea flows smoothly to the next. The result is an essay that is coherent. Consider the boldfaced synonyms and italicized transitional expressions in the following paragraph:

> Good time management is the key to success in college. Setting up **an hour-by-hour breakdown** is the first step. *As* you make your **time plan,** don't forget to include time for meals and for nonschool activities such as exercise. *Once* you establish your **schedule,** you *then* need to follow it closely. *For example,* if you set aside Mondays from 12 to 2 for study time in the library, make sure to follow through on your **commitment.** *When* you follow

your **schedule** carefully, you will find the quality of your work improving.

As you can see, transition holds this paragraph together. For example, **time plan** renames **hour-by-hour breakdown.** In the remaining sentences, two other synonyms, **schedule** and **commitment**, also replace **time plan.** In addition, a number of transitional expressions, including *as, once, then, for example,* and *when,* emphasize the connections between the points.

In the simplest of terms, the foundation for an effective essay consists of numerous specific ideas, details, and examples. With this foundation in place, you develop the essay by making sure that all the information you choose to include is unified and logically and appropriately arranged, with plenty of transition to emphasize the connections between ideas for your reader.

Completing Multiple Drafts

Once you have completed a draft of an essay, your real work has begun. While there is no rule indicating how many preliminary drafts a writer should create before completing that final draft, it is nevertheless unrealistic to expect that you will write the best paper you are capable of on the first try. Athletes and musicians warm up, actors rehearse, and artists paint and repaint—in any field you can name, you'll find that professionals don't expect to do their jobs correctly the first time.

Even when the best among us appear to be completing something effortlessly the first time around, they are often actually making adjustments in their actions as they go along, moving back to retrace small parts of a step just completed as the situation calls for it. A skilled surgeon, for instance, cuts slowly and deliberately, adapting her movements in whatever way necessary to complete the operation successfully; a star professional baseball pitcher pays as much attention to the mechanics of his throwing as he does to the speed, changing this movement or that to place the ball where he wants it.

As a writer, you will find that your papers improve if you complete multiple drafts. Sometimes you will rework your essay paragraph by paragraph to develop your second or third draft. At other times, you may find that your initial drafts have some sections that are already solid. With these more acceptable drafts, you keep the strong material while reworking or eliminating the weaker material. Even with drafts that are initially strong, though, you will probably find that both your introductions and conclusions need reworking draft by draft.

Keep in mind that most first drafts show some degree of promise. Don't shortchange your reader or yourself. Fulfill your promise by carefully and deliberately reworking your initial draft.

Providing Proper Documentation

In addition to the material you generate yourself, you may decide to include information taken from another source to support or illustrate your own points. In these cases, you must always acknowledge your sources; otherwise, you would be guilty of *plagiarism,* the act of taking or stealing someone else's work and passing it off as your own.

When you discover material in another source that would help you make your point, you can include it with your own words in one of three ways. You can present it word for word as it appears, called *direct quotation.* You can also express in a greatly reduced form, called *summary,* or in a version that also includes your own interpretation or explanation of the material, called *paraphrase.*

Regardless of how you choose to present the source material in your paper, you must acknowledge it in two locations in accordance with one of the standard methods of documentation. The two most common styles are the Modern Language Association (MLA) system and the American Psychological Association (APA) method.

In both of these systems, the first citation is set in parentheses immediately following the material you have included. If you are drawing information from a book, using the MLA method, you include the author's last name and the page number—(Lannon 18)—; using APA style, you include the author's last name, a comma, and the year of publication—(Lannon, 2006).

The second place where you must acknowledge your source is at the end of your paper. With the MLA system, this final section is called "Works Cited," and the notation would look like this:

Lannon, John M. Technical Communication, Tenth Edition. New York: Pearson Longman, 2006.

With the APA system, the final section is called "References," and the notation would look like this:

Lannon, J. M. (2006). Technical communication, tenth edition. New York: Pearson Longman.

The complete guidelines for the MLA and APA systems are available on-line and in the reference section of your college library.

Exercises

1. As pages 18–19 indicate, an effective essay is composed of three sections: the introduction, body, and conclusion. Read the following two essays and identify the three sections in each: "The Nose Knows After All" by Bernice Kanner (p. 121) and "Throwing" by Jonathan Walters (p. 286).
2. The part of an essay that expresses the main point is the thesis (p. 20). Its location is determined on the basis of where it will best serve the reader. Identify the theses in "The Man in the Water" by Roger Rosenblatt (p. 195) and "The Triumph of the Good Bad Book" by Stephen Bayley (p. 228), and in a brief paragraph, tell why you feel the writers have chosen these particular locations.
3. As page 23 indicates, one of the most important aspects of an essay is that it be reader-centered rather than writer-centered, that it communicate its ideas to someone other than the writer. Certain documents—for instance, your classroom notes—are likely to be more writer-centered than reader-centered. Take a page of your notes from a class and rewrite this material so that it is reader-centered.
4. A successful essay is effectively organized. Using the material on pages 26–27 to guide you, identify the method of organization in "Exposed Toes" by Diane Riva p. 291 and "The Discus Thrower" by Richard Selzer.
5. One of the best ways to maintain coherence is to include clear transitions to guide your reader. Choose an excerpt of about 300 words from one of your textbooks or a magazine and identify the transitional elements. Refer to the discussion on transition and the list of transitional elements on pages 28–29.

4

Revising: Refining Your Writing

Making Your Writing Polished and Effective

Once you have completed an initial version of your paper, you enter the third stage of writing: *revising.* When you revise, your goal is to reexamine and improve the draft that you've created in the composing stage. Think of revising as a three-step process. When you revise, you

- reassess, noting as objectively as possible what works in your writing and what doesn't;
- redraft, generating new material to address the weaknesses you've identified; and
- edit, tightening your language and proofreading for errors in spelling, diction, usage, and punctuation.

REASSESSING

When you *reassess* a piece of writing, you reexamine the essay for several factors. Keep in mind that an effective essay must be:

- *unified*—all examples and details must be directly connected;
- *coherent*—all of the material must have clear transitions and be expressed in standard English and arranged in logical order; and
- *effectively worded*—all ideas must be specific and concise.

To reassess your draft effectively, you first need to create distance by allowing some time between composing your first or second draft and revising it. By allowing some time—at least a full day—before turning a solid draft into a final draft, you will be better able to see any weaknesses that remain in your content.

Such distancing is necessary because after struggling through several hours to complete a solid draft, you are in no position to evaluate it fairly. You are tired, your mind saturated. You no doubt honestly feel at this point that your paper is as good as you can make it. To continue working on it when you've reached such a point is fruitless. By now, what you intended to express and what you have actually written are all jumbled together, and the whole piece is so familiar and understandable to you that you may incorrectly assume that it will be just as familiar and understandable to your reader.

Imagine, for instance, that you have decided to write an essay about the necessity for Americans to manage their trash better. While in high school, you were an active member of your school's environmental affairs club. During your senior year, the focus of the meetings and the group project was the effect on the environment of the millions of tons of trash that Americans create each day. You learned disturbing facts: Disposable diapers don't break down for more than 200 years; the amount of energy lost when we don't recycle glass products could fuel entire cities; many of this country's landfills are rapidly reaching their limits with far fewer replacement sites available, and potentially dangerous substances can contaminate the surrounding area; and deep-water dumping of trash from major municipalities (such as New York City) is polluting our oceans. By the end of your senior year, you had developed a broad background concerning America's serious trash-management problems.

Because of your involvement in the environmental affairs club, your own reading on the subject, and your resulting strong background in this area, an essay on this subject was a natural choice for you. Your strong background, though, may actually be a drawback. Because the information seems so familiar and matter-of-fact to you, you may mistakenly assume that your reader possesses a similar background. As a result, you may occasionally find yourself writing paragraphs such as this:

> Many of the things we use every day are adding to the growing environmental problems in our country. What we are currently doing doesn't affect us for just today, either. Even if we were to start acting responsibly now, the problems would take hundreds of years to clean up.

If you were to reassess your draft immediately after you completed it, you would probably assume that this paragraph was acceptable because the ideas it suggests are so obvious to you. When you compose and revise, however, you must write so that someone else will understand what you are saying.

A day or more later, with your mind rested, you are better able to discover any parts of your paper that don't express your ideas the way you intended to express them. In other words, a little distance between drafts will enable you to recognize the need to provide the specific examples you were thinking of when you originally wrote the passage.

Although feedback is helpful throughout the entire writing process, the evaluation by an objective reader—a classmate, friend, or family member who you know will be honest and fair about your work, a former instructor whose opinion you respect, or a more experienced student—is especially useful during the reassessing stage. Another reader is obviously far more objective than you could ever be about your writing, so sharing your paper and asking your reader to indicate any remaining problems is a sure way to develop a successful final draft.

You might suggest that your reader use the following "Reader Assessment Checklist."

READER ASSESSMENT CHECKLIST

---

1. Do you understand the point I am making? Does my thesis statement clearly state the topic along with my perspective on it? (*thesis*)
2. Do I stick to that point all the way through? Does the topic sentence of each paragraph relate to the thesis? (*unity*)
3. Are all my ideas and examples clearly connected and easy to follow? (*coherence*)
4. Are the words I've used specific and concise? (*effective language*)
5. Are my introduction and conclusion effective?
6. What changes do you think I should make?

REDRAFTING

Once you have reassessed and identified the problem areas, you need to move back through the writing process to generate and develop information to substitute for, or supplement, the ineffective material. In the paragraph from the paper on environmental issues, the examples are not reader-centered. What, for example, are some of the everyday items that add to the environmental mess? How are today's actions going to affect us in the future? What responsible steps should we take? Why will the problems remain with us for so long?

Once specific examples are provided to answer these questions, the formerly writer-centered passage becomes this reader-centered one:

> Many of the things we use every day are adding to the growing environmental problems in our country. For example, without active recycling programs in place, many plastic and glass items that are used one time only end up taking valuable space in landfills. What we are currently doing doesn't affect us for just today. Many people still don't realize that items such as disposable diapers take more than 200 years to break down and that some styrofoam packaging and cups will last almost forever. Even if we were to start acting responsibly now by recycling and severely limiting our use of plastics, the problems would take hundreds of years to clean up. Many landfills across the country are environmental time bombs, gradually spilling hazardous waste into our water supply.

This redrafted material, with additions shown here underlined, makes the passage effective because it fulfills the reader's needs.

EDITING

Once you have eliminated the weaknesses in your draft, you're ready for the final aspect of the revising stage, *editing*. If your goal with the rest of the writing process is to develop an effective draft, then your goal with the editing step is to polish that draft to ensure that all the promise of the paper appears without any minor flaws to distract the reader. To do so, you need to tighten your writing by eliminating any unnecessary words and then proofread for any remaining errors in spelling, usage, punctuation, and diction.

Tightening Your Writing. One way to eliminate some unnecessary words is to favor the active voice over the passive voice. In the active voice, the subject is the doer of the action; in the passive voice, the subject is acted upon. In most cases, the active voice is more efficient because you generally need fewer words to make your point than with the passive voice. Look at these examples:

Active voice: I recently played the part of Lennie in a production of *Of Mice and Men.*
Passive voice: The part of Lennie was recently played by me in a production of *Of Mice and Men.*

The active-voice version is shorter than the passive-voice version—in these sentences, 15 words versus 17. More important, the active voice is more direct. In the active-voice sentence, your reader knows right from the start who did what, while in the passive-voice version, your reader doesn't know until the end who played the part.

In some cases, however, the passive voice is a better choice. If the actual doer of the action is not known or is less important than some other aspect of the sentence, the passive voice would probably be a better choice, as these examples show:

Passive voice: A twelve-year-old girl was shot last week outside my church.
Active voice: Someone shot a twelve-year-old girl last week outside my church.
Passive voice: Last weekend, the $100,000 experimental solar car was displayed at the mall.
Active voice: Last weekend, the mall displayed the $100,000 experimental solar car.

In the first pair of sentences, the passive voice is the better choice because the assailant is unknown and the focus of the sentence should be the victim. In the second pair of sentences, the passive voice is better because the unique and expensive automobile is clearly more important than where the car was displayed. In most cases, however, you'll probably find that the active voice better communicates your ideas to the reader.

Another way to keep your writing streamlined is to eliminate any *deadwood.* Words like *very* and *really* are examples of deadwood, since they rarely help you clarify a point. What exactly is the difference, for instance, between a person who is attractive and one who is very attractive? In most cases, you should eliminate *very* or *really;* if the modified word itself isn't specific enough, choose a stronger, more specific word rather than try to make another word strengthen a weak word.

Other similar nonspecific expressions include *a lot, definitely, quite, extremely,* and *somewhat.* Make sure that if you use such words, they actually help you make your point. Otherwise, eliminate them.

Another way to make sure your writing is streamlined is to eliminate or alter phrasing that doesn't make its point as succinctly as it could. For instance, *the majority of* is far less efficient than *most; has the ability to* is far less direct than *can.* Here are some other common phrases, along with superior alternative versions:

Deadwood	***Alternative***
due to the fact that	**because**
a large number	**many (or the actual or estimated number)**
in the near future	**soon**
prior to	**before**
completely eliminate	**eliminate**
come to the realization of	**realize**
with the exception of	**except for**
in order that	**so**
at the present time	**now**
take action	**act**
the month of October	**October**
give a summary of	**summarize**
mutual cooperation	**cooperation**
make an assumption	**assume**

Proofreading. The final step in any essay is to *proofread.* Your job is to eliminate any weaknesses that have escaped your scrutiny as you worked through the rest of the writing process. Once you have completed a couple of papers and received some feedback from a reader, you will probably discover a few specific problems that trouble you. With this information, you will be able to develop your own proofreading system that focuses on those problems. Then, rather than trying to find all your errors in one reading, you should proofread your paper more than once, each time looking for one particular error.

Until you know what problems you are most prone to make, use the following list of six common weaknesses as your proofreading guide:

1. **Have you eliminated all ambiguity and awkwardness?** Effective writing communicates one specific message to a reader. In

other words, effective writing is unambiguous. To eliminate ambiguity, you need to make sure that each passage you write makes one point only. The sentence "I can't speak too highly of my high school English teacher" is ambiguous; it could mean that you give your teacher your highest endorsement, but it could also mean that you can't offer much of a recommendation. The sentence "Once John and Joe finished talking, he walked out of the office" is ambiguous because the reader isn't sure who walked out of the office. Eliminating the ambiguity in the first sentence is a simple matter of restating it so that proper praise—or complaint—comes across clearly:

Improved: I have nothing but praise for my high school English teacher.

or

Improved: I have little good to say about my high school English teacher.

And eliminating the ambiguity in the second sentence is merely a matter of specifying who left the office:

Improved: Once John and Joe finished talking, Joe walked out of the office.

Misplaced, dangling, and squinting modifiers are also instances of ambiguous writing. The sentence "As a youngster, my grandmother often took me grocery shopping with her" is incorrect because the modifier *As a youngster* is a *misplaced* modifier. It modifies *my grandmother,* which is logically impossible, since a grandmother cannot also be a child; the phrase belongs with *me.*

Correcting such a sentence means restating part of the sentence so that the proper word is modified, as these versions show:

Improved: When I was a youngster, my grandmother often took me grocery shopping with her.

or

Improved: As a youngster, I often went grocery shopping with my grandmother.

The sentence "Listening to the orchestra, the music was a mixture of classical and New Age" is not correct because there is nothing in the sentence for *Listening to the orchestra* to modify; it is a *dangling modifier.* Correcting such a sentence involves either restating the sentence to eliminate the dangling modifier or making sure there is something in the sentence for *Listening to the orchestra* to modify, as these examples show:

Improved: The music the orchestra played was a mixture of classical and New Age.

or

Improved: Listening to the orchestra, I realized the music was a mixture of classical and New Age.

The sentence, "Edie indicated as she awoke she had smelled smoke in the living room," is ambiguous because *as she awoke* could indicate when Edie made the statement or when she smelled the smoke; it is a *squinting modifier.* To eliminate this ambiguity, you need to move the modifier so that the sentence sends the proper message:

Improved: As she awoke, Edie indicated that she smelled smoke in the living room.

or

Improved: Edie indicated that she smelled smoke in the living room as she awoke.

In addition to eliminating any ambiguity, you must also eliminate any *awkwardness* in your writing. Awkward writing isn't necessarily incorrect. Rather, it is writing that doesn't express ideas as simply, directly, and clearly as it could. The sentence "One seldom encounters distressing situations worse than the extremely painful glare from children under temporary state care who have been informed of another imminent move," while grammatically correct, is too formal and indirect to be fully effective. By retaining the same idea but expressing it in simple, direct, and correct terms, you end up with this version, which does a far better job of making the same point:

Improved: Few things are as sad as the eyes of foster children who have been told that they are being moved to yet another foster home.

2. **Have you made any sentence errors?** The very least your reader expects from you is effective ideas arranged in complete sentence form, that is, in groups of words that contain a subject and verb

and express a complete thought within the context of your essay. Therefore, as you proofread, you need to recheck your work to make sure you have eliminated the three most serious sentence errors: *fragments, comma splices,* and *run-on sentences.*

A *fragment* is an incomplete sentence, recognizable because it does not make sense by itself. You correct a sentence fragment by supplying whatever words are necessary for it to express a complete thought. Look at this brief passage, with the fragment underlined:

Incorrect: Year after year, electric and other utility rates continue to rise. A condition that often affects those people who can least afford to pay. Fortunately, at least in this state, it is against the law for utilities to shut off services to customers for nonpayment during cold-weather months.

To correct this fragment, you either add this fragment to the sentence immediately before it or turn it into a complete sentence by adding to or restating it, as these versions show:

Correct: Year after year, electric and other utility rates continue to rise, a condition that often affects those people who can least afford to pay. Fortunately, at least in this state, it is against the law for utilities to shut off services to customers for nonpayment during cold-weather months.

or

Correct: Year after year, electric and other utility rates continue to rise. Often this situation affects those people who can least afford to pay. Fortunately, at least in this state, it is against the law for utilities to shut off services to customers for nonpayment during cold-weather months.

The second serious sentence error is the *comma splice,* an error in which whole sentences are mistakenly connected with a comma. But commas can't connect—they do the opposite, separating elements within a sentence. Here is an example of a comma splice:

Incorrect: It's still hard for many Americans to imagine that it was once legal for one human being to own another human being on the basis of skin color, society is still suffering from slavery's effects more than a century after its abolition.

To identify a comma splice, you need to examine each comma you have used. If a comma appears between complete sentences, as it does in this example, you must either properly connect or correctly separate the sentences. You may connect the sentences by using a semicolon, the mark of punctuation that does enable you to connect complete sentences, or a comma plus a conjunction, as these versions show:

Correct: It's still hard for many Americans to imagine that it was once legal for one human being to own another human being on the basis of skin color; society is still suffering from slavery's effects more than a century after its abolition.

or

Correct: It's still hard for many Americans to imagine that it was once legal for one human being to own another human being on the basis of skin color, and society is still suffering from slavery's effects more than a century after its abolition.

To separate the sentences properly, you can of course use a period (or, when it's appropriate, a question mark or an exclamation point) at the end of one sentence and begin the next sentence with a capital letter:

Correct: It's still hard for many Americans to imagine that it was once legal for one human being to own another human being on the basis of skin color. Society is still suffering from slavery's effects more than a century after its abolition.

The third major sentence error is the *run-on sentence,* a mistake in which one sentence appears immediately after the next, with nothing to connect or separate them properly. It is therefore like a comma splice without the comma. Here is an example of a run-on sentence:

Incorrect: Over the last decade, the way voters view the major political parties has changed many Americans no longer consider themselves members of either the Democrat or Republican party.

An excellent way to identify run-on sentences is to read your work aloud; an even better method is to have another reader read your work aloud to you. Whoever is reading is likely to stumble at the point where one sentence should end and the next should begin. Once you have identified the break between sentences, you can correct the error the same way you correct a comma splice. That is, you either properly connect the sentences with a semicolon or a comma and a conjunction, or you separate them with an appropriate mark of end punctuation, as these versions show:

Correct: Over the last decade, the way voters view the major political parties has changed; many Americans no longer consider themselves members of either the Democrat or Republican party.

or

Correct: Over the last decade, the way voters view the major political parties has changed, and many Americans no longer consider themselves members of either the Democrat or Republican party.

or

Correct: Over the last decade, the way voters view the major political parties has changed. Many Americans no longer consider themselves members of either the Democrat or Republican parties.

3. Have you made any spelling errors? The mistakes that are most easily recognized by readers are spelling errors. However incorrect an assumption it is, many readers will judge your overall intelligence and writing ability on the basis of your spelling. This isn't fair, but it is reality. Therefore, you need to focus on eliminating all spelling errors.

Actually, unless you suffer from a learning disability such as dyslexia, which can impair your ability to read and write, you can improve your spelling by first identifying your own personal spelling problems. For instance, many people have a few words they use on a regular basis that they consistently spell wrong. Sometimes it's because of a silent letter, as in *psychosis* and *readily.* In other cases, the word is an exception to a guideline that you've learned, such as *leisure* and *neither,* which are exceptions to the "i before e except after c" rule you learned in elementary school. Others may have trouble when the word is one of a pair or group of homophones, words that sound the same, such as *principal* and *principle.* Among the most troublesome of this group of words are possessive pronouns and contractions involving forms of the same pronoun—*your* and *you're; their, they're,* and *there; its* and *it's; whose* and *who's*—and pairs or groups of commonly confused words, such as *affect* and *effect.*

The best way to eliminate these spelling errors from your writing is to keep your own alphabetized list of troublesome words. Each time you come across a word that you or another reader has identified as misspelled, add it to the list. Then, whenever you've completed a draft, run through your own spelling list, checking your paper to ensure that you've properly spelled all of your own personal spelling demons.

Incidentally, when you proofread for spelling, try this method: Read your essay backwards, from last word to first. When you check for spelling errors in the conventional way, you are often distracted from focusing exclusively on spelling by what you are reading. When you scan the essay backwards, however, there is no story to distract you; you are better able to focus on individual words and thus are more likely to find previously overlooked spelling errors.

Finally, if you are using a computer, take full advantage of any spelling or grammar-checking features. Always proofread your paper one more time after using these functions, however, to make sure that all errors have been corrected. Despite all the advances in computer software, a computer still doesn't reason the way a human does. For example, if you write *desert* when you actually mean *dessert,* the computer will not discover the oversight because both *desert* and *dessert* are correctly spelled words.

4. Have you maintained consistency in verb tense? In writing, *tense* refers to the point of time, past, present, or future, indicated by the verb. Actually, each verb in the English language has a total of twelve tenses, a variety that enables writers to translate the actions and conditions of the world to words. The danger with such a wide variety is that a writer may inadvertently shift from one tense to another, thus distracting and potentially confusing the reader.

Many shifts in tense within an essay are of course justified. For example, if you included in your writing a childhood episode to explain some attitude or opinion you have today, it would make sense to shift from the present to the past and then back again. When you proofread, simply make sure you haven't accidentally shifted tenses, especially in the middle of a sentence or paragraph. Look at this example, with the verb shifts underlined:

Incorrect: Suddenly, a small pickup truck crashed through the plate-glass window at the front of the cafeteria. The man driving <u>climbs</u> out of the truck, <u>pulls</u> out an automatic rifle, and began firing. By the time he had finished firing and turned the gun on himself, more than fifty people were dead or severely wounded.

Except for the two underlined present-tense verbs, this episode is written in the past tense. Correcting this problem is simply a matter of changing the underlined present-tense verbs to past tense, as this version shows:

Correct: Suddenly, a small pickup truck crashed through the plate-glass window at the front of the cafeteria. The man driving climbed out of the truck, pulled out an automatic rifle, and began firing. By the time he had finished firing and turned the gun on himself, more than fifty people were dead or severely wounded.

5. **Have you maintained agreement throughout?** As you proofread, you need to check for errors in both kinds of agreement: *subject-verb agreement* and *pronoun-antecedent agreement.* To identify and correct any errors in subject-verb agreement, locate each verb and its subject, making sure that singular subjects have singular verbs and plural subjects have plural verbs. Look at this example, with the faulty subject-verb agreement underlined:

Incorrect: The books on the best-seller list <u>remains</u> on sale through Saturday.

The subject, *books,* is plural; the proper verb choice therefore is *remain,* as this version shows:

Correct: The books on the best-seller list remain on sale through Saturday.

Other problems with subject-verb agreement include sentences in which the verb comes before the subject, as with most sentences beginning with *there* or *here,* and sentences with compound subjects or collective nouns such as *committee* or *audience* used as subjects.

You must also make sure that all pronouns agree with their *antecedents,* the words they refer to or replace. Singular antecedents call for singular pronouns, and plural antecedents require plural pronouns. To correct errors in pronoun-antecedent agreement, check each pronoun, making sure it agrees in number with the word it refers to or replaces. Many of these errors involve the use of singular indefinite pronouns such as *everyone* with the plural pronoun *their,* as this example shows:

> *Incorrect:* When it comes to giving to charity, everyone must be able to satisfy their own conscience.

To eliminate this weakness, you must change one of the pronouns so that the two words match. You might make both singular by changing the sentence this way:

> *Correct:* When it comes to giving to charity, everyone must be able to satisfy her or his [or his or her] own conscience.

As you can see, when referring to a singular pronoun such as *everyone,* you must include both the feminine and masculine personal pronouns to avoid sexist language. Other singular indefinite pronouns that pose the same problem include *everybody, nobody, no one, somebody, someone, anyone,* and *anybody.*

Because such singular pronoun usage may become complicated and awkward, a better solution is to change things a bit so that both pronoun and antecedent are plural, as this version shows:

> *Correct:* When it comes to giving to charity, people must be able to satisfy their own consciences.

When you make both pronoun and antecedent plural, you produce a sentence that is simple, direct, and nonsexist.

6. **Have you kept all elements parallel?** To maintain parallelism in your writing, you must make sure that you present all similar, connected elements in the same form. To correct weaknesses in parallelism, first locate any elements you've presented in pairs or groups, especially those connected by *and* and *or,* and then make sure that the elements are set up the same way. Look at this example, with the nonparallel element underlined:

Incorrect: Copies of this document are available in the local library, at city hall, the statehouse, and in the town newspaper's computer file.

As you can see, four elements, *in the local library, at city hall, the statehouse,* and *in the town newspaper's computer file,* are connected by *and;* unlike the other three, however, the statehouse isn't a prepositional phrase. Correcting the faulty parallelism here is a simple matter of making this element a prepositional phrase, as this version shows:

Correct: Copies of this document are available in the local library, at city hall, at the statehouse, and in the town newspaper's computer file.

Since problems with parallelism can also occur when you connect elements with the correlative conjunctions *both* and *and, either* and *or, neither* and *nor, not only* and *but also,* and *whether* and *or,* double-check for weaknesses in parallelism whenever you use these words. Also check any passage in which you compare elements by using *than* or *as;* make sure that you have expressed the elements of the comparison with the same form.

Although these six types of errors represent the most common problems writers face, you may find that this list doesn't exactly suit your own needs. If you find that you are not prone to one or more of these weaknesses or that you are tripped up by a weakness not listed among these common problems, adapt this list so that it is tailored to your own particular problems. Setting up a consistent, personalized system of proofreading will help you make sure that your final draft is error-free.

PROOFREADING CHECKLIST

---

1. Have you eliminated all ambiguity and awkwardness?
2. Have you corrected any sentence errors?
   ___ sentence fragments?
   ___ comma splices?
   ___ run-on sentences?
3. Have you corrected any spelling errors?
4. Have you maintained consistency in verb tense?
5. Have you maintained agreement throughout?
   ___ subject-verb agreement?
   ___ pronoun-antecedent agreement?
6. Have you kept elements in sequences in parallel form?

The Relationship Between Your Purpose and the Rhetorical Modes

In addition to having a thorough understanding of the writing process itself, you also need to understand the connection between your aim—your purpose—and the patterns or types of writing you use, which are called the *rhetorical modes: narration, description, example, process, definition, comparison and contrast, cause and effect,* and *division and classification.* As noted earlier, people generally write for one of three reasons: to inform, to entertain, or to persuade. In some essays, you'll concentrate almost exclusively on one of these purposes, but in most cases, you'll probably find that your essays fulfill multiple purposes. Most of the time, you don't think about the purpose of your paper, in large part because the assignment you face suggests the purpose you'll fulfill—but the purpose is there nevertheless.

As the next nine chapters demonstrate, you use the rhetorical modes in a variety of combinations to fulfill the purpose in your essay. You'll soon discover that one mode dominates in most papers, with several other modes providing additional support, depending on the specific needs of that assignment. A paper in which you examine two forms of government, for instance, will no doubt feature comparison and contrast as the primary mode, but it is also likely to feature examples to illustrate the types of government, cause and effect to specify how each type evolved, and process to explain how each type functions. All of this happens naturally, most of the time without your even being aware of it, as you work to fulfill the purpose of your essay.

Incidentally, since persuasion is one of the three aims of writing, argument is presented as an aim rather than a mode. When you write an argument essay, you take a stand and attempt to convince the reader that the point of view expressed is valid and reasonable. To argue effectively, you use whatever modes best help you fulfill that intent.

Remember as you work through the remainder of the book that the names of the various modes are merely loose titles rather than all-encompassing categories. In fact, you'll discover some degree of overlap in the modes. *Narration,* for example, involves relating a series of events in order, whereas *process* involves presenting a series of steps in order. *Description* involves using details to make a scene, character, or situation accessible to a reader, whereas *definition* involves using details to specify the elements or characteristics of a scene, character, or situation. Don't worry too much about such overlap; concentrate instead on using the modes to fulfill the purpose of the assignment. If you do, the result will be an effective essay.

Exercises

1. Take another look at the Reader Assessment Checklist on p. 35. Which of these questions do you think you would find most difficult to answer? In a brief paragraph, explain why you feel this way.
2. Of the six common weaknesses discussed on pp. 38–47, and listed on the Proofreading Checklist on p. 47, which one do you find easiest to identify and correct in your writing? Which one do you find most difficult to correct? Why? Explain your answer in a brief paragraph.
3. Find a 150- to 250-word example of what you feel is writing in need of tightening. It could be a portion of a textbook, part of a magazine or a newspaper article, an insurance policy, or a government document. Make a copy of the original passage and then see how many words you can eliminate without changing the meaning of the original.
4. Using the discussion of six common weaknesses (pp. 38–47) to guide you, proofread and correct the following paragraph:

   The trouble when I got to the door of Laura's house. Their, waiting on the porch, is the most biggest retreiver I had ever seen, I didn't know weather to go ahead or turning back, so I just freezed. Meanwhile, snarling and barking and pulling on a chain that didn't look strong enought to hold back a tiny poodle, I watched that dog. It was embarasing to be stuck on the porch like some little coward all I wanted was for my date to come out so we could leave. Instead, her little brother who was about six years old. Comes out and just told the dog to be quite. When the dog immediately become tame, I felt ridiculous, I felt even worst when the rest of her family came out, to. They all just laughed.

5

Narration

The Technique

They are part of the framework of all cultures: the storytellers. Long before there were books or any other documents from which people could learn and be entertained, the storytellers were the teachers and the entertainers. What all cultures and all stories have in common is *narration,* the mode through which a series of events is presented. No matter what your subject and purpose, you'll frequently rely on narration to explain the sequence of some incident or event. Besides using narration as a supporting technique, you will find that certain assignments call for narration as a dominant mode. The essays in this chapter exemplify such writing. To make sure your narrative writing is effective, you must

- present the information in the proper sequence;
- employ appropriate flashbacks and flashforwards;
- recognize the most effective point of view; and
- provide a thorough presentation.

THE PROPER SEQUENCE

The order in which you present a series of events will make a big difference in the way readers experience your narrative journey. You will find *chronological order,* the order in which incidents or events actually occur, an ideal method of arrangement with many of the extended narratives you will write—an essay about your driving test, for example, or a colleague's efforts to improve staff morale. That's because explaining the events in order of time ensures that your audience will easily see and understand what happened first, next, and last.

Take a look at this excerpt from *The Coming Storm: Extreme Weather and Our Terrifying Future* by Bob Reiss, which uses chronological order to retrace the path of a tornado as it causes increasing amounts of destruction in the city of Nashville:

> The tornado, spinning at F2-F3 force, was now moving east along wide, commercial Charlotte Avenue, toward the State Capitol. At the American Red Cross, a wall blew in. The tornado blew the clock off the tower of the Union Station Hotel. It destroyed a wall in the Sheriff's office. It ripped part of the roof off the capitol, and buried valuable fire-fighting equipment under debris at the Metro-Nashville Fire Department headquarters. The Tennessee Oilers' football stadium, one-third complete at the time, suffered damage.
>
> The storm peeled a mural off the Hard Rock Café downtown and tore apart an elevated glass-enclosed crosswalk connecting the Renaissance Hotel and the Church Street Shopping Center. . . . The twister, almost a mile wide, was now heading out of town and into the suburbs, towards Bobby Boyd's office.

FLASHBACKS AND FLASHFORWARDS

Two variations of chronological order can help you add emphasis or suspense to a piece of narrative writing: flashbacks and flashforwards. You'll find these two features especially useful with essays and other documents in which readers need some information outside of the order in which they actually occurred.

When you employ a *flashback,* you suddenly interrupt the chronological flow with an event from the past in order to help the audience understand the significance of some point in the passage. Consider this section from *What a Blessing She Had Chloroform: The Medical and Social Response to the Pain of Childbirth from 1800 to the Present,* which begins in 1929 but then veers back to 1847 to dramatize the roots of an advance in medical care for women:

> "The position of woman in any civilization is an index of the advancement of that civilization; the position of women is gauged best by the care given to her at the birth of her child." So wrote H. W. Haggard in 1929. If so, western European society made a

> significant advance on January 19, 1847, when James Young Simpson, a Scottish obstetrician, administered diethyl ether to facilitate delivery of a child to a woman with a deformed pelvis. This is the first known administration of anesthesia for childbirth. On the same day, Simpson received notice of his appointment as Queen Victoria's "Physician in Scotland." A comment to his brother shows the relative value that Simpson placed on the two events: "Flattery from the Queen is perhaps not common flattery, but I am far less interested in it than in having delivered a woman this week without any pain while inhaling suphuric ether. I can think of naught else."

When you include a flashforward, you also interrupt the chronological flow, in this case interjecting something occurring after the incident under discussion, again with the goal of accentuating the significance of some point within the sequence. Take a look at this brief excerpt from *Great Home Runs of the 20th Century,* the story of Whitey Kurowski's pennant-winning home run on October 5, 1942. The passage begins with a discussion of 1942 but then jumps ahead to a perspective gained only after this year, increasing the drama of the narrative and demonstrating its larger importance to the world of the future:

> The year was 1942. It was not a good year for the world, but it was a glittering year in baseball, particularly for the St. Louis Cardinals.
>
> With the disaster at Pearl Harbor having taken place just a few months earlier on December 7, 1941, and the United States just beginning to emerge from the ravages of the Great Depression and now plunging into a worldwide war, it was a sober time around the country. Baseball, which vowed to remain in operation despite the increasing loss of players to the military draft, was one of the few pleasant diversions still available.
>
> No one could predict it at the time, but the 1942 season would be the last one until World War II ended in which baseball was at full strength. The next three seasons would see the quality of the game deteriorate to a substantially lower level as numerous players were marched off to war and were replaced by a collection of players who were not of major league caliber.

EFFECTIVE POINT OF VIEW

With much of the narration, you will write from a *first-person point of view,* that is, with you as the participant and teller of the story, using *I, me,* and so on. With essays about your own experience, it clearly makes sense to tell the story from this vantage point, as author Annie Dillard does in this brief excerpt from her essay "God in the Doorway":

> One cold Christmas Eve I was up unnaturally late because we had all gone out to dinner—my parents, my baby sister, and I. We had come home to a warm living room, and Christmas Eve. Our stockings drooped from the mantel; beside them, a special table bore a bottle of ginger ale and a plate of cookies.
>
> I had taken off my fancy winter coat and was standing on the heat register to bake my shoe soles and warm my bare legs. There was a commotion at the front door; it opened, and cold wind blew around my dress.
>
> Everyone was calling me. "Look who's here! Look who's here!" I looked. It was Santa Claus. Whom I never—ever—wanted to meet. Santa Claus was looming in the doorway and looking around for me. My mother's voice was thrilled: "Look who's here!" I ran upstairs.

With some narration, though, you will be writing about events that you witnessed or learned about. In these cases, you will write from the third-person point of view, that is, observing and recording the story, using *he, she, they,* and so on. This passage from *The Time Trap,* a book about time management, demonstrates the cool authority of third-person narrative:

> A remarkable example of increased productivity occurred in the management offices of a Canadian airline. The president was in the habit of holding daily staff meetings, each one-and-a-half hours long, without any agenda. No wonder all ten of his top managers labeled "meetings!" as their top time-waster. After learning some better meeting techniques, the president switched the format. Staff meetings would be held only once a week, not every day; they would be limited to one hour, and they would always be run by agenda. Right away the time investment dropped dramatically, from a total of seven and a half hours a week to one hour. After six months, when they had learned how to use the agenda for the powerful tool it is, they had also doubled the results gained from the meetings. So the total productivity of the staff meeting increased fifteen fold.

A somewhat less common point of view is the *second person* (*you* and *your*) *point of view.* This point of view builds its audience right into the presentation, creating, in a sense, a new identity for readers and placing them in a specific "role" in the story. In general, you use this point of view to engage the emotions of readers by asking them to imagine themselves in a situation you've carefully crafted. Keep in mind that in some cases an audience may perceive the second person as aggressive or intrusive, so reserve its use for when you wish to leave an intense impression. This example, from *How to Defend Yourself Against the IRS,* places the audience in the position of a tax-evading businessman:

> Let's say you're in business—you sell garments, or medical services, or cars. . . . Your day starts, continues, and ends with tax consequences.
>
> If you take a business associate or client out to breakfast, you deduct the cost of yours and his. You also deduct the cost of the garage you park in near the restaurant, and tips you give in the garage and restaurant. If you drove straight to your office every day, commutation costs—depreciation on the car, cost of garage, tolls, gas—would not be deductible. So you regularly make interim stops before going to the office—to see a client, or to buy goods, or something similar—and presto, your travel costs become partially deductible.

A THOROUGH PRESENTATION

With any type of writing, your reader depends on you to provide sufficient information. To make sure you meet that need, you need to avoid two main problems: providing too little specific information and becoming sidetracked.

Imagine you are writing an essay about overcoming stage fright. This problem originally developed after your first-grade teacher, angry because you forgot your lines in the spring pageant, left you onstage for what seemed like hours. The overall experience is so vivid for you that the subject is a natural choice for a paper. Ironically, though, because you've lived with the fear day after day, you might tend to undercut your explanation of what your life is like whenever you face any kind of public presentation. But the fear that has become almost routine for you is anything but routine for your reader. Therefore, you must make sure to spell out in thorough detail what happened to you.

The other potential difficulty, the danger of becoming sidetracked, also results from your intimate knowledge of the event. Perhaps you learned some years later that your first-grade teacher suffered the death of a parent shortly before that spring pageant and that his anger with you was a reaction to his own loss. But unless the focus of your paper is to be your reunion with this teacher during which he apologizes for having caused you such pain, you shouldn't include this information.

To ensure that you provide enough information without getting sidetracked, make sure that your narration remains focused on the purpose of your document. Certainly car crashes make for interesting stories in and of themselves, at least in a morbid kind of way. But in this selection from *Unsafe at Any Speed,* activist Ralph Nader stays focused on his major aim: to persuade the reader of the danger inherent in automobile design. He leaves out unnecessary details, giving only enough background about car accidents to prove his point. The result is an effective piece of narrative writing:

> The connection between design defects and driver misjudgment and uncontrollable vehicle behavior is so subtle that neither the accident investigator nor the operator is aware of this connection in collisions. Automatic transmission defects illustrate this point with spectacularly tragic consequences. With more and more vehicles employing automatic transmissions, the occurrence of the "engine powered runaway accident" is rising alarmingly. A vehicle starting from a standstill or at a very low speed careens or lurches completely out of control with startling unexpectancy. For example:
>
> - A young lady enters her garage and gets in her car to go to work. An instant later the car plummets in the wrong direction straight through the back end of the garage.
> - A middle-aged woman is maneuvering her car out of a parked position on a busy main street; suddenly the car shoots forward across the street and crashes fifty feet through a store window, narrowly missing a number of pedestrians and store clerks.
> - An automobile is coming out of a parking garage; abruptly it lurches forward and then careens wildly, killing or injuring pedestrians and patrons of a restaurant.

CHECKLIST FOR USING NARRATION

---

1. Does the document employ **chronological order** or some **other appropriate method of presentation** to clearly indicate the time frame of the events for the audience?

2. Are **flashbacks** and **flashforwards** provided whenever information from outside of the primary sequence is needed?
3. Is the **point of view**—first, second, or third person—appropriate for and consistent with the document's purpose and audience?
4. Are the **mood** and **tone** appropriate for the document?
5. Does the document supply a sufficient **number of examples and details** to keep an audience engaged without becoming sidetracked?

AN ANNOTATED EXAMPLE

LANGSTON HUGHES
Salvation

How terrible it must feel to be a child and be the only one left out of a group. Imagine how much worse it must feel when the group consists of souls who have been granted eternal bliss and have thus earned the admiration of all. This is the situation Langston Hughes presents in this autobiographical essay. One of the most influential voices in modern American literature, Hughes was also a leader of the Harlem Renaissance, the flowering of African American writing, culture, and art in New York beginning in the 1920s. In this piece, Hughes uses narration to bring the reader back to this crossroad of his own youth: his unsuccessful struggle to risk shame by choosing honesty over hypocrisy.

Is it better to stand by your principles or tell a convenient lie?

First-person point of view.

These opening sentences serve as the introduction.

Chronological order is used throughout (note transitional words).

1 <u>I was saved from sin when</u> I was going on thirteen. But not really saved. It happened like this. There was a big revival at my Auntie Reed's church. Every night for weeks there had been much preaching, singing, praying, and shouting, and some very hardened sinners had been brought to Christ, and the membership of the church had grown by leaps and bounds. <u>Then just</u> before the revival ended, they held a special meeting for children, "to

bring the young lambs to the fold." My aunt spoke of it for days ahead. That night I was escorted to the front row and placed on the mourners' bench with all the other young sinners, who had not yet been brought to Jesus.

He spells out his expectations.

My aunt told me that when you were saved you saw a light, and something happened to you inside! And Jesus came into your life! And God was with you from then on! She said you could see and hear and feel Jesus in your soul. I believed her. I had heard a great many old people say the same thing and it seemed to me they ought to know. So I sat there calmly in the hot, crowded church, waiting for Jesus to come to me. 2

Good details.

The preacher preached a wonderful rhythmical sermon, all moans and shouts and lonely cries and dire pictures of hell, and then he sang a song about the ninety and nine safe in the fold, but one little lamb was left out in the cold. Then he said: "Won't you come? Won't you come to Jesus? Young lambs, won't you come?" And he held out his arms to all us young sinners there on the mourner's bench. And the little girls cried. And some of them jumped up and went to Jesus right away. But most of us just sat there. 3

He provides a thorough presentation with plenty of specific examples and good description.

A great many old people came and knelt around us and prayed, old women with jet-black faces and braided hair, old men with work-gnarled hands. And the church sang a song about the lower lights are burning, some poor sinners to be saved. And the whole building rocked with prayer and song. 4

Note the transitional words.

Still I kept waiting to see Jesus. 5

Finally, all the young people had gone to the altar and were saved, but one boy and me. He was a rounder's son named Westley. Westley and I were surrounded by sisters and deacons praying. It was very hot in the church and getting late now. Finally Westley said to me in a whisper: "God damn! I'm tired o' sitting here. Let's get up and be saved." So he got up and was saved. 6

He avoids becoming sidetracked with the story of Westley.

Chronological order is used throughout (note transitional words).

Then I was left all alone on the mourners' 7
bench. My aunt came and knelt at my knees and cried, while prayers and songs swirled all around me in the little church. The whole congregation prayed for me alone, in a mighty wail of moans and voices. And I kept waiting serenely for Jesus, waiting, waiting—but he didn't come. I wanted to see him, but nothing happened to me. Nothing! I wanted something to happen to me, but nothing happened.

I heard the songs and the minister saying: 8
"Why don't you come? My dear child, why don't you come to Jesus? Jesus is waiting for you. He wants you. Why don't you come? Sister Reed, what is this child's name?"

"Langston," my aunt sobbed. 9

"Langston, why don't you come? Why 10
don't you come and be saved? Oh, Lamb of God! Why don't you come?"

Good details.

Now it was really getting late. I began to 11
be ashamed of myself, holding everything up so long. I began to wonder what God thought about Westley, who certainly hadn't seen Jesus either, but who was now sitting proudly on the platform, swinging his knickerbockered legs and grinning down at me, surrounded by deacons and old women on their knees praying. God had not struck Westley dead for taking his name in vain or for lying in the temple. So I decided that maybe to save further trouble, I'd better lie, too, and say that Jesus had come, and get up and be saved.

Note all the transitional words.

So I got up. 12

Suddenly the whole room broke into a sea 13
of shouting, as they saw me rise. Waves of rejoicing swept the place. Women leaped in the air. My aunt threw her arms around me. The minister took me by the hand and led me to the platform.

When things quieted down, in a hushed 14
silence, punctuated by a few ecstatic "Amens," all the new young lambs were blessed in the name of God. Then joyous singing filled the room.

Good details.

The conclusion spells out the significance—the irony of Langston losing faith rather than gaining faith.

That night, for the last time in my life but 15
one—for I was a big boy twelve years old—I cried. I cried, in bed alone, and couldn't stop. I buried my head under the quilts, but my aunt heard me. She woke up and told my uncle I was crying because the Holy Ghost had come into my life, and because I had seen Jesus. But I was really crying because I couldn't bear to tell her that I had lied, that I had deceived everybody in the church, that I hadn't seen Jesus, and that now I didn't believe there was a Jesus any more, since he didn't come to help me.

Your Turn: Responding to the Subject

a. Childhood is full of adventures and experiences that in retrospect seem so clear and simple, sometimes even silly. But that's not the way the experiences felt at the time, when you were delighted or amazed or terrified. For this assignment, focus on one of your childhood recollections—for example, a situation you faced in school, within your family, during a religious service, at a summer camp, during a sporting event, and so on—that you understand differently now as an adult.

b. Adults put children through a number of situations: some, such as religious or social situations, because the adults want the children to follow family tradition; others, such as Little League or dance or music lessons, because these adults think children should be active; and others, such as camp, because adults decide the children want them. For this assignment, focus on one of these stories from your own childhood or one from somebody else's past in which an individual was subjected to something entirely against his or her personal interest.

MARGERY EAGAN

Bond Between Mother, Child Understood After Mom Is Gone

Although it is an inevitable part of life for most people, dealing with the loss of a parent is among the most difficult challenges a child will ever face. In this essay, Boston Herald *columnist Margery Eagan relates her own struggles to deal with the death of her mother. As a featured columnist, Eagan writes on a wide variety of subjects from parenting to politics. Her career has also included stints for* Boston Magazine *and several other newspapers. In addition to her duties as a* Boston Herald *columnist, she currently hosts a daily afternoon talk show in Boston. In this essay, she details the many ways her attitudes, feelings, and reactions have changed since the death, six months earlier, of her mother.*

What does the death of a parent teach us about the relationship between parent and child and about ourselves?

My mother has been dead six months today. I am still searching for the silver lining. 1

So far losing her has brought out some unattractive attributes. Pettiness. Jealously. Irrational envy. 2

I see three generations—grandmother, mother, child—in the toy store, in Filene's junior's department fingering prom gowns on the rack. The toy store grandmother entertains her squealing grandchild at the Lego table, enabling mother to shop peacefully. The Filene's grandmother nods knowingly (where has she seen this before?) when teenager rolls her eyes, dismissing as ridiculous every gown suggestion mother makes. 3

I see these grandmothers looking older and frailer than my own mother ever looked. So why are they still alive when my mother is dead? 4

So far losing my mother has made me resent my mother-in-law as well, though her only sin, like the grandmothers, is living on. 5

She will hear my oldest child sing at her eighth-grade graduation; see my youngest child dance at the preschool promotion. She will likely survive into the college commencement season, too, and the weddings. She will be the grandmother my children remember. 6

Yet my mother was the grandmother who ran alongside my daughter's bike in the Greek church parking lot until, miracle of miracles, she rode her two-wheeler alone. My mother taught her to play double solitaire and rummy, and to bet. My mother pitched underhand for hours to my would-be slugger son. She took him to the airport to watch planes land, to the lake to watch fish jump at dusk. How much will he remember of that? 7

"When the kids wake up, send them to me," she would say to me when we visited her house. "Sleep late." 8

So I stayed in bed until 9:30 or 10 while my mother made yet another bacon-and-pancake breakfast and served it in a highchair or at the kitchen table to a child developing my mother's passion for Sunday crosswords. 9

Now when we go to her house, her bacon press and pancake pans still stand by the stove. In the cupboard are half-used spices and olive oils and the Mott's juice boxes she bought on a final trip to the market last fall. Last year's Mother's Day plants still thrive by the windows. Everything looks the same, but no one is cooking, and her absence hangs like a great, airless weight. 10

We considered it a leap forward in the so-called healing process when one of us—me—took over her traditional place at the kitchen table. 11

"I thought," said my weepy 6-year-old during dinner that night, "she'd be coming back from heaven. But she's not coming back, is she?" 12

I don't mean here to compare my mother's death to some cruel, untimely tragedy, like losing a child or sibling or spouse still young. You are supposed to bury your parents. That's the natural order. My mother was not young. Neither am I. What's surprising is how none of that soothes the wound. 13

When my father died 15 years ago, I felt like an amputee—the chair that once had four legs suddenly had three. When my mother died, I felt the chair pulled out from under me. 14

I remember stroking her dry hair on a hospital gurney and disbelieving it all. I looked at her life and wondered: Was it enough? I remembered the invincible mother who'd once run down a steep hill to rescue me when I'd fallen off our toboggan. She scooped wet snow from inside my boot. Then she carried me way back up the hill, through high, heavy snow; all-powerful, all-knowing, eternally strong—as I have been to my children. 15

My friends and I often debate which is better: to lose parents quickly with no chance to say goodbye, or to have endless goodbyes, even though that means watching them deteriorate slowly and suffer. Since both my parents died in an ambulance, I don't know. 16

But I do know that I wish my mother, a gifted storyteller, had written about her life and left it for us to read. About her marriage, maybe. Or if that were too private, about motherhood and family life, or just about what she'd learned. 17

What she did leave we found on the floor of her closet. She knew we would discover it during the ritualistic, post-mortem sorting of the 88 pumps, the well-worn suits, the wool sweaters that still held the scent of her dusting powder. 18

On the inside cover of her *Complete Works of William Shakespeare* we found her diary of sorts. She wrote down dates of family trips ("Williamsburg, 1961"); of deaths ("my beloved husband, Daniel, 1984"); of births ("my grandson Daniel, 1992"). She warned us not to fight over money, then listed her four favorite sonnets. "Read them," she wrote. 19

No. 71 was first. 20

"No longer mourn for me when I am dead," it begins, "Nay, if you read this line remember not the hand that writ it. For I love you so that I in your sweet thoughts would be forgot, if thinking on me then should make you woe." 21

It was typical of my mother, not one for tears, to advise us from beyond the grave against weeping for her. Yet she must have known the longing would go on and grow deeper, and it does, I think, because the connection between mother and child is so basic, so fierce, primitive and necessary; not extraordinary but ordinary, not intellectual, but physical; and familiar, like a favorite pillow or milk in cereal. Or rain. 22

But like so much else it's only understood best after it's gone. 23

So I was a child like any child, made in a woman, born from her, shaped by her for better, or worse. That woman was my mother, dead six months today, leaving me to mourn for what I have no more. 24

Understanding the Significance

1. In the third paragraph of her essay, Margery Eagan discusses a grandmother, mother, and child. Why do these three generations cause her to feel mixed emotions?
2. Why does Eagan now find herself resentful of her mother-in-law?
3. Why does Eagan feel that the first Shakespearean sonnet her mother chose for her children to read was so typical of her mother's way of viewing life and death?
4. What points does Eagan make about the connection between mother and child?

Discovering the Writer's Purpose

1. What is Eagan saying about the effects of this kind of personal loss on one's perception and attitude about life?
2. In paragraph 7, Eagan presents a series of examples of ways that her mother interacted with Eagan's children. Through these specific details, what point is Eagan making about the significance of her mother's death?
3. Eagan says that the loss of her father made her feel "like an amputee—the chair that had four legs suddenly had three." But when her mother died, she felt that chair ". . .pulled out from under me." Why do you think she refers to the loss of her mother in this way?
4. One of the strengths of Eagan's essay is the number of specific details she includes. Yet the examples themselves are not of great or unusual moments but rather of mundane and ordinary everyday occurrences. What point is she making by focusing on such events?

Examining the Writer's Method

1. Eagan's introduction is effective, even though it is just two short sentences long. What is it about this introduction that serves the reader's needs?
2. This essay features first-person point of view. How would the piece be different if Eagan had instead employed third-person point of view?
3. Rather than tell one story, Eagan presents several brief scenes, saving the vignette about finding and reading through her mother's informal diary for the final third of the essay. Why do you think she presented this particular episode here rather than earlier?
4. How does Eagan's conclusion help her reiterate her thesis?

Considering Style and Language

1. In the third paragraph, when describing the glances that pass between grandmother and granddaughter as the mother checks prospective prom gowns, Eagan includes a brief passage in

parentheses. What point is she making by setting this section off in this way?

2. In the section in which she notes how her mother's house has now changed, she describes her mother's absence as "a great, airless weight." What does this expression mean to you? In what way do these words help to explain how things can sometimes appear as they did before but at the same time be so radically different?
3. Why do you think Eagan chooses to include an actual quote from one of her mother's favorite Shakespearean sonnets rather than to summarize the passage? Do you agree with her choice? Why or why not?
4. What do the following words mean in the context of the writing? *Pettiness* (para. 2); *sin* (para. 5); *dusk* (para. 7); *passion* (para. 9); *gurney* (para. 15); *deteriorate* (para. 16); *ritualistic, post-mortem* (para. 18).

Your Turn: Responding to the Subject

a. In paragraph 13, Margery Eagan makes the following statement relative to the death of her mother: "What's surprising is how none of that soothes me." Do you agree with Eagan? Are there some things that we experience in life that simply can never be soothed? Or does time or love or patience or something else eventually heal our pain? For this assignment, choose an experience of your own or one that you have witnessed or read about and offer your own assessment.

b. Early in her essay, Eagan discusses her feelings whenever she sees three generations out together. She explains how she watches them, describes how they behave with each other, and imagines what they are saying and thinking. For this assignment, think back to a time when you have seen three generations together—child, parent, grandparent. Then, using third-person narration, explain where the scene occurred, and, from what you could tell from your observation, what they were doing, how they reacted to each other, what they were saying and thinking. Finally, suggest what could be learned from this intergenerational interaction.

FRANK MCCOURT

The Bed

Even the most confident and courageous people can feel overwhelmed when facing the prospect of being the newcomer, the square peg, "the other." After all, who among us doesn't want to fit in, if not to be just like everybody else, at least to feel that others accept us despite our differences. Culture, age, gender, sexuality, race, religion, physical appearance—all are factors that, given certain situations, can make someone feel like an outsider. Combine any of these factors with poverty, and the barrier separating the one from the many can seem even less penetrable. Frank McCourt certainly understands this equation. His childhood in Ireland, as recounted in his first memoir, Angela's Ashes, *was marked by extraordinary poverty. As this excerpt from his follow-up memoir,* 'Tis, *McCourt employs narration to show how his desire for a college education in the United States brought him face to face with that barrier, in this case through the act of writing an essay.*

What happens when an event from the past, something that was the source of shame and embarrassment, is suddenly made public?

---

1 The lecturer in English Composition, Mr. Calitri, would like us to write an essay on a single object from our childhood, an object that had significance for us, something domestic, if possible.

2 There isn't an object in my childhood I'd want anyone to know about. I wouldn't want Mr. Calitri or anyone in the class to know about the slum lavatory we shared with all those families in Roden Lane. I could make up something but I can't think of anything like the things other students talk about, the family car, Dad's old baseball mitt, the sled they had so much fun with, the old icebox, the kitchen table where they did their homework. All I can think of is the bed I shared with my three brothers and even though I'm ashamed of it I have to write about it. If I make up something that's nice and respectable and don't write about the bed I'll be tormented. Besides, Mr. Calitri will be the only one reading it and I'll be safe.

The Bed

3 When I was growing up in Limerick my mother had to go to the St. Vincent de Paul Society to see if she could get a bed for me and my brothers, Malachy, Michael, and Alphie who was barely walking. The man at the St. Vincent de Paul said he could give her a docket to go down to the Irishtown to a place that sold second-

hand beds. My mother asked him couldn't we get a new bed because you never know what you're getting with an old one. There could be all kinds of diseases.

The man said beggars can't be choosers and my mother shouldn't be so particular. 4

But she wouldn't give up. She asked if it was possible at least to find out if anyone had died in the bed. Surely that wasn't asking too much. She wouldn't want to be lying in her own bed at night thinking about her four small sons sleeping on a mattress that someone had died on, maybe someone that had a fever or consumption. 5

The St. Vincent de Paul man said, Missus, if you don't want this bed give me back the docket and I'll give it to someone that's not so particular. 6

Mam said, Ah, no, and she came home to get Alphie's pram so that we could carry the mattress, the spring and the bedstead. The man in the shop in the Irishtown wanted her to take a mattress with hair sticking out and spots and stains all over but my mother said she wouldn't let a cow sleep on a bed like that, didn't the man have another mattress over there in the corner? The man grumbled and said, All right, all right. Bejesus, the charity cases is gettin' very particular these days, and he stayed behind his counter watching us drag the mattress outside. 7

We had to push the pram up and down the streets of Limerick three times for the mattress and the different parts of the iron bedstead, the head, the end, the supports and the spring. My mother said she was ashamed of her life and wished she could do this at night. The man said he was sorry for her troubles but he closed at six sharp and wouldn't stay open if the Holy Family came for a bed. 8

It was hard pushing the pram because it had one bockety wheel that wanted to go its own way and it was harder still with Alphie buried under the mattress screaming for his mother. 9

My father was there to drag the mattress upstairs and he helped us put the spring and the bedstead together. Of course he wouldn't help us push the pram two miles from the Irishtown because he'd be ashamed of the spectacle. He was from the North of Ireland and they must have a different way of bringing home the bed. 10

We had old overcoats to put on the bed because the St. Vincent de Paul Society wouldn't give us a docket for sheets and blankets. My mother lit the fire and when we sat around it drinking tea she said at least we're all off the floor and isn't God good. 11

The next week Mr. Calitri sits on the edge of his desk on the platform. He pulls our essays from his bag and tells the class, Not a bad set of essays, some a little too sentimental. But there's one I'd like to read you if the author doesn't mind, "The Bed." 12

He looks toward me and lets his eyebrows go up as if to say, Do you mind? I don't know what to say though I'd like to tell him, No, no, please don't tell the world what I came from, but the heat is in my face already and I can only shrug to him as if I don't care. 13

He reads "The Bed." I can feel the whole class looking at me and I'm ashamed. I'm glad [Alberta] Small isn't in this class. She'd never look at me again. There are girls in the class and they're probably thinking they should move away from me. I want to tell them this is a made-up story but Mr. Calitri is up there talking about it now, telling the class why he gave it an A, that my style is direct, my subject matter rich. He laughs when he says rich. You know what I mean, he says. He tells me I should continue to explore my rich past, and he smiles again. I don't know what he's talking about. I'm sorry I ever wrote about that bed and I'm afraid everyone will pity me and treat me like a charity case. The next time I have to take a class in English Composition I'll put my family in a comfortable house in the suburbs and I'll make my father a postman with a pension. 14

At the end of the class students nod to me and smile and I wonder if they're already feeling sorry for me. 15

Understanding the Significance

1. How does McCourt initially feel about telling the story of the bed that he shared with his brothers during his childhood in an Irish slum? What ultimately convinces him to write the story?
2. Why is McCourt's mother upset about the bed the charitable organization has offered her family?
3. How would you describe Mrs. McCourt's personality and attitude? What example or detail from the excerpt best supports your view and why?
4. McCourt's instructor gives his essay on the bed an A grade and offers him words of encouragement, yet McCourt expresses no happiness. What keeps him from enjoying his success?

Discovering the Writer's Purpose

1. What is McCourt's primary aim for writing this piece: to inform, entertain, or persuade? Explain your position, using examples from the reading to support your answer.

2. How does McCourt make it clear that he believes his background is vastly different from the backgrounds of his classmates?
3. Why do you think McCourt chose to include the essay he wrote rather than just explain what he wrote? How would the impact of the excerpt have been affected if he had chosen that strategy?
4. McCourt doesn't discuss the period between the class when he submitted the essay and the class when his instructor read it aloud. In your view, would the excerpt have been more—or less—effective if he had discussed what he experienced and thought between the two class meetings? Why?

Examining the Writer's Method

1. What do the details McCourt supplies in the second paragraph emphasize? How do they help McCourt tell his story?
2. In the actual essay about the bed, McCourt does not reveal until the closing paragraphs that his father was home but had refused to help his wife and children transport the bed. Why do you think he reserved this information until the end of the story?
3. McCourt's excerpt features two distinct sections, the essay itself, plus a frame that establishes the context for writing the essay and McCourt's reaction. How does the frame affect the reader's understanding of the significance of the episode of the bed?
4. How does the use of chronological order, in both the frame and the essay on the bed, help capture a sense of life for McCourt as a child and McCourt as an adult?

Considering Style and Language

1. In this excerpt McCourt writes from two different perspectives, as an adult and as a child. Which voice did you find more effective and why?
2. Given how McCourt describes his family's situation, do you think his mother is speaking truthfully or ironically in the final sentence of the essay about the bed? How do you think Frank McCourt the child interpreted her words? Explain your reasoning.
3. Throughout both the frame and the essay itself, what methods does McCourt rely upon to record what various people said? Why do you think he made these decisions? Do you agree with his choices?

4. What do the following words mean in the context of the writing? *Domestic* (para. 1); *lavatory, respectable* (para. 2); *docket* (para. 3); *consumption* (para. 5); *pram* (para. 7); *spectacle* (para. 10); *sentimental* (para. 12); *rich* (para. 12).

Your Turn: Responding to the Subject

a. Frank McCourt's writing instructor, Mr. Calitri, asked that his students write about a single, significant object from childhood, specifying that he preferred that it be something from the home. Now you have the same opportunity to tackle the same subject that McCourt and his classmate's faced. For this assignment, write a narrative essay in which you tell the story of a single, significant domestic object from your childhood, using McCourt's essay on the bed he shared with his brothers to guide you.
b. As someone who traveled to the United States at age 19, Frank McCourt certainly understands the many difficulties that immigrants face. For this assignment, focus on the challenge of being an immigrant. You can approach the subject from a variety of directions. If you are an immigrant yourself, you might use narration to focus on one of your own experiences, telling your reader your story. Or if you are the child or grandchild of immigrants, you could use the third person to tell the story of the biggest difficulty someone in your immediate family faced.

HARTLEY NEITA

Old Man Edwards

For a child, a neighborhood is a kind of personal universe encompassing all that is known and all that is needed. The neighbors who share this personal universe are often enormously significant, helping to shape the life experienced there. In Hartley Neita's case, the neighbor whose influence still remains was Mr. Edwards, the old man who lived next to his childhood home in Jamaica. Neita, who served as press officer for two Jamaican prime ministers, is a writer, journalist, and communications consultant. In his view, the lessons learned from Old Man Edwards have had a lifelong influence on the way he views the world.

When we take the time to listen to those around us who have amassed great life experience, what benefits can we gain?

The closest neighbours to my family in the district in which I spent my early years were Mr. and Mrs. George Edwards. To him, my father was Teacher and my mother was Miss Abbie. To them he was Sir George. In our home they referred to him, affectionately, as Old Man Edwards. To us children, he was just Sir. 1

Looking back in time as I write this, I suddenly realize I never met Mrs. Edwards. Her memory is a voice coming from a room inside her house when I shouted goodbye to her. 2

"So long, Son. Give me love to Miss Abbie." 3

Every Saturday morning and every day during the school holidays, I walked across the border between our homes and walked and worked his land with him. My immediate reward at the time was the pretty red-pink mangoes, which always bore high at the top of the trees, and the red and yellow plums, which ripened at the end of the brittle limbs, two joints which he peeled of sugar cane, and two or three fingers of ripe bananas from his buttery. The long-term rewards were the lessons he taught me about the hard work slaved by farmers. 4

Like cutting the trunk of a breadfruit tree or soursop or mango if it refused to bear fruit. Like when to plant gungo peas. Like throwing ashes at the roots of tomatoes, and now I do not remember why. 5

Our part of the country suffered drought for 10 months each year. Except for May and December. The only times it rained in other months was when a storm was near. The soil was therefore tough and hard to plough. So instead of a fork, his favourite tool was a hoe. In 6 the early morning, I walked behind him with a pan of corn grain. He had strung a line with cord already, then he chopped the earth with the hoe and stirred the soil around it. As he went to dig the next hole I threw two grains of corn in the hole and covered them loosely.

When we were finished planting he stopped in the shade of one 7
of the many trees on the farm.

The sun by then was rising towards noon and it was getting hot. 8
So we went to the area in which he grew vegetables. In this area the sun's heat was softened with the cover of fishing nets. He showed me how to use a hand fork to tease up the earth around each plant. Later, I went to the large drum at the corner of his house where rain-water poured from the gutter which rimmed his roof, dipped a pan in it and carried water to sprinkle the vegetables.

During the dry months he pushed a cart with three drums to the 9
schoolyard in the late afternoons after school was closed. My father often joined him. I stood nearby, hearing but never commenting. Old Man Edwards did not depend on the red flag to be hoisted at the Post Office to tell him a hurricane was near. He would sniff the air with his face tilted to the sky.

"Batten down, Teacher," he warned. "It going rain, heavy-heavy." In 10
another of the dry months, he looked at the new moon and said, "It going rain this month." And it always did. My father being a Mico [college] man dismissed these warnings, at first, but later became an apostle.

"For when the horns of the New Moon are parallel to the horizon 11
"The following month would be dry. 12
"When they tilt, 13
"The moon will be pouring water from the sky." 14

It was not old wives talk. It was the wisdom of centuries of 15
African history which his ancestors had brought to Jamaica and never forgotten.

Sometimes, when my father wanted farming advice the two men 16
walked across the schoolyard to the school garden.

They walked through the garden, stopping now and then to pick 17
gormandisers which grew between the stems of the tomatoes and which if left to grow would drain the strength of the plant. They ground the little stragglers in their palms as they walked and talked and then threw them on the heap of leaves and horse and cow manure which fermented in one corner of the garden.

"You need to mulch the vegetable beds," he said. "That's why the 18
plants look weak. I'll bring some guinea grass tomorrow."

So said. So done. Next evening, the two men were on their knees 19
laying out the leaves of the guinea grass between the plants. Old Man Edwards said you must kneel on Mother Earth when you were seeking help from Mother Nature and God.

Understanding the Significance

1. On the basis of the information Neita supplies, what kind of person would you say Mrs. Edwards is?
2. In what ways is Neita rewarded for working with Mr. Edwards?
3. What method did Mr. Edwards follow to recognize the coming of bad weather?
4. In what ways would Mr. Edwards help Neita's father with his gardening?

Discovering the Writer's Purpose

1. In his initial discussion of Mr. Edwards, Neita makes this statement: "To us children, he was just Sir." What does this sentence suggest about Neita's upbringing and the upbringing of other youngsters in his area?
2. In paragraphs 6 through 8, Neita carefully recounts the various tasks that he used to perform as he worked with Mr. Edwards. How would the overall impact of the essay have been affected if he hadn't included this material?
3. Halfway through the essay, Neita switches his focus from his own relationship with Mr. Edwards to his father's relationship with Mr. Edwards. Why do you think he makes this shift?
4. In the concluding paragraph, Neita paraphrases a proverb that Mr. Edwards shares with Neita and his father. What does this saying indicate about Mr. Edwards' view of nature and the environment?

Examining the Writer's Method

1. Neita relies on first-person point of view to introduce Mr. Edwards. How does Neita's use of first-person point of view help his reader better understand the impact that Mr. Edwards had on Neita and his family?
2. Aside from three sentences, including one direct quote, Neita doesn't discuss Mrs. Edwards. So why do you think he includes her in this essay?
3. During his childhood, Neita presumably did many different jobs for Mr. Edwards, yet he spells out only one of the tasks—planting

corn—in detail. Do you agree with his strategy? Explain your reasoning.

4. In your view, how does the use of chronological order help Neita explain the kind of impact that Mr. Edwards had on Neita and his family?

Considering Style and Language

1. In this essay, Neita includes a number of intentional fragments, incomplete sentences presented to create a particular effect. In particular, the fifth paragraph consists entirely of intentional fragments. Why do you think he chose to phrase his ideas this way rather than to express them in complete sentence form? Do you agree with his decision? Why or why not?
2. How would you describe the overall tone that Neita adopts throughout the essay? Do you think it is an appropriate match for his subject? Explain your reasoning.
3. At several points, Neita employs dialect, dialogue that is presented so that it recreates the accent or sound of a particular region. Do you agree with his choice? How would the essay have been affected if Neita had presented Mr. Edwards in grammatically correct form?
4. What do the following words mean in the context of the writing? *Border, brittle* (para. 4); *suffered, drought, loosely* (para. 6); *softened, tease* (para. 8); *hoisted, tilted* (para. 9); *apostle* (10); *old wives tale* (para. 12); *straggler* (para. 14); *heap, fermented* (para. 14); *mulch* (para. 15).

Your Turn: Responding to the Subject

a. Even many years later, Old Man Edwards stands out for Hartley Neita because of what he had to teach and the way he taught it. Think back across your own memories: Who among all the neighbors in your life has had the greatest impact on you, either positively, as Mr. Edwards did to Neita, or negatively? For this assignment, introduce this neighbor and explain in full detail why this person's influence remains.

b. A first job, whether it's a less formal situation like Neita's work for Mr. Edwards or a paid position as a part- or full-time employee, can be the source of lots of lessons. In terms of your own work experience, what did you learn on your first day on the job that you have never forgotten? For this assignment, use narration to tell this story.

Other Possibilities for Using Narration

Here are some additional topics for papers that feature narration. Of course, these subjects are merely starting points. As you work your way through the writing process, adapt or develop the topic you choose so that you fulfill your purpose.

- A time you witnessed a crime
- A trip to the "big city"
- An encounter with the police
- A traumatic experience
- A meeting with an unusual, famous, or otherwise memorable person
- A time that you discovered something wonderful or something shocking about someone you thought you knew well
- The worst phone call you ever received
- An embarrassing episode
- An accident you witnessed
- A trip to the principal's office
- The event in your life that has given you the greatest sense of personal pride
- An experience from driving school
- A family (or school, team, or club) reunion
- An unusual date
- A time that you were caught in a lie

Writing at Work

NARRATION

BLUE MAN GROUP
Tubes

In addition to the uses for narration already demonstrated in this chapter, narration appears in real-world documents whenever a writer needs to explain background or history. Narration is used for exactly this purpose in the following passage, which comes from the program for the theatrical performance of "Blue Man Group—Tubes," a highly enjoyable presentation involving music, video, mime, fluorescent paint, and audience participation. With their recent appearances a in television commercial for the Pentium 4 processors and Grammy nomination for instrumental music (2000), the avant-garde Blue Man Group has received some mainstream attention. This excerpt from the program explains how the group—and the show—evolved.

About the Company

The concept for Blue Man Group emerged out of salon-style meetings hosted in 1987 by Matt Goldman, Phil Stanton, and Chris Wink. Soon the three longtime friends began organizing a series of "happenings" such as "Club Nowhere" and "Funeral for the Eighties," which took place in and around New York's Central Park. Shortly thereafter, they were appearing in performance spaces in the East Village, such as Dixon Place, Performance Space 122 and the Wooster Group's Performing Garage. *1*

"Tubes" first appeared at La MaMa in January 1991, and then appeared later that year at Lincoln Center as part of the SERIOUS FUN! Festival. By this time, the group had grown to include musicians Larry Heinemann and Ian Pai, as well as video designer Caryl Glaab. "Tubes" then moved to the Astor Place Theatre in November, 1991. The La MaMa production won Blue Man Group an Obie Award, and the Astor Place production has won both the Lucille Lortel and Drama Desk awards. In the past two years, Blue Man Group has expanded to include 18 additional performers. *2*

In Boston, Matt Goldman, Phil Stanton, Chris Wink, Shawn Sturnick, Scott Kinworthy, Frank Licari, Nathan Wetherington, and Gideon Banner and the band members will rotate into the show in various combinations, three Blue Men and three musicians at a time. 3

Focusing on the Message and Aim

Answer each of the following questions in a brief paragraph, referring specifically to the passage you've just read.

1. The writer's intent in this passage is to explain the origin of the show. How does the use of narration help the writer fulfill this aim?
2. How does the use of transition help the reader better understand the excerpt? Make a list of the transitional words and explain how they enable the reader to tie together the various points made about Blue Man Group.

3. The first paragraph notes that the show originally began as a "series of 'happenings.'" On the basis of this description, what would you expect to see if you had walked into one of the earlier shows?

Applying the Principles

a. Choose a theatrical performance, a corporation, a sports franchise, your own school, or a similar topic and do some research through print or electronic sources. Then, using the piece about Blue Man Group as a model, create a brief history of the production or organization.
b. Theatrical programs generally include brief biographies of the performers. For this assignment, create a two-paragraph autobiography or a two-paragraph biography of a friend, a family member, one of your instructors, or a local celebrity.

Practical Application: Narration

Congratulations! In yesterday's mail, you received a letter notifying you that on the basis of your grades, you have been nominated by your academic adviser for induction into a prestigious national honor society for students. As the letter explains, the nomination is only the first step. Not all nominees are accepted. Final selection is based on a 300- to 500-word (two typewritten pages maximum) personal statement, written by the nominee on a subject determined by the national organization. This year's nominees have been asked to tell about the best lesson they've been taught, either in school or on the streets.

You immediately go to see your adviser to thank her for recommending you and to seek her advice on writing the personal statement. She graciously offers you a copy of Jacqueline Wright's essay to the same group seeking a fellowship it provides each year. In the essay, Wright outlines her personal philosophy concerning the role of a conductor. Use Wright's "My Road to the Podium and Baton" as a model for approach and format as you create your personal statement on the best lesson you have ever been taught.

My Road to the Podium and Baton

My original decision to become a conductor was largely a result of my own experience as an instrumentalist. As I was finishing up my degrees in music education and flute performance at the University of Rhode Island, I was faced with the question that all undergraduates face: what next? My experiences as a student teacher showed me educating children about music is an incredibly important and worthwhile pursuit, but I also needed to be challenged as a musician. There was the possibility of continuing my flute study, but I was unsure that I really wanted my career to be so solitary. I began to realize that the direction I found most tempting and most challenging was conducting. It was the ideal way of combining all of the different aspects of music I had spent four years studying and perfecting—history, theory, analysis, ear-training, not to mention performing—into a single career.

There was one more aspect of being a conductor that really appealed to me, maybe even more than the personal challenges. I had been so fortunate as a young musician to work mainly with teachers who really cared about students as well as music that I feel a sense of duty to be that sort of teacher for future young musicians. I will always remember a phrase I read in a *Music Educators' Journal* article years ago used to describe a conductor: "servant-leader." The conductor who is a true "servant-leader" is more concerned with the ensemble than with his or her own ego and constantly has the needs of the ensemble members foremost in his or her mind. My conductors at the University of Rhode Island were true "servant-leaders" and my memories of the respect that we, their students, had for them—as well as the joy we took from working with them—drive me in this career.

My will to become a conductor has only intensified as I've encountered more conductors, some of whom do not seem to share my philosophy in the "servant-leader." I have now observed and worked with individuals for whom the students are not a top priority and who have too little trust of or respect for their students. It's easy to imagine what has happened: these individuals have forgotten that there is a subtle difference between conducting and teaching.

Working with professional musicians is an amazing opportunity and one that I hope I will have one day. For obvious reasons, working with students presents very different challenges from working with professionals and they should be treated differently in some ways. This doesn't mean lowered expectations of students; it means knowing their limits so that you can bring them past those limits, rather than expecting them to get there on their own.

While working with professionals appeals to me because of the end product, working with collegiate musicians appeals to me because of the process. Music happens with professional musicians because they are so experienced. Rehearsals with collegiate ensembles are where music is truly made, from notes and phrases up. To me, working with growing musicians is the ideal, because it is the arena in which a conductor can truly make a difference, not just in music but also in lives.

6

Description

The Technique

Since effective writing of any kind depends on the inclusion of specific details, *description* is a mode that you will frequently depend on. More often than not, you'll use description as a supporting technique rather than as the primary mode in an essay. For example, in an essay proposing that existing nuclear power plants should be closed until greater safety measures are developed, you might include a passage that illustrates the actual damage caused by the nuclear disaster at Chernobyl in the former Soviet Union in 1986. But sometimes you will find that a particular assignment calls for a more thorough use of description. An essay about riding out a storm at sea in a small sailboat is a good example of an essay that would be dominated by description, as would an essay about an angry confrontation with an unfair supervisor.

Whether you are using description as support or as the dominant mode in an essay, you need to:

- draw upon sensory details;
- provide a developed and focused description
- rely on both objective and subjective description; and
- apply spatial or emphatic order.

SENSORY DETAILS

Vivid experiences create vivid memories. Think for a moment of the aroma the last time you walked into a bakery or the sensation you felt the last time you plunged into a swimming pool on a hot summer day. Sensory details, what you perceive through sight, hearing, tasting, smelling, and touching, enable you to communicate these experiences to your reader.

An essay about a vacation at a tropical resort, for example, would no doubt benefit from the use of sensory details. The first part of such an essay might focus on your impressions as you arrived at your hotel. In order to make it easier for your reader to walk in your shoes, you might focus on the fragrance of the various flowers, the notes from a distant guitar, the sensation of intense humidity, and so on.

Consider the many sensory details—sight, sound, smell, touch—in the following brief excerpt from *Night of the Grizzlies*. This passage, which concerns a fatal grizzly bear attack in Glacier National Park during the summer of 1967, puts the reader right in the tent with two of the people who were mauled by a grizzly:

> As the little group waited for the help that they now knew was on its way, Roy Ducat slipped in and out of panic but never out of consciousness, and he remembered clearly what had happened. He had been sleeping soundly when all at once he had heard Julie telling him to play dead. While he was still trying to figure out what she was talking about, a single blow from a huge paw knocked both of them five feet away on the ground, and the air was full of an unpleasant smell, as though a dozen dirty sheep dogs had come in from the rain. Roy had landed on his stomach, and out of the corner of his eye, he could see Julie a few feet away. Then he felt something bite deeply into his right shoulder and scrape against the bone, and with a tremendous exercise of will, he neither cried out nor moved. The biting stopped, and Roy opened his eyes long enough to make out the shadow of a bear standing on all fours above the helpless girl and tearing at her body. He shut his eyes tightly in time to feel the bear return, plant its feet firmly in the small of his back, and begin snapping his teeth into his left arm and the backs of both his legs, just below the buttocks. Still he remained silent, and once again the bear returned to the girl.

A DEVELOPED AND FOCUSED DESCRIPTION

To ensure that your reader's experiences are as memorable and vivid as possible with your academic and workplace writing, you need to create a fully developed and focused description. Providing full development involves anticipating your audience's interests, concerns, and questions relative to your subject and then filling in the details necessary to address these needs. And keeping your description focused involves concentrating on the most important interests of your audience as well as your own purpose for the document.

For example, in an essay about your experiences on the first time you were in a hospital examining room, your reader would be especially interested in the specific sights (white tile walls, shiny aluminum storage cabinets, intensely bright examination light), odors (alcohol, bleach, slightly burned coffee from the reception area), and physical sensations (heavy perspiration, stabbing pain in your injured ankle, throbbing through your temples). But your reader wouldn't be especially concerned at this point about the high cost of health insurance or the need for a better triage system in hospital emergency rooms. Supply the details about what you saw, smelled, and felt and leave out any details about extraneous matters, and your description will be complete and focused.

Take a look at the following excerpt from *Just Let the Kids Play: How to Stop Other Adults from Ruining Your Child's Fun and Success in Youth Sports,* which provides thorough description while also maintaining a careful focus. The description zooms in on one particular aspect of youth sports—the behavior of parents—leaving a lasting impression of the damage over-involved parents can inflict on their children:

> Picture the typical youth sports game—a blur of motion and sound. Some parents are busy cheering or chatting among themselves. Others are prowling the sidelines. The prowlers mean business. These parents become field generals, barking orders and commanding their children to excel.
>
> In this world of high volume and hyperventilating, one parent stands out. You can hear him from the parking lot. "Mark your man," he screams to his little boy. Red-faced and nearly breathless, this father runs up and down the sidelines, keeping pace with every play. "See the ball," he growls. And this, his favorite one-liner from the "General Patton Does Soccer" playbook: "Stay within yourself!" The louder he screams, the more he seems to expect from his son.

OBJECTIVE AND SUBJECTIVE DESCRIPTION

When you focus on objects, situations, or people as they appear, without dealing with the impressions they generate, you are using *objective description.* When you focus on the way such things make you feel, you are using *subjective description.* Of course, you use both types of description when you write, generally without giving much thought to which type you are using.

In a passage concerning a carpentry shop you visited as a child, you might provide objective description to note that the shop was filled with racks of lumber, three large power saws, and a workbench covered with various carpentry tools and coffee cans full of nails and screws. In the same piece, you might use subjective description to explain how nervous you felt around the enormous machinery, especially the overhead saw with its exposed blade, and how sweet the sawdust smelled.

In this brief passage from *Night,* Elie Weisel's powerful memoir of his experiences in Nazi death camps, look at how Weisel mixes objective and subjective description as he recounts one evening when he and his father and other prisoners traveled from one camp to the next:

> I lay down and tried to force myself to sleep, to doze a little, but in vain. God knows what I would not have given for a few moments of sleep. But, deep down, I felt that to sleep would mean to die. And something within me revolted against this death. All round me death was moving in, silently, without violence. It would seize upon some sleeping being, enter into him, and consume him bit by bit. Next to me there was someone trying to wake up his neighbor, his brother, perhaps, or a friend. In vain. Discouraged in the attempt, the man lay down in his turn, next to the corpse, and slept too. Who was there to wake him up?

AN APPROPRIATE ORDER

If your reader is to comprehend the sensory details you provide, you must organize these details in an understandable and logical fashion. A couple of common methods of organizing details lend themselves well to descriptive writing. When the description focuses on visual detail, you will often find that *spatial order* serves your purpose. With this arrangement, you choose a starting point in space and then move in a logical fashion—up and down, or left to right—across an item or scene, mimicking the movement of a person's gaze, taking in one part of a whole before moving on to the next. This passage, a brief section from *Stiffed,* a book about American working-class men, relies on spatial order—starting its gaze up high and working its way down—to bring a huge shipyard into focus:

> The shipyard that greeted me fifty years later [after World War II] was a realm of staggering proportions. Overhead, gantry cranes towered, their arms rising and falling like the heads of gigantic horses. The tallest of them all—374 skyscraper feet high and capable of lifting more than four hundred tons (it once hoisted Howard Hughes's "Spruce Goose," the biggest airplane ever built)—was the Titan, the world's largest self-propelled floating crane, known affectionately to the men laboring in its shadow as Herman the German. America's largest war trophy, Herman was captured from the Germans in 1945, partly dismantled, and hauled by barge through the Panama Canal. Below the massive crane gaped its apposite, the gigantic maw of the Moreell dry dock, capable of floating any of the navy's largest aircraft carriers on fifty-six million gallons of seawater.

A second method for arranging a descriptive paper, *emphatic order,* mimics the workings of memory, introducing less vivid details first and saving the most emotional and memorable for last. The following excerpt from *A Delusion of Satan: The Full Story of the Salem Witch Trials,* includes details from a number of different senses that are arranged emphatically, with the text moving from lesser to greater emotional power:

> Almost thirty died. Well over a hundred languished for months in cramped, dark, stinking prisons, hungry and thirsty, never moving from the walls they were chained to, unsure if they would ever go free. Some were tortured by the strange method known as "tying neck and heels," their bodies forced into hoops, necks roped to feet. Others were made to stand without rest during interminable sessions of questioning. Many were even more exquisitely tortured by knowing that their children were left unprovided for when they were seized. Mothers wondered if their babies still lived.

CHECKLIST FOR USING DESCRIPTION

1. Have **sensory** and other **specific details** been provided to meet the needs of the reader?

2. Is the description **fully developed** and **focused**, anticipating audience interests, concerns, and questions without becoming sidetracked?
3. Has **objective description** been appropriately used to provide a more factual and less emotional account of what is being discussed and **subjective description** to focus on its emotional aspects?
4. Is the description appropriately **arranged** to have the greatest effect on the reader?

AN ANNOTATED EXAMPLE

AMY TAN

Fish Cheeks

Amy Tan is probably best known for her best-selling first novel, The Joy Luck Club, *which was nominated for the National Book Critics Circle Award and, in 1993, was made into a movie of the same title. She is also the author of* The Kitchen God's Wife *(1991),* The Hundred Secret Senses *(1993), and* The Bonesetter's Daughter *(2001). She earned a B.A. in English and Linguistics and an M.A. in Linguistics from San Jose State University and completed additional graduate work at the University of California at Berkeley. One theme that she explores in her writing is the relationship between mothers and daughters. Here, Amy Tan uses* description *to capture the sights, sounds, and aromas of her family's traditional Christmas Eve dinner. This time, however, she was embarrassed about the gathering because of the impressions she feared it would create on the young man whose affections she sought.*

How can the presence of an outsider change the way people view family celebrations?

Her first paragraph serves as the introduction, preparing the reader for the story to come.

I fell in love with the minister's son the winter I turned fourteen. He was not Chinese, but as white as Mary in the manger. For Christmas I prayed for this blond-haired boy, Robert, and a slim new American nose. 1

She provides a mixture of objective and subjective description.

When I found out that my parents had invited the minister's family over for Christmas Eve dinner, I cried. What would Robert think of our shabby Chinese Christmas? What would he think of our noisy Chinese relatives who lacked proper American manners? What terrible disappointment would he feel upon seeing not a roasted turkey and sweet potatoes but Chinese food? 2

She provides sensory details about what was seen.

Note both the objective and subjective description.

On Christmas Eve I saw that my mother had outdone herself in creating a strange menu. She was pulling black veins out of the backs of fleshy prawns. The kitchen was littered with appalling mounds of raw food: A slimy rock cod with bulging eyes that pleaded to not be thrown into a pan of hot oil. Tofu, which looked like stacked wedges of rubbery white sponges. A bowl soaking dried fungus back to life. A plate of squid, their backs criss-crossed with knife markings so they resembled bicycle tires. 3

And then they arrived—the minister's family and all my relatives in a clamor of doorbells and rumpled Christmas packages. Robert grunted hello, and I pretended he was not worthy of existence. 4

She provides sensory details about what was seen and smelled.

Dinner threw me deeper into despair. My relatives licked the ends of their chopsticks and reached across the table, dipping them into the dozen or so plates of food. Robert and his family waited patiently for platters to be passed to them. My relatives murmured with pleasure when my mother brought out the whole steamed fish. Robert grimaced. Then my father poked his chopsticks just below the fish eye and plucked out the soft meat. "Amy, your favorite," he said, offering me the tender fish cheek. I wanted to disappear. 5

She provides sensory details about what was heard.

At the end of the meal my father leaned back and belched loudly, thanking my mother for her fine cooking. "It's a polite Chinese custom to show you are satisfied," explained my father to our astonished guests. Robert was looking down at his plate with a reddened face. The minister managed to muster up a 6 quiet burp. I was stunned into silence for the rest of the night.

After everyone had gone, my mother said to me, "You want to be the same as American girls on the outside." She handed me an early gift. It was a miniskirt in beige tweed. "But inside you must always be Chinese. You must be proud you are different. Your only shame is to have shame." 7

She uses her conclusion to emphasize what she learned from the experience.

And even though I didn't agree with her then, I knew that she understood how much I had suffered during the evening's dinner. It wasn't until many years later—long after I had gotten over my crush on Robert—that I was able to fully appreciate her lesson and the true purpose behind our particular menu. For Christmas Eve that year, she had chosen all my favorite foods. 8

Your Turn: Responding to the Subject

a. Amy Tan's essay concerns a childhood recollection of a holiday celebration that didn't go the way she would have hoped. For this assignment, think back to a special celebration from your own childhood—a birthday, holiday gathering, family barbecue, and so on—one that went badly or one that went exactly as you wanted it to, and describe that party.

b. Among the strongest sections of Tan's essay is her detailed description of the various foods served at the Christmas Eve meal to which Robert and his parents had been invited. What is the most elaborate or exotic meal you have ever encountered? For this assignment, use Tan's essay as an example and describe that unusual meal, paying particular attention to the sights, aromas, and tastes you experienced.

RICHARD SELZER

The Discus Thrower

When a surgeon operates, it is to correct some problem a patient is suffering from. But that patient is much more than just the part or system needing repair; alleviating the problem—or being unable to alleviate it—affects the whole person. Richard Selzer, a working surgeon, is certainly aware of this, as his essay shows. In addition to his medical career, Selzer has enjoyed a successful writing career with both fiction and essays, including Confessions of a Knife *(1979), from which the following selection is taken,* Raising the Dead: A Doctor's Encounter with His Own Mortality *(1995), and* The Exact Location of the Soul: New and Selected Essays *(2001), as well as articles in such periodicals as* Harper's, Esquire, *and* Redbook. *His work often draws upon the world of medicine and his vantage point as a physician. In this essay, his description brings to life a patient he calls the "discus thrower," enabling the reader to understand that this patient's behavior each morning was a result of the patient's frustration and isolation brought about by his condition.*

How should a person facing grief and pain respond to these feelings?

I spy on my patients. Ought not a doctor to observe his patients by any means and from any stance, that he might the more fully assemble evidence? So I stand in the doorways of hospital rooms and gaze. Oh, it is not all that furtive an act. Those in bed need only look up to discover me. But they never do. 1

From the doorway of Room 542 the man in the bed seems deeply tanned. Blue eyes and close-cropped white hair give him the appearance of vigor and good health. But I know that his skin is not brown from the sun. It is rusted, rather, in the last stage of containing the vile repose within. And the blue eyes are frosted, looking inward like the windows of a snowbound cottage. This man is blind. This man is also legless—the right leg missing from midthigh down, the left from just below the knee. It gives him the look of a bonsai, roots and branches pruned into the dwarfed facsimile of a great tree. 2

Propped on pillows, he cups his right thigh in both hands. Now and then he shakes his head as though acknowledging the intensity of his suffering. In all of this he makes no sound. Is he mute as well as blind? 3

4 The room in which he dwells is empty of all possessions—no get-well cards, small, private caches of food, day-old flowers, slippers, all the usual kick-shaws of the sickroom. There is only the bed, a chair, a nightstand, and a tray on wheels that can be swung across his lap for meals.

5 "What time is it?" he asks.

6 "Three o'clock."

7 "Morning or afternoon?"

8 "Afternoon."

9 He is silent. There is nothing else he wants to know.

10 "How are you?" I say.

11 "Who is it?" he asks.

12 "It's the doctor. How do you feel?"

13 He does not answer right away.

14 "Feel?" he says.

15 "I hope you feel better," I say.

16 I press the button at the side of the bed.

17 "Down you go," I say.

18 "Yes, down," he says.

19 He falls back upon the bed awkwardly. His stumps, unweighted by legs and feet, rise in the air, presenting themselves. I unwrap the bandages from the stumps, and begin to cut away the black scabs and the dead, glazed fat with scissors and forceps. A shard of white bone comes loose. I pick it away. I wash the wounds with disinfectant and redress the stumps. All this while, he does not speak. What is he thinking behind those lids that do not blink? Is he remembering a time when he was whole? Does he dream of feet? Of when his body was not a rotting log?

20 He lies solid and inert. In spite of everything, he remains impressive, as though he were a sailor standing athwart a slanting deck.

21 "Anything more I can do for you?" I ask.

22 For a long moment he is silent.

23 "Yes," he says at last and without the least irony. "You can bring me a pair of shoes."

24 In the corridor, the head nurse is waiting for me.

25 "We have to do something about him," she says. "Every morning he orders scrambled eggs for breakfast, and, instead of eating them, he picks up the plate and throws it against the wall."

26 "Throws his plate?"

27 "Nasty. That's what he is. No wonder his family doesn't come to visit. They probably can't stand him any more than we can."

28 She is waiting for me to do something.

29 "Well?"

"We'll see," I say. 30

The next morning I am waiting in the corridor when the kitchen delivers his breakfast. I watch the aide place the tray on the stand and swing it across his lap. She presses the button to raise the head of the bed. Then she leaves. 31

In time the man reaches to find the rim of the tray, then on to find the dome of the covered dish. He lifts off the cover and places it on the stand. He fingers across the plate until he probes the eggs. He lifts the plate in both hands, sets it on the palm of his right hand, centers it, balances it. He hefts it up and down slightly, getting the feel of it. Abruptly, he draws back his right arm as far as he can. 32

There is the crack of the plate breaking against the wall at the foot of his bed and the small wet sound of the scrambled eggs dropping to the floor. 33

And then he laughs. It is a sound you have never heard. It is something new under the sun. It could cure cancer. 34

Out in the corridor, the eyes of the head nurse narrow. 35

"Laughed, did he?" 36

She writes something down on her clipboard. 37

A second aide arrives, brings a second breakfast tray, puts it on the nightstand, out of his reach. She looks over at me shaking her head and making her mouth go. I see that we are to be accomplices. 38

"I've got to feed you," she says to the man. 39

"Oh, no you don't," the man says. 40

"Oh, yes I do," the aide says, "after the way you just did. Nurse says so." 41

"Get me my shoes," the man says. 42

"Here's oatmeal," the aide says. "Open." And she touches the spoon to his lower lip. 43

"I ordered scrambled eggs," says the man. 44

"That's right," the aide says. 45

I step forward. 46

"Is there anything I can do?" I say. 47

"Who are you?" the man asks. 48

In the evening I go once more to that ward to make my rounds. The head nurse reports to me that Room 542 is deceased. She has discovered this quite by accident, she says. No, there had been no sound. Nothing. It's a blessing, she says. 49

I go into his room, a spy looking for secrets. He is still there in his bed. His face is relaxed, grave, dignified. After a while, I turn to leave. My gaze sweeps the wall at the foot of the bed, and I see the place where it has been repeatedly washed, where the wall looks very clean and very white. 50

Understanding the Significance

1. What is it that Richard Selzer finds so fascinating about this patient?
2. In telling this story, what is Selzer trying to say about the practice of medicine?
3. Why does Selzer include his dialogue with the discus thrower?
4. How does Selzer emphasize this man's isolation?

Discovering the Writer's Purpose

1. With little exception, Selzer keeps himself—and his emotions—out of the piece. How do you think this writing would have been different had he broken down that barrier and allowed more of his feelings to come through in his dealings with the discus thrower?
2. It is clear that Selzer and the nurses who care for the discus thrower hold different opinions about this patient. Specify the differences in their points of view.
3. The nurse who reports the discus thrower's death says his passing is "a blessing," an expression that people sometimes use when someone who has suffered before death finally dies. Considering all that Selzer relates about this patient, including the frustration of dealing with him day after day, what do you feel the nurse might mean by this expression?
4. After reading this essay, how do you feel about the discus thrower? Which emotions does he trigger in you—pity, sadness, frustration, anger, or some combination? Why?

Examining the Writer's Method

1. Throughout the essay, Selzer provides a number of vivid sensory details. What point do you feel Selzer makes by using these sensory details?
2. Selzer's use of subjective description accounts for much of the power in this essay. Of the subjective description that Selzer provides, which image affected you most? Why?
3. Selzer ends his essay with a striking piece of description: He enters the room where his now-dead patient lies and then notes that the

wall the patient had used as a target "looks very clean and very white." What message do you think Selzer is trying to impart with this description?

4. Selzer never explains why the patient erupts in laughter after throwing his plate. Why do you think the discus thrower laughs when his plate of scrambled eggs hits the wall?

Considering Style and Language

1. From what you can infer, how does Selzer feel about patients like the discus thrower? Explain.
2. Throughout the essay, Selzer describes the discus thrower from the viewpoint of an objective observer. Does he break away from this stance at any point? Explain.
3. In paragraph 34, Selzer provides this description of how the man laughs when he realizes that his breakfast plate has hit its target: "It is a sound you have never heard. It is something new under the sun. It could cure cancer." What does he mean? Why did he choose this type of description rather than saying he "laughs hilariously" or "howls" or "guffaws"?
4. What do the following words mean in the context of the writing? *Furtive* (para. 1); *vigor, vile, bonsai* (para. 2); *shard* (para. 19); *hefts* (para. 32); *accomplices* (para. 38); *dignified* (para. 50).

Your Turn: Responding to the Subject

a. As Selzer explains in the second sentence, he observes while he works. His essay stems from his efforts to "spy" and "gaze" on the people he serves, an excellent method for developing a paper. For this assignment, follow Selzer's lead and spend some time observing people involved in or served by your current job, or think back to the people you were in contact with in some previous job. Then focus on a specific figure whose actions or words remain with you today.

b. Choose a place where you regularly spend time—one of your classes, the school cafeteria, the library, a health club—and describe the various ways that people behave there.

JAMAICA KINCAID

My House

"Location, location, location." It's a kind of mantra in the world of real estate, suggesting that the value of a piece of property is always tied to where it can be found. The exact same house can cost thousands more—or less—based simply on where within a city or town or zip code it is located. But few people would disagree that real value depends on far more than just its location to give a house its special quality, its character, its essence, making it a home. That's the point that Jamaica Kincaid, best known for her coming-of-age novel Annie John *and her essays in* The New Yorker, *makes in the following excerpt from* My Garden (Book). *Here, the Antiguan-born Kincaid, one of the most compelling literary voices of the current age, relies on a fully developed presentation, including both objective and subjective description and compelling sensory details, to make her audience understand the love she has for her house.*

Why is it that some inanimate objects—houses, parks, geographical spots—can inspire devotion so deep that it could be called love?

I love the house in which I live. Before I lived in it, before I was ever 1 even inside it, before I knew anything about it, I loved it. I would drive by, seeing it sitting on its little mound, seeming far away (because I, we, did not own it then), mysterious in its brown shingles, its red shutters, surrounded by the most undistinguished of evergreens (but I did not know they were undistinguished then), humble-seeming, and that is how it drew attention to itself, by seeming humble. I longed to live in this house, I wanted to live in this house. I was a grown-up woman by that time, I had already had my first child and should have by then settled the question of where I should live and the kind of place I should live in, for that sort of settling down is an external metaphor for something that should be done inside, a restfulness, so that you can concentrate on this other business, living, bringing up a child. But I would see this house and long for it. It was especially visible in winter, for then the other trees that were not among the undistinguished evergreens were bare of leaves and the house would become more visible. These other trees, too, were without horticultural interest, common maples, the kind that seed themselves everywhere, choking each other out, distorting each other's trunk, chokecherry. In the winter the house is particularly beautiful when it is surrounded by snow, and the little mound on which it stands falls away from it, down into a meadow, and I would imagine my children (I had one child when I first saw the house but I knew I would have more, I always wanted to have more than one child, and the reason is completely selfish, but with children are there any other kinds of reasons) sliding down this slope in snowsuits, on sleds. This is now a sight I see quite regularly on a winter's day when there is snow on the ground and from the very same windows from which I view the mountain named after an Anthony.

A house has a physical definition; a home has a spiritual one. My house I can easily describe: it is made of wood (Douglas-fir beams, red cedar shingles), it has four bedrooms, a sleeping porch, two and one-half bathrooms, a kitchen which flows into the large area where we eat our meals, a living room, a sunroom, a room over the garage where my husband works, another room in which I work. That is my house. My home cannot be described so easily; many, many things make up my home. 2

The house in which I now live was built in 1935 by a man named Robert Woodworth for himself and his wife, Helen, and their three children. I am very conscious of this fact, for almost every day something makes me so: the view of Mount Anthony, those uninteresting evergreens, when something, the plumbing, breaks and has to be repaired, the low cost of heating such a large house (it is well insulated), the room in which I write. He died in the room in which I write. A barometer, which he might have consulted every day, still hangs in the same place he must have put it many years ago. I have no real interest in the weather, only as it might affect my garden, and so I regard the barometer as a piece of decoration on the wall. Robert Woodworth was a botanist and taught this subject at a nearby college. He invented time-lapse photography. I do not know if the exciting and unusual collection of trilliums, jack-in-the-pulpit, squirrel corn, Solomon's seal, and mayapple that are in a bed just outside the kitchen window are the very same ones that appear in his films on time-lapse photography. He tended a vegetable garden and also raised chickens. There was a henhouse right near the vegetable garden, but I tore it down after much agonizing, for it was a beautiful Vermont-like structure, which is to say, simple, calling attention to itself by its very simplicity, just like the house. I loved the henhouse. I believe I was not around to see it actually being dismantled. 3

* * *

I cannot now remember the day on which the house we used to live in was sold; and I cannot remember the day on which Robert Woodworth's house became our house. I can only remember that not one of the heirs' domiciles could accommodate Helen's piano. It was 4 offered to us for purchase, but we could hardly afford the down payment on the house and so had to decline. It now sits in our living room waiting for permanent settlement with one of Helen's grandchildren. My children practice their piano-lesson assignments on it all the time. Many quarrels are had over Helen's piano. They do not like to practice their piano lessons, apparently no child who lives in the culture of piano playing and who has imposed on him and her the love of music through the piano ever likes practicing the piano. And so this piano is yet another reminder of the people we call the Woodworths.

If you must go through your life being reminded of people you have never met, Bob and Helen Woodworth would be the ideal people with whom to have this experience. At Robert Woodworth's memorial service there were many people from the small village of North Bennington. Some of them were colleagues of his from the college where he taught, others were just local people whom he had known from being a resident of the village. I'm not sure they noticed how many of their memories of Robert Woodworth were like this: "Bob and I were chopping wood" or "I gave Bob some wood" or "That day Bob called me about some wood." I was sitting in the audience and I believe I was the only person who had never met Bob Woodworth, and so that must have been why I noticed that there were a lot of memories about wood connected to a man named Woodworth. I desperately wanted to stand up and point out the connection between the wood and the name of the person being commemorated. I did not. All the people who talked about him mentioned how close he was to Helen and how much they all loved Helen, too. He played Dixieland music with a group of men every Tuesday night. One night, the last Tuesday night before he died, he said goodbye to them and one man said to him, "See you next week, Bob," and Robert Woodworth said, "I don't think so." And that was true. He died sometime between that Tuesday night and the next Tuesday night when they would meet. The man he had the exchange with told that story at his memorial service. After we bought the house, we went through it and found a lot of wood ready for the fireplace in the basement. In the basement also was a wood-burning stove and it was hooked up to the furnace. We realized that the entire house could be heated with wood, but no one in my family is capable of cutting it. 5

When Dr. Woodworth died in the room in which I now write, he was alone. Helen had died two years earlier. His spirit does not haunt the room. His spirit does not haunt the house. One night, during the first winter we spent in the house, I was lying in my bed, when suddenly I smelled smoke. I ran into every room, I ran into the attic, I ran into the basement, trying to see where the smell of smoke was 6 coming from, trying to see if I could find the thing burning. The smell of smoke was not to be found in any other part of the house, only in my bedroom. The phenomenon of the smell of smoke occurs only in the wintertime and only in that one room.

When I lived in the yellow house, I used to pass other houses and imagine myself in them. I used to see the other houses and love some of them; sometimes I wished I lived in them. Some of them were very beautiful all by themselves, or they were beautiful and in an extraordinary setting to boot. I never do that anymore. I never want to live anywhere else or in any other house. 7

Understanding the Significance

1. According to Kincaid, how do the different seasons of the year enhance the beauty of her house?
2. What connection between Dr. Woodworth and the garden does Kincaid suggest?
3. What opinion does Kincaid hold of the people who originally owned her house? What in the excerpt gives you this impression?
4. How has living in her house affected her attitude about living elsewhere?

Discovering the Writer's Purpose

1. How would you describe Jamaica Kincaid's primary purpose in this writing? In your view, what aspects, examples, and details help her fulfill this aim?
2. In her opening paragraph, Kincaid describes her house as "humble-seeming." What do you think she is suggesting about the nature of beauty by using this phrase?
3. Kincaid didn't know the former owners of her home well, yet in many of the references to them, she includes their first names rather than just calling them Mr. and Mrs. Woodworth. Why do you think she chose this strategy? How does it affect the overall effectiveness of the excerpt?
4. Near the end of the excerpt, Kincaid says that Dr. Woodward's spirit does not haunt her writing room or the house. Yet in the same paragraph, she discusses the inexplicable odor of smoke in her bedroom. In your view, what is Kincaid suggesting about the previous owner's ghost?

Examining the Writer's Method

1. Kincaid opens the excerpt with this sentence: "I love the house in which I live." How does her use of description throughout the excerpt support and reinforce this sentence?
2. What method of organization does Kincaid employ to describe her house for her audience? Why do you think she made this choice?
3. Of the sensory details that Kincaid includes, which one do you find strongest or most effective? Why?
4. Kincaid supplies a number of specific details about Dr. Robert Woodward, the man who built and lived in the house before Kincaid and her husband bought it. Are more of them subjective or objective? How does this combination of details help the reader get a better sense of the former owner?

Considering Style and Language

1. How would you describe Kincaid's overall tone in her document? Do you think this tone is an appropriate match for what she is describing for her reader? Explain your reasoning.
2. Early in the piece, Kincaid discusses a henhouse that she had torn down, saying that "it was a beautiful Vermont-like structure, which is to say, simple, calling attention to itself by its very simplicity. . . ." Why do you think she chose to describe the structure this way?
3. Kincaid noticed that many of the memories mourners shared about Dr. Woodward involved wood, a point that she wanted very much to share with everyone but ultimately decided not to. Why do you think she included this detail in her discussion of Dr. Woodward's memorial service?
4. What do the following words mean in the context of the writing? *Undistinguished, humble, metaphor* (para. 1); *conscious, barometer, botanist, agonizing; domicile, culture* (para. 4); *exchange* (para. 5); *phenomenon* (para. 6).

Your Turn: Responding to the Subject

a. "A house has a physical definition; a home has a spiritual one." Jamaica Kincaid makes this point early in this excerpt. For this assignment, write a personal essay in which you interpret her words and draw on the powers of description to create a clear image of the homes and houses of your life.

b. The hit cable-network show *Trading Spaces* features people who agree to allow a radical makeover of a room in their home and to participate in making over a room in someone else's home. For this assignment, think of a room in a friend's home, an area at school, the break room at work, and so on, and write an essay in which you specify how you would remake this space.

STEPHEN KING

A Walk Seriously Interrupted

It's an undeniable fact: life in the twenty-first century is inherently dangerous. Unfortunately, insulating yourself completely from this danger is impossible. No matter how carefully you plan and no matter how many precautions you take, horrible accidents can occur, sometimes while you are involved in an activity that is normally danger-free, for instance, taking a walk along a country road. That's what Stephen King was doing on June 19, 1999, when Bryan Smith, distracted by a dog riding in his van, veered off the road and slammed into King, shattering his legs, fracturing his hip, breaking four ribs, chipping his spine in eight places, and nearly ending his life. In this passage from On Writing: A Memoir of the Craft, *King, author of such hugely popular works as* The Shining, Misery, *and* The Green Mile, *employs a focused combination of objective and subjective description, including powerful sensory details, to take his reader along through his own personal nightmare.*

What goes through a person's mind when circumstances bring that individual to the very edge of death?

Smith sees I'm awake and tells me help is on the way. He speaks calmly, even cheerily. His look, as he sits on his rock with his cane drawn across his lap, is one of pleasant commiseration: *Ain't the two of us just had the shittiest luck?* it says. He and Bullet left the campground where they were staying, he later tells an investigator, because he wanted "some of those Marzes-bars they have up to the store." When I hear this little detail some weeks later, it occurs to me that I have nearly been killed by a character right out of one of my own novels. It's almost funny. 1

Help is on the way, I think, and that's probably good because I've been in a hell of an accident. I'm lying in the ditch and there's blood all over my face and my right leg hurts. I look down and see something I don't like: my lap now appears to be on sideways, as if my whole lower body had been wrenched half a turn to the right. I look back up at the man with the cane and say, "Please tell me it's just dislocated." 2

"Nah," he says. Like his face, his voice is cheery, only mildly interested. He could be watching all this on TV while he noshes on one of those Marzes-bars. "It's broken in five I'd say maybe six places." 3

"I'm sorry," I tell him—God knows why—and then I'm gone again for a little while. It isn't like blacking out; it's more as if the film of memory has been spliced here and there. 4

When I come back this time, an orange-and-white van is idling at the side of the road with its flashers going. An emergency medical technician—Paul Fillebrown is his name—is kneeling beside me. He's doing something. Cutting off my jeans, I think, although that might have come later. 5

I ask him if I can have a cigarette. He laughs and says not hardly. I ask him if I'm going to die. He tells me no, I'm not going to die, but I need to go to the hospital, and fast. Which one would I prefer, the one in Norway–South Paris or the one in Bridgton? I tell him I want to go to Northern Cumberland Hospital in Bridgton, because my youngest child—the one I just took to the airport—was born there twenty-two years before. I ask Fillebrown again if I'm going to die, and he tells me again that I'm not. Then he asks me if I can wiggle the toes on my right foot. I wiggle them, thinking of an old rhyme my mother used to recite sometimes: *This little piggy went to market, this little piggy stayed home*. I should have stayed home, I think; going for a walk today was a really bad idea. Then I remember that sometimes when people are paralyzed, they think they're moving but really aren't. 6

"My toes, did they move?" I ask Paul Fillebrown. He says they did, a good healthy wiggle. "Do you swear to God?" I ask him, and I think he does. I'm starting to pass out again. Fillebrown asks me, very slowly and loudly, bending down into my face, if my wife is at the big house on the lake. I can't remember. I can't remember where any of my family is, but I'm able to give him the telephone numbers of both our big house and the cottage on the far side of the lake where my daughter sometimes stays. Hell, I could give him my Social Security number, if he asked. I've got all my numbers. It's just everything else that's gone. 7

Other people are arriving now. Somewhere a radio is crackling out police calls. I'm put on a stretcher. It hurts, and I scream. I'm lifted into the back of the EMT truck, and the police calls are closer. The doors shut and someone up front says, "You want to really hammer it." Then we're rolling. 8

Paul Fillebrown sits down beside me. He has a pair of clippers and tells me he's going to have to cut the ring off the third finger of my right hand—it's a wedding ring Tabby gave me in 1983, twelve years after we were actually married. I try to tell Fillebrown that I wear it on my right hand because the real wedding ring is still on the third finger of my left—the original two-ring set cost me $15.95 at Day's Jewelers in Bangor. That first ring only cost eight bucks, in other words, but it seems to have worked. 9

Some garbled version of this comes out, probably nothing Paul Fillebrown can actually understand, but he keeps nodding and smiling as he cuts that second, more expensive, wedding ring off my swollen right hand. Two months or so later, I call Fillebrown to thank him; by then I understand that he probably saved my life by administering the correct on-scene medical aid and then getting me to the hospital at a speed of roughly one hundred and ten miles an hour, over patched and bumpy back roads. 10

Fillebrown assures me that I'm more than welcome, then suggests that perhaps someone was watching out for me. "I've been doing this for twenty years," he tells me over the phone, "and when I saw the way you were lying in the ditch, plus the extent of the impact injuries, I didn't think you'd make it to the hospital. You're a lucky camper to still be with the program." 11

The extent of the impact injuries is such that the doctors at Northern Cumberland Hospital decide they cannot treat me there; someone summons a LifeFlight helicopter to take me to Central Maine Medical Center in Lewiston. At this point my wife, older son, and daughter arrive. The kids are allowed a brief visit; my wife is allowed to stay longer. The doctors have assured her that I'm banged up, but I'll make it. The lower half of my body has been covered. She isn't allowed to look at the interesting way my lap has shifted around to the right, but she is allowed to wash the blood off my face and pick some of the glass out of my hair. 12

There's a long gash in my scalp, the result of my collision with Bryan Smith's windshield. This impact came at a point less than two inches from the steel driver's-side support post. Had I struck that, I likely would have been killed or rendered permanently comatose, a vegetable with legs. Had I struck the rocks jutting out of the ground beyond the shoulder of Route 5, I likely also would have been killed or permanently paralyzed. I didn't hit them; I was thrown over the van and fourteen feet in the air, but landed just shy of the rocks. 13

"You must have pivoted to the left just a little at the last second," Dr. David Brown tells me later. "If you hadn't, we wouldn't be having this conversation." 14

The LifeFlight helicopter lands in the parking lot of Northern Cumberland Hospital, and I am wheeled out to it. The sky is very bright, very blue. The clatter of the helicopter's rotors is very loud. Someone shouts into my ear, "Ever been in a helicopter before, Stephen?" The speaker sounds jolly, all excited for me. I try to answer yes, I've been in a helicopter before—twice, in fact—but I can't. All at once it's very tough to breathe. 15

They load me into the helicopter. I can see one brilliant wedge of blue sky as we lift off; not a cloud in it. Beautiful. There are more 16 radio voices. This is my afternoon for hearing voices, it seems. Meanwhile, it's getting even harder to breathe. I gesture at someone, or try to, and a face bends upside down into my field of vision.

"Feel like I'm drowning," I whisper. 17

Somebody checks something, and someone else says, "His lung has collapsed." 18

There's a rattle of paper as something is unwrapped, and then the someone else speaks into my ear, loudly so as to be heard over the rotors. "We're going to put a chest tube in you, Stephen. You'll feel some pain, a little pinch. Hold on." 19

It's been my experience (learned when I was just a wee lad with infected ears) that if a medical person tells you you're going to feel a little pinch, they're going to hurt you really bad. This time it isn't as bad as I expected, perhaps because I'm full of painkiller, perhaps because I'm on the verge of passing out again. It's like being thumped very high up on the right side of the chest by someone holding a short sharp object. Then there's an alarming whistle in my chest, as if I've sprung a leak. In fact, I suppose I have. A moment later the soft in-out of normal respiration, which I've listened to my whole life (mostly without being aware of it, thank God), has been replaced by an unpleasant *shloop-shloop-shloop* sound. The air I'm taking in is very cold, but it's air, at least, *air,* and I keep breathing it. I don't want to die. I love my wife, my kids, my afternoon walks by the lake. I also love to write; I have a book on writing that's sitting back home on my desk, half-finished. I don't want to die, and as I lie in the helicopter looking out at the bright blue summer sky, I realize that I am actually lying in death's doorway. Someone is going to pull me one way or the other pretty soon; it's mostly out of my hands. All I can do is lie there, look at the sky, and listen to my thin, leaky breathing: *shloop-shloop-shloop.* 20

Ten minutes later we set down on the concrete landing pad at CMMC. To me, it seems to be at the bottom of a concrete well. The blue sky is blotted out and the *whap-whap-whap* of the helicopter rotors becomes magnified and echoey, like the clapping of giant hands. 21

Still breathing in great leaky gulps, I am lifted out of the helicopter. Someone bumps the stretcher and I scream. "Sorry, sorry, you're okay, Stephen," someone says—when you're badly hurt, everyone calls you by your first name, everyone is your pal. 22

"Tell Tabby I love her very much," I say as I am first lifted and then wheeled, very fast, down some sort of descending concrete walkway. All at once I feel like crying. 23

"You can tell her that yourself," the someone says. We go through a door; there is air-conditioning and lights flowing past overhead. Speakers issue pages. It occurs to me, in a muddled sort of way, that 24 an hour before I was taking a walk and planning to pick some berries in a field that overlooks Lake Kezar. I wouldn't pick for long, though; I'd have to be home by five-thirty because we were all going to the movies. *The General's Daughter,* starring John Travolta. Travolta was in the movie made out of *Carrie,* my first novel. He played the bad guy. That was a long time ago.

"When?" I ask. "When can I tell her?" 25

"Soon," the voice says, and then I pass out again. This time it's no 26
splice but a great big whack taken out of the memory-film; there are a few flashes, confused glimpses of faces and operating rooms and looming X-ray machinery; there are delusions and hallucinations fed by the morphine and Dilaudid being dripped into me; there are echoing voices and hands that reach down to paint my dry lips with swabs that taste of peppermint. Mostly, though, there is darkness.

Understanding the Significance

1. In the opening paragraph, King describes Bryan Smith, the man who hit King with his van. After hearing Smith speak, King notes that Smith could qualify as "a character right out of one of my own novels." What is he suggesting about Smith's character and behavior?
2. As King describes the various steps EMT Paul Fillebrown takes to treat him, he also explains that he still wears his original wedding ring. He notes that this ring cost a mere $8 "but it seems to have worked." What does he mean?
3. When he calls EMT Fillebrown some months after the accident, what does King learn about his state of health when Brown arrived on the scene?
4. Although King notes several reasons for wanting to live, what does he realize as he is being treated on the LifeFlight helicopter flying him for more specialized treatment?

Discovering the Writer's Purpose

1. In your view, what point is Stephen King making in this document about the nature of trauma? What material in the excerpt makes you come to this judgment?
2. In the tenth paragraph, King includes the average speed that the ambulance carrying him to the hospital traveled. Why do you think he included this detail?

3. King notes that his children and wife visit him before his flight, but he doesn't include the details of the conversation. Why do you think he made this decision? Do you agree with his choice? Explain your reasoning.
4. In the final three paragraphs, the discussion is far less coherent than in the rest of the excerpt, jumping quickly from one image to the next. By following this strategy, what is King suggesting about the effect of his injuries?

Examining the Writer's Method

1. What type of description dominates in King's piece, objective description or subjective description? Upon what do you base your reasoning?
2. In your view, which of the sensory details that King supplies does the best job of explaining what it is like to be badly injured? Why is it so effective?
3. Clearly, King's accident was truly horrific, yet King tells the story in a fairly matter-of-fact fashion. Why do you think he chose to follow this strategy? Do you agree? Why or why not?
4. In your view, is King's final paragraph an effective conclusion for the document? Explain your reasoning.

Considering Style and Language

1. How would you describe King's overall tone in this excerpt? In your view, does the tone match the seriousness of the incident he is describing?
2. King employs *onomatopoeia*—a figure of speech that uses words that captures the sound something makes—in two cases. The first describes what he could hear in his lungs (*shloop-shloop-shloop*) and the other captures the sound of the helicopter (*whap-whap-whap*). Why do you think he chose this means of expression?
3. Throughout the entire excerpt, King uses a number of direct quotations. Why do you think he chose to record the actual words he and other figures in the episode used rather than to rely on paraphrase? Do you agree with his decision? Explain your reasoning?
4. What do the following words mean in the context of the writing? *Commiseration* (para. 1); *wrenched* (para. 2); *noshes* (para. 3); *hammer* (para. 8); *garbled* (para. 10); *rendered, shy* (para. 13); *pivoted*

(para. 14); *gesture* (para. 16); *thumped, alarming* (para. 20; *whack, glimpses, looming, delusions* (para. 26)

Your Turn: Responding to the Subject

a. In the final paragraphs of this excerpt, King mentions that actor John Travolta played a supporting role in *Carrie,* a movie with a number of scary moments. For this assignment, think of a movie, television show, amusement park ride, and so on, that scared you, and write an essay in which you use description to capture what you felt.

b. If it were not for the quick and capable work of EMT Paul Fillebrown, Stephen King might have died. Most of us have witnessed the actions of an EMT, either as an unfortunate victim of an accident or as an involved or interested bystander to someone else's accident. For this assignment, focus on the situation involving EMT services that you experienced or witnessed and employ description to express this full sense of what you went through or saw.

Other Possibilities for Using Description

Here are some additional topics for a paper that features description. As you work through the writing process, adapt and develop the subject you choose in whatever way necessary to help you turn the general idea into an effective essay.

- Your earliest memory
- A normally busy place, now deserted
- A memorable sunrise or sunset you've witnessed
- Backstage during a play or performance
- An unusual person you've met
- What you see in a painting or photograph
- A family heirloom or antique
- An unusual room you've visited
- The scene at a concert or athletic event
- A physical injury or bout with illness
- A distinctive, renowned, or unique restaurant, deli, bakery, or bar

- An accident scene
- A special place—an amusement park, a zoo, a swimming area—that you remember from your childhood
- What you envision as you listen to a piece of music
- The feeling of being alone

Writing at Work

DESCRIPTION

THE DREAM TEAM CHILDREN'S CHARITY
Press Release: Too Many Cooks?

Bringing a situation, scene, or individual into focus is a primary requisite for much real-world writing. And when such focus is called for, it is description that helps to provide it. Description plays a major role in the product specifications included in a computer manual. Description is also central in a nurse's notes detailing a patient's condition and in an environmental group's newsletter concerning the opening of a newly developed hiking trail. The following piece, a press release from a charitable organization about an upcoming fund-raising event, is another example of the part description plays in the writing we encounter on a day-to-day basis. Here description captures some of the sights, tastes, and aromas that will mark the event with the hope of motivating people to attend and make financial donations.

Focusing on the Message and Aim

Answer each of the following questions in a brief paragraph, referring specifically to the press release on the opposite page.

1. This document contains a number of passages of subjective description. Which of these sections do you think is most effective? Why?
2. Why do you think the writer chose to present some of the information, including some of the description, in the form of direct quotation? Do you agree with this choice? Explain your reasoning.
3. The goal of this press release is to encourage people to make donations. In your judgment, does the document fulfill this aim? What leads you to this conclusion?

The Dream Team Children's Charity, Inc.

177 Forster Drive East
Springfield, IN 54354-0342

Tel. 888 976-2948
Fax 888 976-2944

www.DREAMCHILD.org

For Immediate Release

For more information, contact Laura Fleming, 888 976-2949
lfleming@DREAMCHILD.org

Too Many Cooks? Not When It Comes to Children's Charity

Springfield, IN—On Friday, May 11, chefs and their staffs from ten of Springfield's top restaurants will meet at the Meredith Convention Center for a noontime cook-off. For a donation of $15, patrons will be treated to a gourmet luncheon. A panel of local officials, including Channel 3 anchor Palmer Layton, Mayor Christine Lee, and members of the popular band Newtonia, will taste the specialty meals—tender, succulent Chicken Marsala to fiery Vindaloo curry to tangy Cajun jambalaya, and many other delicious dishes—and then name the Cook-Off Champion. All proceeds will go to the Dream Team Children's Charity, Inc., a fund that provides financial support for seriously ill children and their families.

Antonia Freido, Executive Director of Dream Team, says that she came up with the idea after seeing the popular *Iron Chefs* program on the Food Channel. "I thought to myself, why can't we do something like that here? We have such terrific restaurants in town. Just think of The Factory, an old rehabbed mill building with a huge piece of machinery full of shiny gears—now it's a four-star restaurant with a nationally known chef. The sweet aroma of garlic cooking throughout that building is heavenly. So why not have all these great restaurants compete in fun and raise some money at the same time?" She made a few phone calls, and within an hour, ten chefs had agreed to participate.

Ticket sales so far have been excellent, Ms. Freido reports, with the first seating already sold out and nearly two-thirds of the second seating taken. A number of Springfield companies have made additional financial donations, which has her brimming with hope. "With a little luck, we'll exceed our first-year goal of raising $50,000."

Applying the Principles

a. You have recently joined **Gourmet to Go**, located at 30 New Park Street in your city. This new company, set to open in two weeks, specializes in meals to go that can be frozen for later use. The twist here is that the meals are gourmet delights, prepared by the customers themselves with the help of an award-winning chef with over 15 years' experience preparing meals at five-star restaurants in New York, Chicago, and New Orleans. The typical meal costs about half of what the same dish would cost in a restaurant, and clients have the fun of a night out during which they prepare a great meal to be enjoyed at some future time and learn a trick or two about cooking. Since communications is one of your new job duties, you have been selected to prepare a press release to be sent to area newspapers, announcing the grand opening of Gourmet to Go. Using the press release about the cook-off as a guide in terms of focus and length, prepare a document that introduces the public to this innovative company.

b. Think of a restaurant that you have patronized recently and imagine that you have been asked to write a restaurant review that considers food, service, facilities, atmosphere, and so on. Take another look at the way description is used in the press release about the cook-off and then prepare a review of about 300 words.

Practical Application: Description

A month ago you became an intern at Fine, Howard, and Fine, a small advertising and marketing firm. Your first two weeks on the job were a blur as you tried to learn as much as you could about the advertising business. It's a good thing that you have paid close attention, because your supervisor has just pulled you aside to give you your first real assignment: to help develop the copy for the advertising campaign of Diego Valdez House, the region's fastest growing chain of gourmet coffee bars.

Mr. Maxwell Folger, CEO of Diego Valdez House, Inc., was impressed with the successful advertising campaign that Timothy Matos of Fine, Howard, and Fine had developed for Azores Resorts, and he has provided a copy of the successful print advertisement than ran in several travel magazines and newspapers last year. Your supervisor has asked you to develop a statement of approximately 300 words that captures the aroma and atmosphere of a Diego Valdez House coffee bar, much as Matos had captured the sense of the Azorean Island resort. Use Matos's copy as a model in terms of approach and format.

Your Azorean Getaway

The Ponta Delgada Island Resort is a quaint white-washed Iberian-style hotel located on the lush island of São Miguel. The brisk mornings are pleasantly spent enjoying a cup of freshly ground coffee on your warm sunbathed beach-side verandah. As you bask in the salty-sweet smell of an Atlantic breeze, the haunting melodies of the Fado, the traditional Portuguese folk music, pull your attention from the hypnotic murmur of the sea to a distant vision of the countryside. In the songs, the tormented wails of an unseen voice sound out loud the quiet desperation of the people, the Açorianos.

Our tour guides will show you the lamented places described in these songs, the sights of love gone astray. The boiling crystal-clear waters of Furnas, the blue and green lagoons of Sete Cidades, and the daunting heights of Pico de Vara exist, it seems, simply to provide the perfect setting for drama and romance of the highest order.

Yet this is only half of what the island has to offer, for hidden in the vast canopy of greenery are tiny villages, each with its own unique flavor. There you can sample rich cheeses, bold homemade wines, and the famous cozido (meat and vegetables boiled on the volcanic earth). The savory smell of the boiling meats is so intense that it even overwhelms the primeval incense of volcanic sulfur.

Finally, as the mild evening sun sets into the ocean, the cobblestone streets of the charming little city lead you back to the coastline. Your long day ends in a walk along black sand beaches that seem almost to vanish in the total darkness. Sometimes, it feels as if you will, too.

7

Example

The Technique

As might be expected, *example* is frequently used as a supporting technique in writing. In an essay against capital punishment, for instance, providing cases of innocent individuals who were wrongfully executed would clearly reinforce the point that with capital punishment, mistakes cannot be rectified. In some cases, though, an assignment—a paper about the difficulties involved in hunting for a job—will call for example to be the dominant mode.

Whether example is a supporting mode or the dominant technique, you need to

- use specific examples;
- provide relevant examples;
- include multiple and varied examples to make your point; and
- provide an effective arrangement.

SPECIFIC EXAMPLES

In order to make the assertions you include in your writing convincing and your explanations clear, you must anticipate the reader's needs and supply specific supporting examples to address them. Specific examples provide concrete and detailed answers to the key questions: *who, what, when, where, why,* and *how.* This brief excerpt from *Noodling for Flatheads: Moonshine, Monster Catfish, and Other Southern Comforts* illustrates the practice of moonshining—illegal liquor production—in the American South. It provides highly specific examples to support the assertion that many moonshiners have had to "modernize their methods" to avoid arrest:

> When helicopters began to scan the forest, moonshiners camouflaged their stills with maple-leaf stencils. When motorboats puttered down streams in search of wood fires and exposed water pumps, moonshiners switched to propane and submersible pumps. When agents prowled the woods with infrared scopes, night-vision goggles, and motion-detecting cameras, moonshiners got the same equipment.
>
> These days the biggest stills have moved indoors—whether in tobacco barns, chicken houses, or purpose-built structures—where water and heat are easy to come by. They're often hidden underground or behind false walls. And they may pump their liquor to a separate, inconspicuous building for loading. (A few years ago a still in northern Georgia was found in a basement, at the bottom of a hidden staircase. When you turned on the tap upstairs, moonshine came out.)

RELEVANT EXAMPLES

Relevant examples closely represent and relate to your subject and aim. To ensure that your examples are relevant, you must keep your focus narrow. In an essay about the federal government's efforts to reduce water pollution, for example, you would certainly want to discuss how cities and towns must now upgrade sewer systems and treatment plants to block any raw wastewater from entering waterways. Because it is directly related to the changes mandated by the federal government, discussion of the expense of such measures—$150 million or more in order for some older cities to comply—would definitely be relevant.

At the same time, be sure to rely on commonplace, easily understood examples, and always avoid disingenuous or atypical ones. Certainly you could come up with at least one example to support any wild assertion ("My girlfriend once got into a car accident, so all women must be bad drivers"), but doing so wouldn't be convincing or ethical.

Consider this paragraph from *No Foreign Food: The American Diet in Time and Place,* which carefully underscores the relevance of each example to the concept that people often closely associate food with tradition and comfort:

> Because we eat for many reasons other than fueling the body, the selection of foods, their times of consumption, and the combinations in which they are consumed reflect tradition as much as need and availability. This can most easily be seen in times of stress, when all of us tend to return to our own particular comfort foods. The military, for example, attempts to provide a "traditional" Thanksgiving meal to troops in the field in order to raise morale . . . The corollary among travelers to other countries is the search for hamburgers, french fries, and pizza even if those foods are not frequently consumed by them at home. The comfort provided by familiar foods somehow makes it easier for them to cope with sometimes overwhelmingly unfamiliar places. Conversely, foreign locals patronize expatriate American restaurants in the belief that the cachet of a Big Mac will somehow make them more akin to America and Americans. The concepts of inertia, or tradition, and comfort are immutably linked.

MULTIPLE AND VARIED EXAMPLES

As pages 24–25 show, an essay that paints a full picture for a reader is one that is fully developed or amplified. A series of short examples can often powerfully illustrate a single concept or assertion, and extended examples, whether in the form of anecdotes, case studies, or other scenarios can add to the depth of your presentation, making it that much more likely that your reader will understand and accept your overall point.

In addition, the presence of examples from several different sources—your own experiences, the experiences of others, the viewpoints of experts, data and statistics—demonstrates that you have put time and thought into the issues you discuss. And, from a practical standpoint, if one kind of example fails to elucidate or convince, another kind may still do it.

This passage from a book called *Delicate Threads* puts forth the idea that befriending children with special needs can be beneficial to students without disabilities. It offers examples of four different types of benefits to the nondisabled students to demonstrate to the audience that these friendships are indeed special and life affirming:

> Charles Peck, Jodi Donaldson, and Michelle Pezzoli (1990) reported . . . [many benefits] . . . following interviews with high-school aged students who had developed personal relationships with students with severe disabilities. . . . First, many of the students made com-

ments indicating growth in their understanding and appreciation of their personal characterizations. The researchers called this category "self-concept." Responses found in this category included, "I feel good about myself," and "I learned who I was." The second type of benefit found was titled "social cognition," and referred to students' increased understanding of the feelings underlying the behavior of their schoolmates with disabilities (e.g., "they have feelings, too, and they need to have the same things we do") and of human differences (e.g., "he was coming from a completely different world, which was good, because I learned a lot and he learned a lot"). The third and fourth types of benefits found were reduced fear of human differences (e.g., "you get to meet a whole range of people—so you're not afraid of the unknown anymore") and tolerance of other people (e.g., "I've treated my own friends better . . . I haven't been as cold to people").

AN EFFECTIVE ARRANGEMENT

As with all essays, how the material in an example essay is presented is important. Sometimes you will write an essay focusing on a single episode or experience as an example, using chronological order as the method of arrangement. Occasionally, your essay will be composed of multiple examples, each having about the same degree of impact, so the order of arrangement is less of a concern. In other cases, however, some of the examples are more striking or powerful than others. As page 27 illustrates, *emphatic order,* in which you build up to your strongest example, is the most effective way to arrange such a paper.

Consider an essay discussing situations in which dishonesty is justified. In such a paper, emphatic order would ensure that the main point is most effectively supported. For instance, showing enthusiasm for a gift you don't actually like would be a strong example, and pretending not to hear someone's off-color language would be a stronger one. Stealing to save someone from starvation would clearly be the strongest example of all, however, since it deals with life and death. Saving it for last allows the paper to build in intensity and thus maintain the reader's interest.

Here is a brief excerpt from a psychology text written by Carol Tarvis and Carole Wade, in which they use emphatic order to present different interpretations of common hand gestures:

> Even the simplest gesture is subject to misunderstanding and offense. The sign of the University of Texas football team, the

Longhorns, is to extend the index finger and the pinkie. In Italy and other parts of Europe this gesture means a man's wife has been unfaithful to him—a serious insult! Anita Rowe, a consultant who advises businesses on cross-cultural customs, tells of a newly hired Asian engineer in a California company. As the man left his office to lead the first meeting of his project team, his secretary crossed her fingers to wish him luck. Instead of reassuring him, her gesture thoroughly confused him: In his home country, crossing one's fingers is a sexual proposition.

CHECKLIST FOR USING EXAMPLE

1. Are the examples used **specific**, providing concrete, specific illustrations that tell *who, what, when, where, why,* or *how* to support the aim of the document?
2. Are the examples **relevant**—that is, the most representative of and closely related to the subject and purpose?
3. Have **multiple examples** of the subject under discussion been supplied to illustrate and substantiate the point being made?
4. Are the examples drawn from a **variety of sources**—for instance, from your own experience, the experiences of others, from experts, and so on—in order to portray the subject accurately and fulfill the purpose of the document?
5. Are the examples **effectively arranged** so that they have the most impact?

AN ANNOTATED EXAMPLE

STEVEN PINKER

Horton Heared a Who

Steven Pinker is currently Professor of Psychology in the Department of Brain and Cognitive Sciences at the Massachusetts Institute of Technology, where he is also Director of the Center for Cognitive Neuroscience. A graduate of McGill University in his native Canada, he earned his Ph.D. in psychology from Harvard. Since joining the faculty at MIT, he has been cited for outstanding undergraduate and graduate teaching. His writings have frequently appeared in a number of publications, including The New Yorker, Time, Slate, *and* The New York Times. *Pinker is also the author of several books, including* Language Learnability and Language Development *(1984),* How the Mind Works *(1997), and* Words and Rules: The Ingredients of Language *(1999), from which this writing has been adapted. In this piece, Pinker relies on example to provide a thorough explanation of the way English has evolved.*

With something as complex as the English language, how do people ever learn to use words according to the commonly accepted rules?

He provides several examples to illustrate the point he makes at the end of his introduction.

1 Kids say the darndest things. "We holded the baby rabbits." "The alligator goed kerplunk." "Horton heared a Who!" These lapses, you might dimly recall, have something to do with irregular verbs. But please don't stop reading just yet. Children's errors are not just anecdotes for grandparents or reminders of long-forgotten grammar lessons. They're windows into the workings of language, history and the human mind.

He supplies several examples of regular verbs.

2 Verbs in English come in two flavors. Regular verbs like *walk* and *smell* form the past tense by adding *-ed:* Today I walk, yesterday I walked. English has thousands of them, and new ones arise every day, thanks to our ability to apply rules instinctively. When people first heard *to spam, to mosh* and *to diss,* they did not run to the dictionary to look up the past tenses; they knew they were *spammed, moshed* and *dissed*.

He presents several examples of irregular verbs.

3 Even children do it. Told that a man likes to *wug,* they will say yesterday he *wugged*. Children are not sponges; they're constantly creating sentences and words, never more clearly or charmingly than when they encounter the second flavor of verb, the quirky irregulars. The past tense of *spring* is *sprang,* but the past of *cling* is not *clang* but *clung,* and the past of *bring* is neither *brang* nor *brung* but *brought.* English has 180 irregulars, a ragtag list that kids simply must memorize.

But when an irregular word is still fresh in the mind, it is fragile. If a child's memory cannot cough up *held* quickly enough, he or she adds *-ed* by default and says *holded* instead. 4

He offers several illustrations of how people process language.

Irregular and regular verbs embody the two underlying tricks behind the gift of articulate speech: words and rules. A word is a memorized link between a sound and a meaning. The word *duck* does not look, walk or quack like a duck. But we can use it to convey the idea of a duck because we all once learned to connect the sound with the idea. 5

We also combine words into bigger words and sentences, using the second trick of language, rules. Journalists say that when a dog bites a man, that isn't news but when a man bites a dog, it is. Rules let us convey news by reshuffling words. 6

He presents examples of various languages that developed from Indo-European.

Regular and irregular verbs today have their roots in old border disputes between words and rules. Many irregulars can be traced back over 5,500 years to a mysterious tribe that came to dominate Europe, western Asia and northern India. Its language, Indo-European, is the ancestor of Hindi, Persian, Russian, Greek, Latin, Gaelic and English. It had rules that replaced vowels: the past of *senkw-* (*sink*) was *sonkw-*. 7

Language as it evolves is like the game of Broken Telephone, in which a whispered phrase gets increasingly distorted as it passes from lip to ear. Eventually speakers no longer discern the rule behind a motley set of mangled verbs. They just memorize them as a list, as do subsequent generations. These are the irregulars, the fossils of dead rules. 8

He offers examples from older forms of English to illustrate his point.

The irregulars are vulnerable too because they depend on fallible memory. If a verb declines in popularity, speakers may not hear its irregular form often enough to fix it securely in memory. They fall back on *-ed,* changing the language for following generations. That is why forms from Chaucer's time such as *chide–chid* and *writhe–wrothe* turned into *chided* and *writhed*. 9

You can feel that force of history acting today. *Smote, slew, throve* and *forsook* sound odd, and few people use them. In a century, they'll probably go the way of *chid* and *wrothe.* 10

Do irregular and regular verbs really come out of a dictionary in one part of the brain and a grammar in another? Perhaps. Neuroimaging techniques suggest that regular and irregular forms may trigger signals in different parts of the brain. Some neurological patients seem to have damaged dictionaries: they strain to retrieve words but speak in fluent sentences; like children, they say *heared* and *holded.* 11

He uses the conclusion to reemphasize his point about irregular verbs and their effect on how the human mind deals with language.

Why pay so much attention to the lowly irregular verb? I see these studies as part of a trend that biologist E. O. Wilson calls "consilience": the bridging of science and humanities through an understanding of how the mind works. A slip of the child's tongue may link the migrations of great prehistoric tribes to the brain-imaging technologies of the next millennium. 12

Your Turn: Responding to the Subject

a. In paragraph 8, Pinker makes the following statement: "Language as it evolves is like the game of Broken Telephone, in which a whispered phrase gets increasingly distorted as it passes from lip to ear." What Pinker says about language is true of communication in general—that the meaning of what we say often becomes twisted as it passes from one person to another. For this assignment, focus on situations in which others interpreted differently the intent of what someone said.

b. One interesting part of communication is the wide variety of accents that English-speaking people from across the U.S. have. In many cases, people who live only a few towns away from each other are clearly distinguishable from each other by the ways they speak and the expressions they use. For this assignment, concentrate on some of the different ways you have heard people "say" English.

BERNICE KANNER

The Nose Knows After All

Close your eyes and inhale: What is it? Is it food cooking? Flowers blooming? Garbage fermenting? Whether the aromas are pleasant or withering, they fill up a huge part of our consciousness. And our sense of smell is far stronger than most of us realize. According to some experts, the memories that last the longest are those that result from odor. So it should come as no surprise that business and industry would try to find a way to take full advantage of this sensation. In the following essay, Bernice Kanner turns to example to make her reader see how organizations are using odors to add a new dimension to the work- and marketplace.

In what ways do the distinctive odors and aromas that surround us affect us?

Marketers have long known that customers browse longer and buy more in shops with floral fragrance, and that supermarkets whose bakeries emit the scent of fresh-baked bread sell more of everything. 1

The smell of peppermint is known to stimulate, lavender to relax and citrus to uplift. Nowadays, casinos are playing a good bet by piping in not only oxygen to keep gamblers awake, but also a whiff of peppermint and vanilla to keep them enthralled. Their chips have come in: Slot machine play is up. 2

Smell is the most evocative of the senses and until recently, the least utilized. Years ago Vance Packard, author of "The Hidden Persuaders," the most famous book about marketing hijinks in history, would have decried using the old schnoz as a malicious mind game, subliminal weaponry that posed a threat more dire than the Evil Empire. 3

Today, we accept being led by the nose as the common course, as prevalent and unnoticed as acid rain. 4

Researchers at the University of Liverpool recently discovered that scents such as those of ink, cheese, fruit and wine elicit far more detailed memories than do words or pictures. 5

British Airways injects the subtle scent of new-mown grass into passenger lounges at its terminals, so as to bring the outside inside to frazzled and cynical flyers. 6

Luxury automaker Rolls-Royce has taken the scent-sational step of treating its new cars with a chemical solution that mimics the 7 scent of its illustrious 1965 Silver Cloud—the new-car smell isn't what its caliber of buyer wants. The vintage model smell suggests the automaker hasn't replaced much of the wood once used in the cars' interiors with molded plastic.

However, acknowledging the regional preferences of smell, automakers in Japan try to eliminate the smell of fine leather interiors because many Japanese people dislike the smell of leather. *8*

"Odors alter brain wave activity and produce emotional responses that can influence us positively or negatively," says Sarah Harrop, director of the Aroma Co. in the United Kingdom, which scents the British Airways lounges. Scents can do more than put shoppers in the mood to buy. They can increase brand value by creating a more pleasant environment. *9*

Indeed, a study by the Smell & Taste Treatment and Research Foundation in Chicago determined scent can often mean the difference between a browser and a buyer. *10*

Eighty-four percent of consumers [were] asked to rate two identical pairs of Nike sneakers—one showcased in an unscented room and the other in a room that had been sprayed with floral scent. They claimed that the sneakers in the scented room were superior to the others. *11*

They even admitted they would be willing to pay $10 more for the sneakers that didn't smell like, well, sneakers. *12*

Annette Green, president of the New York–based Fragrance Foundation and Olfactory Research Fund, says marketers now recognize the nose can improve our whole quality of life and are learning to use scents in very innovative ways. *13*

Automakers, for example, are testing the power of scents to prevent road rage and perk up weary drivers. Other companies are investigating behavioral aromatherapy to calm stressed workers. *14*

In New Zealand and Europe, companies have trademarked product scents and even sued makers of smell-alikes. *15*

There's even talk down the road of tampering with the human genome to alter our natural aromas genetically, so that we'll be able to smell younger, fresher or sexier naturally. *16*

Perhaps sooner than that, scents will emerge from the Web. DigiScents, of California Technologies, has created the iSmell device. This device plugs into a computer and offers 128 basic smells, intact or blended, and wafted through via fan. *17*

DigiScents plans to begin marketing this device to consumers soon, and has signed a deal with Procter & Gamble to scent its site. Cyrano Sciences, also based in California, is marketing a similar "portable nose" to the food industry. *18*

Something else to sniff out: personalized scents. The latest status symbol is a unique signature fragrance, instead of a designer brand *19* found in department stores. At the Paris-based House of Creed, perfumers customize fragrances after in-person consultations about one's lifestyle. The deal is that Creed won't sell that scent to anyone else for five years.

But not everyone is sniffing pretty. Anti-fragrance activists in 20
North America are irked by what they call the invasiveness of secondhand scents and are moving to limit their use, claiming they threaten sufferers of asthma, allergies and chemical sensitivities.

Some institutions such as the University of Minnesota's School of 21
Social Work and Denver's National Jewish Medical and Research Center have declared themselves fragrance-free. In Halifax, Nova Scotia, every public building and many private businesses have voluntarily gone fragrance-free.

Understanding the Significance

1. In what ways has the gambling industry embraced the idea that what we breathe affects our behavior?
2. Kanner states in the fourth paragraph that the public is willingly "led by the nose," that the use of fragrances is now "as prevalent and unnoticed as acid rain." What point is she making about how people today react to attempts by business and government to manipulate their attitudes and feelings?
3. Why do the makers of Rolls-Royce automobiles add a scent that replaces what is often referred to as "new-car smell"?
4. What do scientists investigating odors hope that future manipulation of the human genome will make possible some day?

Discovering the Writer's Purpose

1. Kanner opens her essay with two specific examples involving scents. Why do you think she chose these particular examples?
2. Both paragraphs 9 and 14 provide the names and affiliations of people commenting on the power of fragrance. What is the significance of this information? What would the effect have been if these details had not been included?
3. In paragraphs 11 and 12, Kanner discusses surveys involving sneakers. As you see it, what does this example indicate about our reaction to the odor associated with some common items?

4. By including the example about plans to use the Internet to deliver scents, what is Kanner implying about how widespread the use of aromas may be in the future?

Examining the Writer's Method

1. In your view, are the examples Kanner includes sufficiently specific and relevant? Explain your reasoning.
2. In the ninth paragraph Kanner includes a single direct quotation. Why, do you think, does she use Ms. Harrop's actual words rather than rely on paraphrase as she does with the other examples? Do you agree with strategy? Why or why not?
3. In paragraph 21, Kanner notes that activists opposed to the use of scents at work or in public areas object to its "invasiveness." What does this word suggest about aromas? How does this connotation contribute to the point Kanner is making about this innovation?
4. An overwhelming number of examples that Kanner supplies are positive. Why do you think she chose to keep most of the examples that show the downside of aromas until the final two paragraphs? How would her essay have been different if she had begun it with these examples?

Considering Style and Language

1. At times the tone in this piece is light-hearted while at others it is far more serious. What does this shift suggest to you about the subject of the increasing use of aromas?
2. The paragraphs about the experiment involving the reaction to two pairs of Nike sneakers include specific percentages and monetary amounts. Why do you think Kanner chose to include these specific details rather than discuss the experiment in more general detail?
3. Now that you've read through her essay, what would you say Kanner's attitude is about the matter of scents and their effects on us? What details or examples make you think so? Why?
4. What do the following words mean in the context of the writing? *Browse* (para. 1); *stimulate, uplift, enthralled* (para. 2); *evocative, hijinks, malicious, subliminal* (para. 3); *prevalent* (para. 4); *elicit* (para. 5); *frazzled, cynical* (para. 6); *mimic, illustrious, caliber, vintage* (para.

7); *olfactory, innovative* (para. 13); *perk, aromatherapy* (para. 14); *tampering, genome, genetically* (para. 16); *wafted* (para. 17); *signature* (para. 19); *activist, irked, invasiveness* (para. 20).

Your Turn: Responding to the Subject

a. In her essay, Kanner focuses on a number of ways that companies have focused on aromas and fragrance to help sell their products. For this assignment, think of other techniques that marketers use to convince people to buy. Identify at least four and then turn to example to explain these different marketing strategies.

b. Kanner opens her essay with two examples—floral fragrances and fresh-baked bread—with such positive impressions that people purchase more when they encounter them. In your life, what aromas or fragrances rank as the most pleasant and positive you have experienced? For this assignment, focus on at least four of these scents and explain the power they have over you.

STEVEN DOLOFF

Let's Offer a Good Word on Politics

Steven Doloff is Professor of English and Humanities at Pratt Institute in New York City. His essays on culture and education have appeared in a number of publications including the New York Times, *the* Philadelphia Inquirer, *the* Boston Globe, *the* Chicago Sun-Times, *and the* Chronicle of Higher Education. *In this essay, which was originally published in* Newsday, *Doloff offers a pointed commentary on how those in positions of power often deliberately say one thing while they mean something quite different. Specifically, he identifies a number of particularly flagrant examples, and, in the tradition of rhetoricians and philosophers of the past, he labels and explains them. The result is a biting warning to listen very carefully to what our leaders tell us, since it might not be the same thing as the truth.*

When it comes to some people in power, what different verbal techniques do they employ so that they won't be inconvenienced by concerns of ethics or honesty?

The 19th-century German philosopher Arthur Schopenhauer once suggested that "it would be a very good thing if each trick could receive some short and obviously appropriate name, so that when a man used this or that particular trick, he could at once be reproved for it." 1

Actually, long before Schopenhauer, classical Roman rhetoricians had done just that, coining names for devious political debating tactics such as *argumentum ad hominem* ("arguing against the person"), attacking an opponent's character instead of addressing the issue at hand; and *petitio principii* ("begging the question"), posing a question that assumes an unproved point. 2

Unfortunately, these classical terms for oratorical flimflam are familiar today only to academics and a few professional writers. And, even more unfortunately, modern public officials find new scams to add to their bag of traditional verbal tricks. Clearly, we could use some simple and convenient Americanisms to quickly identify and denounce contemporary political humbug. Here are some: 3

Redlegging: When an incumbent (or his/her spokesperson) implies or outright declares political critics of his/her policies are unpatriotic. 4

5 Sitting on one's hat: When a public figure emphatically denies he/she intends to enter a particular political race (until it looks like there's a reasonable chance to win).

6 Pixelating: Staging media photo opportunities that frame politicians with emotionally evocative scenery (flags, aircraft carriers, Mt. Rushmore, etc.).

7 Chickenwinging: When a politician deliberately understates or waffles on his opposition to an incumbent's policy (because it would entail voicing a politically unpopular, if valid, criticism) until it is strategically safe (or advantageous) to be blunt.

8 Shroud waving: When a politician evokes the memory of a national tragedy as a means of eliciting emotional receptivity for an unrelated policy or proposal.

9 Calling a club a spade: When a politician sanctimoniously calls attention to his/her own moral backbone for voicing some unpopular truth while actually misrepresenting or distorting that truth.

10 Sheep shifting: When a politician retroactively revises the rationale for a policy (like, say, a popular military action) because ongoing events belie that rationale and suggest instead unstated, more controversial (or lupine) motives for the policy.

11 Barber polling: When a politician carefully shapes (shaves?) his positions on issues so as to smoothly wrap them around public opinion polls.

12 Gilding the lemon: When a politician redoubles the defense of a failing policy because the wonks can't figure out a way for him/her to withdraw gracefully from it.

13 Opening out of town: When a Hollywood celebrity starts a media circus by getting himself elected to public office in order to guarantee maximum box office for his next picture, or second term (whichever comes first).

14 What are the chances that the common use of such new terms will cast fear into the hearts of devious public officials and chasten the rhetoric of future political contests? Zip. Let's not flimflam ourselves.

15 But it just might be worth our while to be able to call the good plays from the bad as we watch these contests, and know when to boo.

Understanding the Significance

1. Doloff opens his essay with a statement by German philosopher Arthur Schopenhauer. Why does Schopenhauer advise coming up with names for the deceitful and dishonest ways that some people behave?

2. What is Doloff's concern about argumentum ad hominem, begging the question, and other behaviors that the ancient Greeks and Romans identified and labeled?
3. In the body of his essay, Doloff presents a list of terms, each consisting of a title and an explanation. In your view, which title most accurately and closely matches its description? Explain your reasoning.
4. What value does Doloff see in being able to identify these behaviors by name?

Discovering the Writer's Purpose

1. How does the statement by Schopenhauer in the opening paragraph help to prepare the reader for Doloff's main point?
2. In the second paragraph, Doloff introduces and explains two of what today are often referred to as logical fallacies: argumentum ad hominem and begging the question. (See page 313 for a more complete explanation.) Why do you think Doloff includes these two fallacies if he doesn't discuss them any further?
3. In your view, has Doloff listed his examples in emphatic order or are the examples more or less equal in terms of significance? What makes you think so?
4. In what way does Doloff's conclusion reinforce the main point he raises in his introduction?

Examining the Writer's Method

1. Why do you think Doloff included a direct quotation in his opening paragraph rather than simply paraphrasing what Schopenhaer had said? Do you agree with his choice? Why or why not?
2. Which of Doloff's examples is the most specific and relevant? Explain your reasoning.
3. This essay originally appeared in *Newsday,* a daily newspaper with wide readership. In your view, has Doloff made his examples accessible to the wide variety of readers that read a typical newspaper? What about the examples leads you to this conclusion?
4. In the next to last paragraph, Doloff employs a variation of a rhetorical question, followed by a single word: "Zip." Why do you

think he followed this strategy rather than present the information in simple statement form?

Considering Style and Language

1. In this essay, Doloff relies a great deal on connotation to make his attitude about these offenses clear. Pick the three words from the essay that you think express Doloff's overall attitude, and explain your choices.
2. Doloff structures each of his examples the same way, a title followed by a fragment. Why do you think he followed this pattern rather than present them in complete sentence form? Do you agree with his choice? Why or why not?
3. In several spots, Doloff's writing is tongue in cheek, that is, deliberately ironic or facetious for humorous effect. Where do you find this humor most effective in his essay? What makes this particular element stand out among the rest?
4. What do the following words mean in the context of the writing? *Appropriate, reproved* (para. 1); *classical, coining, devious, tactics* (para. 2); *oratorical, flimflam, scam, denounce, humbug* (para. 3); *incumbent* (para. 4); *evocative* (para. 6); *waffle, entail* (para. 7); *shroud, evoke, elicit* (para. 8); *sanctimoniously* (para. 9); *retroactively, rationale* (para. 10); *wonks* (para. 12); *devious, chasten* (para. 14); *while* (para. 15).

Your Turn: Responding to the Subject

a. Doloff focuses on the different ways that politicians and public officials twist language to draw attention away from their actual views or behavior or to mislead the public. But it's not just in public life and politics that people manipulate the truth for their own purposes. For this assignment, think of another setting, the workplace, the dating scene, the classroom, and so on, in which people occasionally fail to be truthful and straightforward. Then, as Doloff has done, identify at least five deceptive behaviors, and write an essay in which you name and explain them.

b. In the third paragraph, Doloff uses the term *Americanisms* to refer to modern-day manipulations on the part of U.S. politicians and public officials. But in a broader sense, Americanisms could refer to any behaviors, qualities, habits, and so on that are uniquely or peculiarly the territory of people living in the United States. For this assignment, identify at least four examples of characteristics or beliefs that typify or mark U.S. residents. Then turn to the power of example to write an essay in which you explain these Americanisms to your reader.

BOB KERR

The Best Story Turned Out to Be No Story at All

As a newspaper reporter for more than thirty years, Bob Kerr clearly knows how to record a scene accurately. But, as Kerr found out while serving as a Marine Corps combat correspondent during the Vietnam War, recording the scene accurately doesn't always guarantee that the article will appear in print, especially when the scene recorded runs contrary to the way the military would like it to have run. Besides focusing on this particular example, however, Kerr, who for close to fifteen years has served as a featured columnist for the Providence Journal, *also includes a series of additional examples to illustrate a simple fact: For many, the Vietnam experience provided more than just the absolute horror of war; there were moments of beauty, of absurdity, of humanity.*

What would cause a combat correspondent's superiors to reject a story that favorably presented an episode involving two Marines who had taken an enemy soldier prisoner?

The man was a North Vietnamese soldier. He sat on a pile of ammunition crates on a brutal day in September of 1968, an enigmatic smile playing across his face as he waited to be taken away. He seemed to be wondering if he had done the right thing. 1

He was the centerpiece of the best war story I was ever a part of. I was a Marine combat correspondent. As much as anyone, that man summed up the experience of reporting on Vietnam while having to ignore its casualties. 2

I have written about him before, and on this quarter-century anniversary of the dreary, defeated end of the war, he seems the most enduring image to pull from that incredible jumble of images that make up the Vietnam scrapbook. He came to stand for the separate truth we were often issued, along with the salt tablets and bush hats. 3

They revisit us now and then, these people who were part of a time when we were taken as far from old comforts and beliefs as we could ever get. A smell, a sound, a passing face or stupid comment can be enough to connect us to a small but lasting piece of ourselves. 4

Sometimes, there is a feeling that we should make it all mean 5
something—find out the role Vietnam plays in making us the people we've become. But most of the time, I think, there is a simple gratitude that we were able to survive the great adventure of our generation, hold on to the memories, and enjoy that slightly crazy edge we've all been granted by historians, moviemakers, and standup comics.

The memories are dark and cruel, funny and drunken. I was given 6
a wonderful window on Vietnam when the Marine Corps made me a combat correspondent and allowed me to move about with a freedom some generals didn't enjoy. I was able to stop and watch and listen sometimes.

Every Christmas now, somewhere in the giving frenzy, I think 7
about the beautiful little girl in Cam Lo village, near Quang Tri. She had great big eyes and a joyous laugh, and we couldn't help watching her as she waited by the side of a Marine truck for her turn to reach up and receive one of the brightly wrapped packages sent by Americans to children in Vietnam. She carried her package to the shade of a tree, tore it open, and took out . . . a pair of white figure skates. She held them up, clearly mystified by the metal blades stuck to what appeared a perfectly good pair of shoes. She dragged them along the dirt street. A Navy corpsman who was treating villagers in a makeshift clinic looked over and said, "Don't those bozos back in the world know anything about this place?"

In a Montagnard village, where a Marine sergeant was living and 8
working with the villagers, we sat in a low-roofed hut around the body of a man who had died after a long life and before the war had reached him. Rice wine was passed in small shells as the men of the village talked in low voices. I wasn't sure if we Marines were welcome there, or merely tolerated. There was always in Vietnam the question of whether a deep distrust or hatred of Americans was hidden behind a forced show of friendship.

On a fire-support base in I Corps, the northernmost section of 9
South Vietnam, Viet Cong sappers worked their way through perimeter wire at night by flashing tiny flashlights on and off, to blend in with the ever-present fireflies. They moved from bunker to bunker, throwing in satchel charges. The next morning, we carried a body onto a relief helicopter. It had no face and was being taken back for dental identification. As we rode away, the people lined up along the sides of the helicopter studiously avoided looking at the body that lay between us.

At Cua Viet, on the South China Sea, a bunch of kids we had 10
picked up in Quang Tri swam and ran on the beach and waited for us to throw them over our mighty Marine shoulders and into the ocean. A friend said it could have been a Sunday afternoon at the beach back

home. And for a few hours, it almost seemed like it. Simple contact like that always made the most sense.

11 At the Vandegrift Combat Base, not far from Khe Sanh, North Vietnamese soldiers fished in the river by dropping in grenades, then skimming the dead fish off the top of the water.

12 There were times on operations when there was no contact with the enemy, and we would sit on a hillside and look out at the most beautiful place many of us had ever seen.

13 There were other times when there was contact and 18- and 19-year-olds would react magnificently in the middle of the madness. Say what you will about the Marine Corps, it has great job training.

14 In August of 1969, shortly before coming home, I was made a "brig chaser" and told to escort another 19-year-old to the brig in Da Nang. He had been convicted of being an accessory to murder for having held open a hooch door while another Marine threw in a fragmentation grenade and killed their company commander. It was a time when "fragging" had become a new and frightening threat on the U.S. bases. The kid was facing 25 years in prison at Leavenworth. As we sat by the side of the airstrip waiting for a helicopter, he pleaded with me to look the other way and let him escape. I reminded him that we were in Vietnam and his options were limited. We never did get a helicopter that day, and I was relieved of having to take him to the brig. If he later went on to serve his full sentence, he would have gotten out in the mid-90s.

15 I tell people I had a good year in Vietnam. It sounds strange, considering how twisted and twisting the experience is supposed to have been. But I did get to see a lot of country that was a long, long way from Grosse Pointe, Mich.—and, on the best days, learn things about that country that had nothing to do with the war.

16 I had some of the best times of my life in Vietnam, with some of the best people I've ever known.

17 But there was, of course, that day when I saw that North Vietnamese soldier sitting on the ammunition crates, and reality shifted.

18 It was the same day on which I had scrambled to find my helmet during a mortar barrage, only to discover that I was sitting on it. It was the day, too, when I had looked out from a descending helicopter, saw men lying on ponchos in the landing zone, and wondered how they could be sleeping in the middle of the action. I was new "in country."

19 I heard about the two Marines who had taken the North Vietnamese soldier prisoner. I was told he had a weapon, and they didn't. It sounded like a story to me. My news instincts were just beginning to take shape.

I found the prisoner and his captors. The two Marines were eager 20
to tell me the story:

As Marines will do, they had taken the canteens from their entire 21
squad and headed for a nearby stream to fill them. They carried the canteens on a wire held between them. They didn't carry their M-16s.

The North Vietnamese soldier stepped out from the side of the 22
trail and pointed his AK-47 at them. The Marines thought they were dead—could feel their bodies giving in to the paralyzing fear of it.

But instead of dying, they took the man prisoner. They were 23
young and excited, and told the story with rich detail. They told of how they had used their four or five words of Vietnamese and some careful gestures to negotiate for their lives.

"I saw the barrel of his rifle start to lower just a little bit," said one 24
of them.

They said they had talked of "beer," making drinking motions to 25
indicate that there was some cold brew waiting if the soldier decided to go the American way.

They took an unlikely prisoner. The story—of unarmed Marines 26
taking an armed enemy soldier prisoner—spread quickly through the Marines on the parched hillside. I took it all down in the plastic-wrapped notebook pulled from the side pocket of my camouflage trousers.

I couldn't talk to the prisoner. He was going to be put on a heli- 27
copter and taken somewhere to be questioned—I could make no demands about my right to get his side of the story. I was a Marine combat correspondent, a "military journalist"; there were restrictions. It is something I think about now, as I do my newspaper job with a freedom I didn't have then.

I wrote the story about the capture after I got back to Dong Ha. I 28
thought it was great testimony to Marine ingenuity.

It was sent off in the daily news packet to the American military 29
press center in Da Nang, where all our stories were reviewed before being sent to divisional newspapers, Stars and Stripes, sometimes stateside newspapers.

It came back a couple of days later with the words Marines would 30
not go for water without their weapons written across the top.

So it hadn't happened. I had been out there, seen the prisoner, 31
and talked to the two Marines, and I was pretty sure that it had happened.

But in that year, when the truth of things was starting to get skewed 32
on almost every level, my story of Marines drawing on incredible reserves to save their lives was declared inappropriate and inoperative.

A sergeant told me it was good that this lesson in Marine reality 33
happened early in my tour. It would guide me in the future, he said.

And it did. From then on, I knew that the bad stuff—Marines with their faces missing, Marines tossing grenades at their own officers—would be something for the civilian press to uncover. But not me. I was upbeat. Under orders, I could turn a flat-out rout into a strategic retreat. *34*

It invited a play on that old, salty bit of Marine wisdom that if the Marine Corps had wanted you to have something, the Corps would have issued it. Including, apparently, the truth. *35*

Understanding the Significance

1. What advantage did Kerr enjoy as a Marine Corps combat correspondent that most people serving in Vietnam didn't?
2. One episode Kerr relates involves a young man charged as an accessory in the murder of his commanding officer. The young man pleaded with Kerr to help him escape; Kerr reminds him that "his options were limited." What does Kerr mean?
3. How did the two unarmed Marines manage to capture the North Vietnamese soldier who was carrying an AK-47 ?
4. Why was Kerr's story of the incident rejected by his superiors in the military press center in Da Nang?

Discovering the Writer's Purpose

1. In paragraph 8, Kerr tells the story about sitting with a number of villagers around the body of another villager who had died of natural causes. What point about people in general do you think Kerr is making by telling this story?
2. Kerr tells the story of his helicopter ride during which he states that he saw men on the ground below, lying on ponchos, "sleeping in the middle of the action." What is he actually seeing? Why do you think he presented the story this way?
3. As Kerr relates how the young, unarmed Marines captured the armed North Vietnamese soldier, he includes the following direct quotation, one of only two in the entire piece: "I saw the barrel of his rifle start to lower just a little bit." If Kerr had used a paraphrase instead of this direct quotation, how would the passage have been different?

4. In paragraph 30, Kerr discusses how his article was returned with a superior's comments written across the top. What point is he trying to make about the way the military handled the truth as Kerr knew it to be?

Examining the Writer's Method

1. The first of the specific examples that Kerr provides involves the gift of ice skates to a young Vietnamese girl. In what way is this example relevant to the point Kerr is making about his experiences in Vietnam?
2. Despite the overall focus of his piece, Kerr includes many more positive examples than negative ones. Of these positive examples, which one do you find most effective and why?
3. Kerr indicates his primary focus in his introduction and then supplies several examples of his everyday existence in Vietnam. How would his piece have been different if he had focused exclusively on the story of the capture of the North Vietnamese soldier?
4. The last two paragraphs of Kerr's essay serve as his conclusion. What point do these paragraphs make, and how do they relate to the point he expresses in his introduction?

Considering Style and Language

1. Kerr introduces the North Vietnamese soldier, the focus of his main story, in the first two paragraphs, which serve as his introduction. However, he doesn't give any indication of exactly what this story entails. How does this strategy encourage his audience to read on?
2. In paragraph 9, Kerr explains how some Viet Cong soldiers had infiltrated the U.S. encampments. In the same paragraph, he discusses carrying the remains of an American soldier to a relief helicopter as Vietnamese citizens "studiously avoided looking at the body that lay between us." What point is he making by tying these two incidents together?
3. In paragraph 13, Kerr notes that the Marine Corps "has great job training." What does he mean, given the examples he has provided?

4. What do the following words mean in the context of the writing? *Enigmatic* (para. 1); *dreary* (para. 3); *makeshift* (para. 7); *studiously* (para. 9); *magnificently* (para. 13); *barrage* (para. 18); *gesture, negotiate* (para. 23); *skewed, inoperative* (para. 32).

Your Turn: Responding to the Subject

a. *Propaganda* is defined as the systematic dissemination of information of a given doctrine or system of beliefs. The U.S. military rejected Bob Kerr's original story because it didn't fit the view it wished to portray about the readiness of its soldiers. Therefore, this essay is about propaganda, or rather, about the truth that underlies the propaganda—the real story behind the official story. For this assignment, discuss a situation or situations for which there were two versions: the story that people were told and the story as it actually occurred.

b. Kerr's essay centers on a single example of the power the U.S. government has to control the lives of individuals. In fact, for better or worse, government at all levels has a great deal of influence over how people live their lives. For this assignment, provide examples of ways that government at the local, state, and federal levels is involved in the day-to-day lives of its citizens.

Other Possibilities for Using Example

Here are some additional topics from which you might develop a paper that features example. Keep in mind that these are only general starting points. Make whatever changes necessary to develop the idea into a full essay:

- Negative political advertisements
- College challenges
- Highway dangers
- Shortcomings in today's high schools
- Urban myths
- Fads
- Duties as a pet owner
- Hints for incoming college students

- Pet peeves
- Outstanding leaders—historical or current—in a field (literature, entertainment, sports, medicine, scientific research)
- Boring hobbies
- Diets
- Corruption in society, government, or religion
- Superstitions
- Proper manners

EXAMPLE

BRISTOL COMMUNITY COLLEGE
FAQ

One principle that is true of successful workplace writing is that it provides plenty of support in the form of numerous simple, clear, and direct cases or illustrations. In other words, it features example. In a detailed listing of stocks making up a particular investment portfolio, for instance, example plays a central role. It also dominates in a print advertisement introducing an updated selection of laptop computers and in a memorandum detailing ways to make recycling in the office more efficient. In the following passage, which is part of Bristol Community College's (Massachusetts) web page, example plays a vital role. Here, in the form of questions and answers, example serves to clarify the questions most frequently asked about Bristol Community College and the educational opportunities it provides.

Frequently Asked Questions

What is Bristol Community College?
BCC is a comprehensive public community college, offering 65 degree and certificate programs. You can make BCC's many resources work for what you need, whether it's short-term training in the latest computer technology, or a full degree.

What degrees and certificates does BCC offer?
Click here for a complete list of all programs of study at Bristol Community College.

Who can attend BCC?
Everyone! Whether you need your high school equivalency, a college degree, high-tech computer training for career enhancement, or courses that make your leisure time more enjoyable, you can find it at BCC. We even have courses especially for children, in our "Kids College" program.

How do I apply?

If you're interested in enrolling in a degree program, start with the Admissions office, ext. 2179 or by email. They can send you a catalog or other information you need, including an application form. The College offers rolling admission, which means you can apply at any time during the year. Students are accepted to begin in September, January, or the summer. Application to competitive degree programs, including Child Care, Clinical Laboratory Science, Complementary Healthcare, Dental Hygiene, Healthcare Information, Nursing and Occupational Therapy Assistant will receive priority consideration if a complete application package is received by January 15

Why go to a community college when I can go right to a four-year college?

Earning the first two years of your baccalaureate degree at BCC is an affordable alternative to the high tuition and living expenses you would have to pay at a residential college. With excellent teaching faculty and educational resources available at BCC, we can assure that your first two years will give you a top-notch education.

Do I need to take any special testing for admission?

Bristol Community College does not require the Scholastic Aptitude Test (S.A.T.) All incoming freshman will complete a computerized placement test in Reading, English, Arithmetic, and Algebra.

Must I choose a program of study before I enroll?

If you're unsure about your career direction, you can choose to enroll in the Liberal Arts and Sciences, or enroll as a non-degree student. You can also seek career advice from the Career Planning office.

How do I apply for financial assistance to attend college?

The Financial Aid office can help you file the Free Application for Federal Aid, and also to apply for the many scholarships and grants offered through the BCC Foundation.

When is the campus open?

Generally, the campus is open when classes are in session—from 7:30 a.m. to approximately 10 p.m. Hours change during holidays and in the summer. For more information, contact the Switchboard by dialing 0, or Campus Security by dialing ext. 2218. For hours in the Learning Resources Center, dial ext. 2105. For information on the Arts, dial A-R-T-S (ext. 2787). For more information on hours of operation, click here.

Do you have other questions? Send us your question, and a way we can contact you, by email, phone, or mail.

Focusing on the Message and Aim

Answer each of the following questions in a brief paragraph, referring specifically to the passage you've just read.

1. One of the main reasons a person would seek out any college's web pages would be to get as full a portrait as possible of the institution itself and what it has to offer a prospective student. How does this section of Bristol Community College's web page help to provide that complete picture?
2. Why do you think the questions and answers that constitute the examples are presented in the order in which they appear?
3. In your view, which of the examples would be most encouraging to someone with a traditional educational background and which would be most encouraging to someone whose educational background is weak or nontraditional? Why?

Applying the Principles

a. Using the same question-and-answer technique shown here, prepare a one-page list of what you believe to be the top ten concerns that students attending your institution for the first time would likely have.
b. One of the biggest challenges for people planning to attend post-secondary school is paying for it. For this assignment, prepare a section to be added to the web page suggesting at least five specific examples of ways students can finance their college education.

Practical Application: Example

Last year, your uncle began a small mail-order business from his home. His specialty is a gift item perfect for birthdays and anniversaries: old newspapers—not facsimiles but actual old newspapers—each in a clear plastic case. The concept has been such a hit that your uncle has taken a partner, moved the business out of his house and into a small office, and hired you to work there part time. Your job is take orders over the phone, contact the suppliers at the warehouses where the old papers are kept and cataloged, and record the transactions.

Right from your first day on the job, you have been amazed at how old-fashioned and inefficient your uncle's method of operation is. Everything, from ordering to keeping inventory to writing the copy for advertisements, is done by hand—paper and pencil. It is obvious to you that if this business is going to grow, it needs to be streamlined, and the perfect way to do so is to computerize.

When you suggest this innovation to your uncle, he is hesitant. He doesn't know much about computers, he explains, and he isn't convinced that spending money on a computer system at this point even makes sense. But he is willing to consider discussing the prospect with his partner if you will prepare a 300- to 500-word report on ways that computerizing will help a small business such as his. To give you an idea of what he is looking for, your uncle gives you the following report prepared by business consultant Jessica A. Fletcher on ways that small businesses can cut expenses without compromising quality. Now get to work, using Fletcher's report to guide you in terms of *approach* and *format.*

Reduce Costs—Increase Quality

Any type of business can increase profits by increasing sales or reducing costs. Methods for increasing sales need to be considered on an individual basis for each situation because every business is different. However, there are several ways every business can reduce costs without reducing efficiency.

Saving money by cutting your company's cost expense must be based on the concept of an organized, planned program. First of all, adequate financial records must be maintained through a proper accounting system in order to ascertain and analyze costs. Rather than hiring an accountant, purchasing a software package such as Peachtree Accounting or Quicken that can be specifically tailored to your company's needs is more cost-effective and equally time-effective. In addition, your taxes can be done by using a similar program, like Kiplinger's Tax Cut series.

In short, the owner-manager must understand the nature of expenses and how expenses interrelate with sales, inventories, cost of goods sold, gross profits, and net profits in order to effectively be able to reduce expenditures.

When thinking of ways to reduce costs, consider the following:

- **Computerize your business**
  Aside from the accounting aspect, a computer can be used to create and produce your own letterheads, invoices, and memos—the list is endless. You can even use the computer now as a marketing tool by using the Internet. The savings in time and money will by far outweigh the initial cost of becoming computerized. If you aren't proficient with a PC, there are generally inexpensive courses offered at your local community college.
- **Cut out the middle man**
  A perfect example is to stop paying a payroll service—use direct deposit. Electronic banking for most businesses is free or offered for a minimal fee from most major banks. The money you will save in comparison to using a paper check system is quite substantial.
- **Advertise your business**
  There are several places to advertise that are relatively inexpensive and yet can generate a great response. Consider all of your options besides the obvious phone book, TV, and billboards. Don't forget local possibilities, such as mailers, or other companies' methods of advertising, such as the back of menus or health newsletters. And don't forget the Internet. It's a great way to spread the name of your business around.
- **Work smarter not harder**
  Make sure you are working to your full potential. Is your work space adequate? Are supplies accessible and useful in saving time? Remember—time is money.

There is really no end to the ways a small business can lower costs. And when a business does so, quality does not have to suffer. In fact, by becoming cost-efficient, your business may actually discover new avenues of service to offer to your clients, thereby benefiting all parties concerned. In the end, your business can't afford not to.

8

Process

The Technique

As with the rest of the modes, *process* often serves as a supporting technique in an essay. A paper concerning the first night working at a pizza parlor, for example, might include the initially confusing list of steps involved in preparing the pizza. An essay about the dangers of the use of anabolic steroids might include a section that details the physical and emotional changes a user experiences following a cycle of use.

Process will also sometimes be the primary focus of an essay, and it can be classified in one of three ways. One type is a set of instructions (often called *how-to writing*), which explains how to do something; the second type, *process analysis,* outlines how a condition or activity occurred; and the third type, *process narrative,* spells out how you or somebody else completed some task or action. Regardless of the focus you choose when you use process, you must make sure to

- keep the writing clear and direct;
- divide the process into simple, logical steps;
- specify what to expect and what to avoid; and
- rely on linear order.

CLARITY AND DIRECTNESS

Your reader always depends on you to make an essay clear and direct, but in no case is that need greater than with a paper that focuses primarily on process. No matter how familiar a process may seem to you as a writer, you must take into account that the reader may have a very limited understanding of it. And the more complex or technical the subject, the greater the chance that the reader won't know much about it. Therefore, you must fully explain all specialized terms and steps. A paper about how nitrites in prepared foods can trigger serious allergic reactions wouldn't be effective without the explanation that nitrites are preservatives added to such items as hot dogs, bologna, and some Chinese food.

When giving a set of instructions, an additional way to ensure that the writing communicates the various steps effectively is to address the reader directly through use of the *imperative mood,* commonly referred to as *command.* In the imperative mood, the subject of the sentence is not stated but is understood to be the person reading the piece.

Note the use of the imperative mood in this brief excerpt from Herbert Benson's *Beyond the Relaxation Response:*

> Starting with your feet and progressing up to your calves, thighs, and abdomen, relax the various muscle groups in your body.
>
> Loosen up your head, neck, and shoulders by gently rolling your head around and shrugging your shoulders slightly. As for your arms and hands, stretch and then relax them, and then let them drape naturally into your lap. Avoid grasping your knees or legs or holding your hands tightly together.

SIMPLE, LOGICAL STEPS

With a paper featuring process as a dominant mode, the gap between what you and your reader know is often greater than it is with other types of writing. After all, a reader generally seeks out a process writing piece in order to gain a greater understanding of some task, condition, or phenomenon. When you write a process paper, you are essentially an expert presenting information to someone less knowledgeable, so you must make sure to break the process into easily understandable steps and then explain each step fully.

For example, you could describe how people see by explaining that it is the process by which an image is viewed by the eye and translated by the brain, but such an explanation would be vastly inadequate. A far better method would be to break the process of vision into these four steps:

1. Light enters the lens of the eye and strikes specialized photoreceptor cells—called rods and cones—in the retina, the tissue at the back of the eye.
2. The light stimulates the photoreceptor cells to record the image within the range of the lens.
3. The photoreceptor cells send the visual message captured on the retina along the optic nerves to the visual cortex, the vision center of the brain.
4. The visual cortex translates the signals into a mental image.

With the process divided into smaller units like these, all that remains is to provide supporting examples or explanations so that the purpose and function of the various elements that allow us to see are clear for the reader.

The following passage from *Conscious Divorce: Ending a Marriage with Integrity* deals with a process that people often give little thought to: listening. The excerpt breaks down this skill into easily followed steps that will turn anyone into a good listener:

> First of all, you should strive to convey respect, empathy, and genuineness when speaking or listening. Respect can be expressed by showing courtesy and attentiveness, making direct eye contact, and using open body language. Do not cross your arms or legs or sit sideways or with a shoulder to the other person, but sit in a relaxed and receptive manner. Respect also means not passing judgment and remembering the information shared. Show empathy by nodding as the person speaks, using direct eye contact and similar facial expressions as the person talking. We are empathetic when we use active listening, giving responses such as, "That must have been really hard to do," or "I can understand why you feel that way."

SPECIFIC OUTCOMES AND NEGATIVE INSTRUCTIONS

If your process involves startling changes or surprising results, make sure to tell your audience what to expect. Otherwise, learners new to a process may assume such changes mean that something has gone wrong. For instance, if performing a kickboxing movement will cause a pulling sensation in the hamstring, a feeling that will dissipate with repeated practice, let your reader know that the sensation will fade. With this point identified, your reader will be less worried about a long-term injury.

Notice how this excerpt from *The Bread Lover's Bread Machine Cookbook* minimizes any concerns that novice bakers might have by pointing out that variations in dough texture are normal:

> The bread machine has a slow clockwise rhythm that blends the dough properly, turning for about three minutes (if the blade was turning more vigorously at this point, flour would be flying up against the lid and over the sides onto the heating element). The yeast gets distributed and moistened during this mixing. The gluten in the flour begins to be moistened by the liquids, and all the ingredients become evenly distributed. The dough can look anywhere from batterlike to dry and crumbly at this point, depending on the recipe, and there may be lots of lumpy, unincorporated bits of flour in the corners of the pan; this is okay. In the center of the mass, around the blade, there will be the beginnings of a dough ball coming together.

If, on the other hand, you suspect that your audience may make a mistake that would derail an important process—particularly with safety or health issues—consider providing negative instructions. In other words, tell your audience what *not* to do. This section from Kate Orman's *Domestic Violence Webpage* gives a number of negative instructions to help parents of abused women protect their daughters from harm:

1. **Don't be critical of her.** Be encouraging and supportive.
2. **Try not to criticize her boyfriend or partner,** as this may only serve to make her defensive and stop her from telling you honestly how she feels. Let her know that his behavior is unacceptable, that no one has the right to abuse her, and that it is not her fault.
3. **Let her know you care about her** and are concerned about her safety.
4. **Try not to tell her what to do,** as she may have experienced this from her boyfriend.
5. **Think carefully and listen to your teenager before deciding to take action yourself.** Your initial reaction might be to try to stop

her from seeing him, or to want to report the abuse to the police. But forcing her to break up the relationship before she herself is ready to do that can be counterproductive. She may secretly still try to see her boyfriend, or stop talking to you openly. And there may be repercussions for her if she suddenly stops seeing her boyfriend, or if the police become involved, especially if he has threatened her about this.

LINEAR ORDER

One attribute that distinguishes process writing from other types of writing is that it often features *linear order,* meaning that the steps are presented in the order in which they occur or must be completed. A paper dealing with how a hurricane develops or an essay on how the impeachment of President William Clinton occurred are examples of subjects that would be arranged in linear order.

Not all papers with process as a dominant mode feature linear order, of course. An essay explaining how to lose weight and tone up would contain such elements as taking the stairs rather than using elevators or escalators; walking; jogging; swimming; eliminating snacks between meals; cutting back on fatty foods; and so on. But successfully completing the process doesn't require that these steps be done in a particular order.

Taking a photograph properly with a 35-millimeter camera, however, does require adherence to linear order. First you adjust the focus, then you change the setting to allow the proper amount of light through the lens, and then you push the shutter button to take the picture. Linear order is called for here because if these steps were rearranged in any other way, the resulting photograph would not likely be particularly pleasing.

In this brief excerpt from *The Education of Koko,* their fascinating book dealing with a study of the language abilities of apes, psychologist Francine Patterson and writer Eugene Linden use linear order to describe part of the daily routine that Koko, the female lowland gorilla who is the primary subject of the study, follows:

> I wake Koko up at 8:00 or 8:30 a.m. if she has not already been roused by Michael's [another gorilla involved in the study] antics. Following a breakfast of cereal or rice bread (rice and cereals plus raisins baked into a cake), milk, and fruit, Koko helps with the daily cleaning of her room. She enjoys going over both her room

and Michael's with a sponge. Often these cleaning sessions end when Koko, seized by some urge, rips the sponge to shreds.

Then, some mornings, she sits on a chair before an electric teletype keyboard in the kitchen for a thirty-minute lesson in the production of English. Gorillas cannot generate the sounds necessary to speak, but through this Auditory Language Keyboard, which is linked to a voice synthesizer, we have given Koko a device that enables her to talk as well as generate signs. Other mornings, we videotape or audiotape our work with flash cards.

CHECKLIST FOR USING PROCESS

1. Is the presentation **clear** and **direct**, with the **command—you**—used when appropriate?
2. Is the process separated into simple, logical steps?
3. Does the document inform readers **what to expect** concerning potentially surprising changes?
4. Does the document include **negative instructions** to make it clear what *not* to do?
5. Is the process presented in linear order?

AN ANNOTATED EXAMPLE

DIANE ACKERMAN

Why Leaves Turn Color in the Fall

Diane Ackerman has enjoyed a prolific and varied writing career. A graduate of Pennsylvania State University and Cornell University, Ackerman is a highly acclaimed poet as well as the author of a number of successful nonfiction texts that explore the world of science and natural history, including The Moon by Whale Light, and Other Adventures among Bats, Penguins, Crocodilians, and Whales *(1991) and* The Rarest of the Rare: Vanishing Animals, Timeless Worlds *(1995). She is also the author of* A Natural History of Love *(1994), a collection of essays examining the phenomenon of romantic love. In addition, she has directed the writing program at Washington State University, been a writer in residence or visiting writer at several colleges, such as the College of William and Mary and Columbia University, served as a staff writer for the* New Yorker, *and hosted the PBS series,* Mystery of the Senses. *This selection, taken from her 1992 text* A Natural History of the Senses, *details how the color change associated with fall occurs.*

How is the brilliant green that signifies spring and summer transformed into the rainbow of colors that characterizes fall?

Goldfinch, yellow, *and* red-winged *are key words, signaling the color change to be discussed in the body of the paper.*

The opening paragraph serves as an overview of the entire process—from green leaves to bare limbs.

This piece is process analysis, *so it is presented using third-person point of view.*

Note the use of a rhetorical question to signal the focus of the essay.

The stealth of autumn catches one unaware. Was that a goldfinch perching in the early September woods, or just the first turning leaf? A red-winged blackbird or a sugar maple closing up shop for the winter? Keen-eyed as leopards, we stand still and squint hard, looking for signs of movement. Early-morning frost sits heavily on the grass, and turns barbed wire into a string of stars. On a distant hill, a small square of yellow appears to be a lighted stage. At last the truth dawns on us: Fall is staggering in, right on schedule, with its baggage of chilly nights, macabre holidays, and spectacular, heart-stoppingly beautiful leaves. Soon the leaves will start cringing on the trees, and roll up in clenched fists before they actually fall off. Dry seedpods will rattle like tiny gourds. But first there will be weeks of gushing color so bright, so pastel, so confettilike, that people will travel up and down the East Coast just to stare at it—a whole season of leaves. 1

Where do the colors come from? Sunlight rules most living things with its golden edicts. When the days begin to shorten, soon after the summer solstice on June 21, a tree reconsiders its leaves. All summer it feeds them so they can process sunlight, but in the dog days of summer the tree begins pulling nutrients back into its trunk and roots, pares down, and gradually chokes off its leaves. A corky layer of 2

How the tree prepares for winter is presented.

cells forms at the leaves' slender petioles, then scars over. Undernourished, the leaves stop producing the pigment chlorophyll, and photosynthesis ceases. Animals can migrate, hibernate, or store food to prepare for winter. But where can a tree go? It survives by dropping its leaves, and by the end of autumn only a few fragile threads of fluid-carrying xylem hold leaves to their stems.

The process of green fading away, revealing actual color, is described.

A turning leaf stays partly green at first, 3
then reveals splotches of yellow and red as the chlorophyll gradually breaks down. Dark green seems to stay longest in the veins, outlining and defining them. During the summer, chlorophyll dissolves in the heat and light, but it is also being steadily replaced. In the fall, on the other hand, no new pigment is produced, and so we notice the other colors that were always there, right in the leaf, although chlorophyll's shocking green hid them from view. With their camouflage gone, we see these colors for the first time all year, and marvel, but they were always there, hidden like a vivid secret beneath the hot glowing greens of summer.

How color changes occur differently in different geographical regions is explained.

The chemical process of color change is presented.

The most spectacular range of fall foliage 4
occurs in the northeastern United States and in eastern China, where the leaves are robustly colored, thanks in part to a rich climate. European maples don't achieve the same flaming reds as their American relatives, which thrive on cold nights and sunny days. In Europe, the warm, humid weather turns the leaves brown or mildly yellow. Anthocyanin, the pigment that gives apples their red and turns leaves red or red-violet, is produced by sugars that remain in the leaf after the supply of nutrients dwindles. Unlike the carotenoids, which color carrots, squash, and corn, and turn leaves orange and yellow, anthocyanin varies from year to year, depending on the temperature and amount of sunlight. The fiercest colors occur in years when the fall sun-

light is strongest and the nights are cool and dry (a state of grace scientists find vexing to forecast). This is also why leaves appear dizzyingly bright and clear on a sunny fall day: The anthocyanin flashes like a marquee.

The process as it affects different species is noted.

5 Not all leaves turn the same colors. Elms, weeping willows, and the ancient ginkgo all grow radiant yellow, along with hickories, aspens, bottlebrush buckeyes, cottonweeds, and tall, keening poplars. Basswood turns bronze, birches bright gold. Water-loving maples put on a symphonic display of scarlets. Sumacs turn red, too, as do flowering dogwoods, black gums, and sweet gums. Though some oaks yellow, most turn a pinkish brown. The farmlands also change color, as tepees of cornstalks and bales of shredded-wheat-textured hay stand drying in the fields. In some spots, one slope of a hill may be green and the other already in bright color, because the hillside facing south gets more sun and heat than the northern one.

6 An odd feature of the colors is that they don't seem to have any special purpose. We are predisposed to respond to their beauty, of course. They shimmer with the colors of sunset, spring flowers, the tawny buff of a colt's pretty rump, the shuddering pink of a blush. Animals and flowers color for a reason—adaptation to their environment—but there is no adaptive reason for leaves to color so beautifully in the fall any more than there is for the sky or ocean to be blue. It's just one of the haphazard marvels the planet bestows every year. We find the sizzling colors thrilling, and in a sense they dupe us. Colored like living things, they signal death and disintegration. In time, they will become fragile and, like the body, return to dust. They are as we hope our own fate will be when we die: Not to vanish, just to sublime from one beautiful state into another. Though leaves lose their green life, they bloom with urgent colors, as the woods grow mum-

mified day by day, and Nature becomes more carnal, mute, and radiant.

How the name of the season evolved is explained.

7 We call the season "fall," from the Old English feallan, to fall, which leads back through time into the Indo-European phol, which also means to fall. So the word and the idea are both extremely ancient, and haven't really changed since the first of our kind needed a name for fall's leafy abundance. As we say the word, we're reminded of that other Fall, in the garden of Eden, when fig leaves never withered and scales fell from our eyes. Fall is the time when leaves fall from the trees, just as spring is when flowers spring up, summer is when we simmer, and winter is when we whine from the cold.

8 Children love to play in piles of leaves, hurling them into the air like confetti, leaping into soft unruly mattresses of them. For children, leaf fall is just one of the odder figments of Nature, like hailstones or snowflakes. Walk down a lane overhung with trees in the never-never land of autumn, and you will forget about time and death, lost in the sheer delicious spill of color. Adam and Eve concealed their nakedness with leaves, remember? Leaves have always hidden our awkward secrets.

Another rhetorical question is used to begin the discussion of the next aspect of the process.

The steps involved in the separation of leaf from branch are presented.

9 But how do the colored leaves fall? As a leaf ages, the growth hormone, auxin, fades, and cells at the base of the petiole divide. Two or three rows of small cells, lying at right angles to the axis of the petiole, react with water, then come apart, leaving the petioles hanging on by only a few threads of xylem. A light breeze, and the leaves are airborne. They glide and swoop, rocking in invisible cradles. They are all wing and may flutter from yard to yard on small whirlwinds or updrafts, swiveling as they go. Firmly tethered to earth, we love to see things rise up and fly—soap bubbles, balloons, birds, fall leaves. They remind us that the end of a season is capricious, as is the end of life. We especially like the way leaves rock,

A comparable process is included.

careen, and swoop as they fall. Everyone knows the motion. Pilots sometimes do a maneuver called a "falling leaf," in which the plane loses altitude quickly and on purpose, by slipping first to the right, then to the left. The machine weighs a ton or more, but in one pilot's mind it is a weightless thing, a falling leaf. She has seen the motion before, in the Vermont woods where she played as a child. Below her the trees radiate gold, copper, and red. Leaves are falling, although she can't see them fall, as she falls, swooping down for a closer view.

The concluding paragraph emphasizes the eternal nature of the seasons.

At last the leaves leave. But first they turn 10
color and thrill us for weeks on end. Then they crunch and crackle underfoot. They shush, as children drag their small feet through leaves heaping along the curb. Dark, slimy mats of leaves cling to one's heels after a rain. A damp, stuccolike mortar of semidecayed leaves protects the tender shoots with a roof until spring, and makes a rich humus. An occasional bulge or ripple in the leafy mounds signals a shrew or a field mouse tunneling out of sight. Sometimes one finds in fossil stones the imprint of a leaf, long since disintegrated, whose outlines remind us how detailed, vibrant, and alive are the things of this earth that perish.

Your Turn: Responding to the Subject

a. In this piece, Ackerman explains a process in nature that we observe and appreciate but often don't fully understand. For this assignment, choose another aspect or element of nature that we experience or witness without, for the most part, considering how that aspect or element came to be. For instance, how does rain or snow form? How does beach erosion or beach transformation occur? How do various animals in cold climates prepare for winter? How does the Gulf Stream or an atmospheric condition such as El

Niño change weather patterns? How does the lunar cycle occur? Because of your own academic background or interests, you may already understand the process you choose. If you lack the specialized information that would help you explain this process, however, plan to do a little research in the library or on the Internet so that you will be prepared to explain the various steps to your reader.

b. In the sixth paragraph of this excerpt, Ackerman suggests that the change in the color of leaves gives us hope that we, too, will become more vibrant as we move through our cycle of life. The idea that we pass through stages of life is one that has always captivated philosophers and writers. Here, for instance, is how Shakespeare characterized the cycle of life in his wonderful pastoral comedy *As You Like It:*

All the world's a stage,
And all the men and women merely players.
They have their exits and entrances,
And one man in his time plays many parts,
His acts being seven ages. At first, the infant,
Mewling and puking in the nurse's arms.
Then the whining schoolboy, with his satchel
And shining morning face, creeping like a snail
Unwillingly to school. And then the lover,
Sighing like furnace, with a woeful ballad
Made to his mistress' eyebrow. Then a soldier,
Full of strange oaths and bearded like the pard,
Jealous in honour, sudden and quick in quarrel,
Seeking the bubble reputation
Even in the cannon's mouth. And then the justice,
In fair round belly with good capon lin'd
With eyes severe and beard of formal cut,
Full of wise saws and modern instances;
And so he plays his part. The sixth age shifts
Into the lean and slipper'd pantaloon,
With spectacles on nose and pouch on side;
His youthful hose, well sav'd, a world too wide
For his shrunk shank, and his big manly voice,
Turning again toward childish treble, pipes
And whistles in his sound. Last scene of all,

That ends this strange eventful history,
Is second childishness and mere oblivion,
Sans teeth, sans eyes, sans taste, sans everything.
(Act II, Scene 7, lines 138–165)

For this assignment, consider the stages of life we go through, either as Shakespeare spells them out or as you envision them. Then explain how you think people progress from one phase to the next.

JOSHUA PIVEN AND DAVID BORGENICHT

How to Land a Plane

"Do not attempt to undertake any of the activities described in the book yourself."

That's the warning in the Preface of The Worst-Case Scenario Survival Handbook, *the thoroughly enjoyable text by Joshua Piven and David Borgenicht. And with pieces with titles such as "How to Survive if Your Parachute Fails to Open," "How to Wrestle Free from an Alligator," and "How to Jump from a Moving Car" included in the text, it's no wonder that the first word of the Preface, in huge red letters, is* WARNING. *The author's intent, then, is not for people to try any of these activities themselves. Rather, they want their readers to understand the steps that an experienced professional in a particular field might take when faced with one of these situations so that they can follow the same steps should they be in that situation themselves, as unlikely as that might be. This writing provides a step-by-step guide to landing a small plane should the pilot become unable to fly it any longer.*

How would an individual with no flying experience safely land a small aircraft should the pilot suddenly become incapacitated?

These instructions cover small passenger planes and jets (not commercial airliners). 1

1. **If the plane has only one set of controls, push, pull, carry, or drag the pilot out of the pilot's seat.** 2
2. **Take your place at the controls.** 3
3. **Put on the radio headset (if there is one).** 4
   Use the radio to call for help—there will be a control button on the yoke (the plane's steering wheel) or a CB-like microphone on the instrument panel. Depress the button to talk, release it to listen. Say "Mayday! Mayday!" and give your situation, destination, and plane call numbers, which should be printed on the top of the instrument panel.
4. **If you get no response, try again on the emergency channel—tune the radio to 121.5.** 5
   All radios are different, but tuning is standard. The person on the other end should be able to talk you through the proper landing procedures. Follow their instructions carefully. If you cannot

reach someone to talk you through the landing process, you will have to do it alone.

5. **Get your bearings and identify the instruments.** 6
Look around you. Is the plane level? Unless you have just taken off or are about to land, it should be flying relatively straight.

YOKE. This is the steering wheel and should be in front of you. It turns the plane and controls its pitch. Pull back on the column to bring the nose up, push forward to point it down. Turn left to turn the plane left, turn right to turn it right. The yoke is very sensitive—move it only an inch or two in either direction to turn the plane in flight. While cruising, the nose of the plane should be about three inches below the horizon. 7

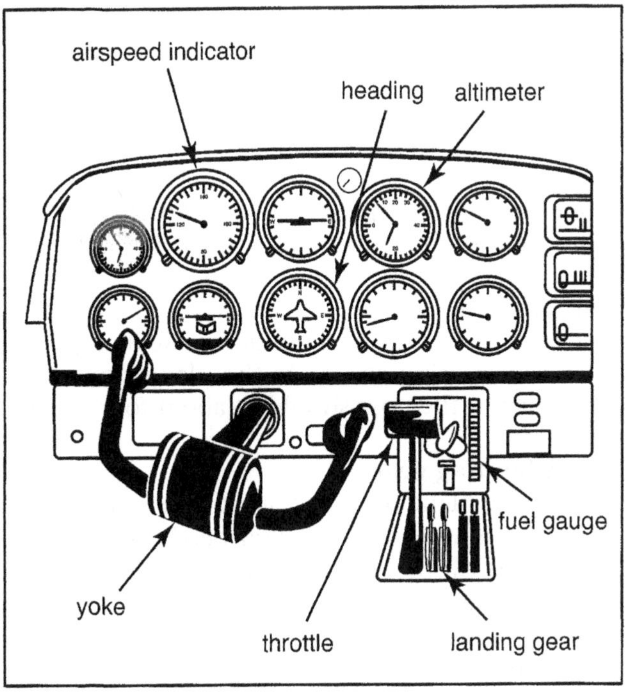

ALTIMETER. This is the most important instrument, at least initially. It is a red dial in the middle of the instrument panel that indicates altitude: the small hand indicates feet above sea level in thousand-foot increments, the large hand in hundreds. 8

HEADING. This is a compass and will be the only instrument with a small image of a plane in the center. The nose will point in the direction the plane is headed. 9

AIRSPEED. This dial is on the top of the instrument panel and will 10
be on the left. It is usually calibrated in knots, though it may also
have miles per hour. A small plane travels at about 120 knots while
cruising. Anything under 70 knots in the air is dangerously close to
stall speed. (A knot is 1¼ miles per hour.)

THROTTLE. This controls airspeed (power) and also the nose atti- 11
tude, or its relation to the horizon. It is a lever between the seats and
is always black. Pull it toward you to slow the plane and cause it to
descend, push it away to speed up the plane and cause it to ascend.
The engine will get more or less quiet depending on the direction the
throttle is moved.

FUEL. The fuel gauges will be on the lower portion of the instru- 12
ment panel. If the pilot has followed FAA regulations, the plane
should have enough fuel for the amount of flying time to your intended destination plus at least an additional half hour in reserve.
Some planes have a reserve fuel tank in addition to the primary one,
but do not worry about changing tanks.

FLAPS. Due to their complexity, wing flaps can make the plane 13
harder to control. Use the throttle to control airspeed, not the flaps.

6. **Begin the descent.**
   Pull back on the throttle to slow down. Reduce power by about 14
   one-quarter of cruising speed. As the plane slows, the nose will
   drop. For descent, the nose should be about four inches below the
   horizon.
7. **Deploy the landing gear.** 15
   Determine if the plane has fixed or retractable landing gear. Fixed
   landing gear is always down so you need do nothing. If it is retractable, there will be another lever between the seats near the
   throttle, with a handle that is shaped like a tire. For a water landing, leave the landing gear up (retracted).
8. **Look for a suitable landing site.** 16
   If you cannot find an airport, find a flat field on which to land. A
   mile-long field is ideal, but finding a field of this length will be
   difficult unless you are in the Midwest. The plane can land on a
   much shorter strip of earth, so do not bother to look for the "perfect" landing site—there is no such thing. Bumpy terrain will also
   do if your options are limited.
9. **Line up the landing strip so that when the altimeter reads one** 17
   thousand feet the field is off the right-wing tip.
   In an ideal situation, you should take a single pass over the field
   to look for obstructions; with plenty of fuel, you may want to do

so. Fly over the field, make a big rectangle, and approach a second time.

10. **When approaching the landing strip, reduce power by pulling back on the throttle.** 18
    Do not let the nose drop more than six inches below the horizon.
11. **The plane should be one hundred feet off the ground when you are just above the landing strip, and the rear wheels should touch first.** 19
    The plane will stall at fifty-five to sixty-five miles per hour, and you want the plane to be at just about stall speed when the wheels touch the ground.
12. **Pull all the way back on the throttle, and make sure the nose of the plane does not dip too steeply.** 20
    Gently pull back on the yoke as the plane slowly touches the ground.
13. **Using the pedals on the floor, steer and brake the plane as needed.** 21
    The yoke has very little effect on the ground. The upper pedals 22 are the brakes, and the lower pedals control the direction of the nose wheel. Concentrate first on the lower pedals. Press the right pedal to move the plane right, press the left pedal to move it left. Upon landing, be aware of your speed. A modest reduction in speed will increase your chances of survival exponentially. By reducing your groundspeed from 120 to 70 miles per hour, you increase your chance of survival threefold.

Be Aware

- A well-executed emergency landing in bad terrain can be less hazardous than an uncontrolled landing on an established field. 23
- If the plane is headed toward trees, steer it between them so the wings absorb the impact if you hit.
- When the plane comes to a stop, get out as soon as possible and get away—and take the pilot with you.

Understanding the Significance

1. The first five paragraphs of this writing urge the reader to take several steps before ultimately trying to land a plane independently. What point is being made about the task of making an emergency landing?

2. Paragraph 7 includes a caution about the sensitivity of the yoke. Why is this particular point emphasized?
3. Information about fuel is provided in paragraph 12. What does this information indicate about the degree of caution the FAA demands of pilots of small planes and jets?
4. The final paragraph opens with the following statement: "A well-executed emergency landing in bad terrain can be less hazardous than an uncontrolled landing on an established field." In your own words, what does this sentence mean?

Discovering the Writer's Purpose

1. Paragraph 6 of this essay opens with the following order to the reader: "Get your bearings...." What point is being made about what a person must do in order to succeed in this kind of emergency situation?
2. Why are definitions of the various controls outlined in paragraphs 1–13 included?
3. In the discussion of the throttle in paragraph 11, why is mention made of the sound of the engine?
4. In your view, what is the real point being made in paragraph 16 about finding a suitable area to land a plane?

Examining the Writer's Method

1. How do the first five paragraphs of this piece function as its introduction?
2. The various controls with which a person would have to be familiar in order to make an emergency landing are listed in paragraphs 6–13. In your view, why are they presented in this particular order?
3. Paragraph 13 discusses the role of wing flaps but indicates that they should not be used to control airspeed during an emergency landing. If the wing flaps aren't to be used in this procedure, why do you think they are mentioned?
4. The hallmarks of good process writing are that the steps are clear and direct and that they are presented in simple, logical fashion. In what ways does paragraph 22 match this description?

Considering Style and Language

1. Linear order plays an important role in this writing. In your view, which paragraph contains the most effective use of linear order? Why?
2. How would you describe the tone of this writing?
3. The purpose of a conclusion is to bring a piece of writing to a logical, complete, effective close. How does paragraph 23 fulfill this role?
4. What do the following words mean in the context of the writing? *Pitch* (para. 7); *increment* (para. 8); *calibrated* (para. 10); *deploy* (para. 15); *obstruction* (para. 17); *exponentially* (para. 22).

Your Turn: Responding to the Subject

a. One unstated premise behind *The Worst-Case Scenario Survival Handbook* is that planning is the only way to survive unusual, life-threatening situations such as a failing parachute or an attacking alligator. For this assignment, think of another rarely occurring circumstance and then, using the essay on landing a plane as an example, write a set of instructions on how to survive this extreme situation.

b. Clearly, the secret to success when it comes to many situations is to avoid panicking. But how can a person avoid panicking? For this assignment, write a set of instructions explaining how to stave off panic and maintain a sense of calm.

JILL GRIFFIN

Growing a Loyal Customer

When it comes to purchasing goods and services, U.S. consumers almost always have a choice. Think of the brand name items you have bought, credit card companies you do business with, restaurants you patronize. What made you select these companies in particular? And, if you've done business with them on previous occasions, what keeps you coming back? The answers to these questions are vitally important to the companies involved. After all, unless they attract and keep your business and the business of others, they will soon be out of business themselves. Courting a customer base and then maintaining and increasing it does not happen by accident. As this brief excerpt from Jill Griffin's Customer Loyalty: How to Earn It, How to Keep It, *success in this area occurs when companies systemize their approach. Note how heavily Griffin relies on process, specifically a carefully outlined set of stages effectively arranged, to show what a business should do to stay in business.*

What's the best way for a company to cultivate and hold the interest of its customers?

How can other companies engender the same loyalty that Harley-Davidson has developed? To understand the process, consider nature and the lessons it provides. In my seminars, I show a slide of an acorn and ask my participants what an acorn becomes over time. An oak tree, of course. It doesn't happen in a day, a week, a month, or even a year—it's a long, step-by-step progression. 1

People grow into loyal customers by stages as well. The process is accomplished over time, with nurturing, and with attention to each stage of growth. Each stage has a specific need. By recognizing each of these stages and meeting those specific needs, a company has a greater chance of converting buyers into loyal customers and clients. Let's look at each of these stages one by one: 2

STAGE 1: SUSPECT. Suspects include everyone who might possibly buy your product or service. We call them suspects because we believe, or "suspect," they might buy, but we don't know enough yet to be sure. 3

STAGE 2: PROSPECT. A prospect is someone who has a need for your product or service and has the ability to buy. Although a prospect has not yet purchased from you, he or she may have heard about you, read about you, or had someone recommend you to him or her. Prospects 4 may know who you are, where you are, and what you sell, but they still haven't bought from you

STAGE 3: DISQUALIFIED PROSPECT. Disqualified prospects are those 5
prospects about whom you have learned enough to know that they do not need or do not have the ability to buy your products.

STAGE 4: FIRST-TIME CUSTOMER. First-time customers are those who 6
have purchased from you one time. They can be customers of yours and still be customers of your competitor as well.

STAGE 5: REPEAT CUSTOMER. Repeat customers are people who have 7
purchased from you two or more times. They may have bought the same product twice or bought two different products or services on two or more occasions.

STAGE 6: CLIENT . A client buys everything you have to sell that he 8
or she can possibly use. This person purchases regularly. You have a strong, ongoing relationship that makes him or her immune to the pull of the competition.

STAGE 7: ADVOCATE . Like a client, an advocate buys everything you 9
have to sell that he or she can possibly use and purchases regularly. In addition, however, an advocate encourages others to buy from you. An advocate talks about you, does your marketing for you, and brings customers to you.

STAGE 8: INACTIVE CUSTOMER OR CLIENT. An inactive customer or client 10
is someone who was once a customer or client but has not bought from you in a period of time longer than the normal purchase cycle.

The Profit Generator System and the Customer Stages

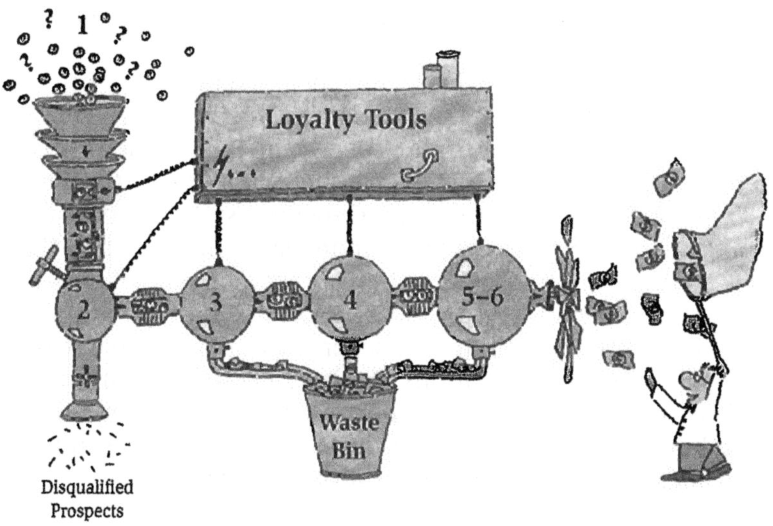

Source: Copyright 1991 by Jill Griffin and Griffin Group, reprinted with permission of John Wiley & Sons, Inc.

How the Profit Generator System Works

In my marketing seminars, I use the image of the Profit Generator system to illustrate the marketing challenges every company must address to be profitable. 11

The Profit Generator system works like this: An organization funnels *suspects* into its marketing system, and these people are either qualified as high-potential *prospects* or disqualified. Disqualified prospects are filtered out of the system, while qualified prospects remain inside. The sooner a disqualified prospect is filtered out, the better for you. Wasting time and money on suspects who will not buy or are unable to buy cuts dramatically into your profits, so you want to identify disqualified suspects as quickly as possible. Qualified prospects are then focused upon with the goal of turning them into *first-time customers*, then *repeat customers*, and eventually *clients* and *advocates*. While moving them through the Profit Generator system into higher levels of loyalty, you also want to encourage customers to buy regularly from you and stop buying from your competition. Without proper care, first-time customers, repeat customers, clients, and advocates can become *inactive*, causing a company substantial losses in sales and profits. You'll notice that the globes representing each customer stage become progressively larger. This is because, despite the fact that the number of customers in each stage is smaller than that in the preceding stage, the further along in the system the customer gets, the more bottom-line profit the organization can enjoy. 12

Every business has customers and clients that fall into some if not all of these categories. A residential real estate company has homeowners as clients. These homeowners could transition through five stages: suspect, prospect, lister, seller, and advocate. A hotel chain catering to corporate travelers has the travel departments of major corporations as clients. Their customer stages could be suspect, prospect, first-time booker, repeat booker, client, and advocate. While the actual names of the customer stages may be modified, most organizations have customers that evolve through a similar transition. 13

Other applications to the Profit Generator system vary as well. For example, in many industries buyer monogamy (i.e., whether that person is buying only from you or is also buying from a competitor) is the client-stage litmus test. In some sectors like state government that cannot buy exclusively from one seller, this may not be a reasonable requirement. In those situations, the best a company can hope for is that it is one of two or three sellers used exclusively by that buyer. Depending on the nature of your business, these stages can be modified to address the specifics of your own buying situation. 14

The rule of thumb in working within the Profit Generator system is that the goal for you within each stage of development is to "grow" the relationship into the next stage of development. The goal of interacting with a prospect is to turn a prospect into a first-time customer, a repeat customer into a client, a client into an advocate. Once you reach the advocate stage, your job is to keep that person buying and referring. As we saw earlier with the definition of loyalty, a company can enjoy real profits when the customer has evolved into the latter stages of the Profit Generator process. Failure to "grow" customers to those advanced stages robs the company of profits and valuable referrals. 15

Understanding the Significance

1. According to Griffin, what is the connection between acorns and customer loyalty?
2. In terms of the stages Griffin presents, how does an advocate differ from a client?
3. In the explanation of the Profit Generator system, Griffin states that disqualified prospects should be filtered out of the system as quickly as possible to avoid "[w]asting time and money." In what ways could a disqualified prospect cost an organization money?
4. As Griffin explains it, what should be the basic goal of anyone using the Profit Generator system?

Discovering the Writer's Purpose

1. Griffin begins her piece with a *metaphor,* a figure of speech involving the comparison of two dissimilar things for the sake of clarifying meaning. Why do you think that Griffin chose to use the metaphor of nature—the acorn to the oak tree—to explain how businesses should function?
2. Griffin carefully outlines the different levels of clients or customers in paragraphs 3–10. By presenting the information this way, what is she suggesting about understanding complex issues?
3. By including a description and discussion of disqualified prospects, what do you think Griffin suggesting about the realities of doing business?

4. In your view, what does Griffin want her audience to understand about the ways successful companies do business? What aspects or examples in the document have helped you reach this conclusion?

Examining the Writer's Method

1. Griffin opens this excerpt with a question. Why do you think she made this choice to introduce her process? Do you agree with her strategy? Explain your reasoning.
2. The hallmarks of effective process writing are clarity and directness. Where in Griffin's piece do you find the writing most clear and direct? What makes you come to this conclusion?
3. In paragraph 12, Griffin outlines the process involved in using the Profit Generator system. Why do you think she chose to present the steps in declarative sentence form rather than to use the imperative? Do you agree with her choice? Why or why not?
4. In the next to the last paragraph, Griffin makes the following statement: "In some sectors, like state government that cannot buy exclusively from one seller, this may not be a reasonable requirement." Why is this negative instruction vital to understanding the process that she is presenting?

Considering Style and Language

1. How would you describe Griffin's tone in this piece? What words, phrases, images, and so on lead you to this conclusion?
2. In Stage 1, according to Griffin, a potential customer is a suspect. This term usually carries a more negative connotation. How does her explanation help to create a more positive connotation?
3. The excerpt features a visual entitled "The Profit Generator System." In what ways does this visual enhance the document, making it easier to understand the process?
4. What do the following words mean in the context of the writing? *Engender, seminar* (para. 1); *nuturing* (para. 2); *funnels, filtered, progressively, preceding* (para. 12); *transition, catering, evolve* (para. 13); *litmus test, exclusively* (para. 14)

Your Turn: Responding to the Subject

a. In a way, Griffin's excerpt is all about cultivating and maintaining interest in something. For this assignment, first focus on one of your own hobbies or interests, carefully considering how you came to develop your interest in it. Then use process to lay out steps you would take to persuade someone else to develop the same level of interest in your subject.

b. Loyalty, Griffin explains, is the key if businesses are to generate and hold onto clients. But it isn't just in business that loyalty is important. Loyalty is at the core of most relationships. For this assignment, think of a particular relationship and then write an essay in which you outline a process to create and maintain loyalty in that relationship.

MALCOLM X WITH ALEX HALEY

Education

For most people, it's hard to imagine a more brutal, dehumanizing, demoralizing circumstance than imprisonment. So it is equally difficult for most people to imagine that much positive can occur for those experiencing those circumstances. But this writing, an excerpt from The Autobiography of Malcolm X, *deals with such a positive occurrence. Here, famed Black Muslim activist Malcolm X recalls how after recognizing the power of the spoken and written word and his own weaknesses in this regard, he set out to educate himself, a single word at a time. Malcolm X, born Malcolm Little, spent the years after his prison education working to eliminate oppression of blacks by the U.S. government. He was assassinated in 1965. Alex Haley, who worked with Malcolm X on* The Autobiography, *is best known for his Pulitzer Prize–winning bestseller,* Roots, *detailing his family's history, beginning with the capture in Africa and subsequent enslavement in America of his great-grandfather.* Roots *was later adapted to become one of the most acclaimed television mini-series ever created.*

How is it possible to achieve intellectual freedom while imprisoned?

It was because of my letters that I happened to stumble upon starting to acquire some kind of a homemade education. *1*

I became increasingly frustrated at not being able to express what I wanted to convey in letters that I wrote, especially those to Mr. Elijah Muhammad. In the street, I had been the most articulate hustler out there—I had commanded attention when I said something. But now, trying to write simple English, I not only wasn't articulate, I wasn't even functional. How would I sound writing in slang, the way I would say it, something such as, "Look, daddy, let me pull your coat about a cat, Elijah Muhammad—" *2*

Many who today hear me somewhere in person, or on television, or those who read something I've said, will think I went to school far beyond the eighth grade. This impression is due entirely to my prison studies. *3*

It had really begun back in the Charlestown Prison, when Bimbi first made me feel envy of his stock of knowledge. Bimbi had always taken charge of any conversations he was in, and I had tried to emulate him. But every book I picked up had few sentences which didn't contain anywhere from one to nearly all of the words that might as *4* well have been in Chinese. When I just skipped those words, of course, I really ended up with little idea of what the book said. So I had come to the Norfolk Prison Colony still going through only book-reading motions. Pretty soon, I would have quit even these motions, unless I had received the motivation that I did.

5 I saw that the best thing I could do was get hold of a dictionary—to study, to learn some words. I was lucky enough to reason also that I should try to improve my penmanship. It was sad. I couldn't even write in a straight line. It was both ideas together that moved me to request a dictionary along with some tablets and pencils from the Norfolk Prison school.

6 I spent two days just riffling uncertainly through the dictionary's pages. I'd never realized so many words existed! I didn't know which words I needed to learn. Finally, just to start some kind of action, I began copying.

7 In my slow, painstaking, ragged handwriting, I copied into my tablet everything printed on that first page, down to the punctuation marks.

8 I believe it took me a day. Then, aloud, I read back, to myself, everything I'd written on the tablet. Over and over, aloud, to myself, I read my own handwriting.

9 I woke up the next morning, thinking about those words—immensely proud to realize that not only had I written so much at one time, but I'd written words that I never knew were in the world. Moreover, with a little effort, I also could remember what many of these words meant. I reviewed the words whose meaning I didn't remember. Funny thing, from the dictionary's first page right now, that "aardvark" springs to my mind. The dictionary had a picture of it, a long-tailed, long-eared, burrowing African mammal, which lives off termites caught by sticking out its tongue as an anteater does for ants.

10 I was so fascinated that I went on—I copied the dictionary's next page. And the same experience came when I studied that. With every succeeding page, I also learned of people and places and events from history. Actually the dictionary is like a miniature encyclopedia. Finally the dictionary's **A** section had filled a whole tablet—and I went on into the **B**'s. That was the way I started copying what eventually became the entire dictionary. It went a lot faster after so much practice helped me to pick up handwriting speed. Between what I wrote in my tablet, and writing letters, during the rest of my time in prison I would guess I wrote a million words.

11 I suppose it was inevitable that as my word-base broadened, I could for the first time pick up a book and read and now begin to understand what the book was saying. Anyone who has read a great deal can imagine the new world that opened. Let me tell you something:

from then until I left that prison, in every free moment I had, if I was not reading in the library, I was reading on my bunk. You couldn't have gotten me out of books with a wedge. Between Mr. Muhammad's teachings, my correspondence, my visitors—usually Ella and Reginald—and my reading of books, months passed without my even thinking about being imprisoned. In fact, up to then, I never had been so truly free in my life.

Understanding the Significance

1. What motivated Malcolm X to seek some kind of education?
2. After several false starts, what did Malcolm X finally decide was the best way to begin his prison studies?
3. In your own words, what was the process that Malcolm X followed as he educated himself?
4. How did his newly acquired education help Malcolm X deal with his incarceration?

Discovering the Writer's Purpose

1. In paragraph 2, Malcolm X includes a direct quotation. Why is this a better choice than a paraphrase of the same information?
2. What point is Malcolm X making about knowledge with his story of Bimbi in paragraph 4?
3. In paragraph 9, Malcolm X provides an entry he still remembered from the first page of the dictionary. Why do you think he includes this particular detail?
4. What does Malcolm X mean with his final sentence: "In fact, up to then, I never had been so truly free in my life?"

Examining the Writer's Method

1. The opening two paragraphs of this piece serve as the introduction. In what way do these paragraphs prepare the reader for the rest of the essay that follows?
2. How does the use of linear order in this writing help make Malcolm X's struggle to learn easier to understand?

3. In several paragraphs, Malcolm X details the process he followed as he learned to read. In which of these sections do you think he most effectively presents the information in simple, logical steps? Explain.
4. How does Malcolm X's conclusion relate to the point he raises in his introduction?

Considering Style and Language

1. Malcolm X concludes paragraph 2 with a rhetorical question. How does this device help him to make his point?
2. In paragraph 6, Malcolm X explains that, out of confusion about how to begin his self-education, he decided to begin copying the first page of the dictionary. He uses the word *copy* again in the next paragraph, and then switches to the word *written*. What is the difference between the words as they are used in this writing?
3. In the final paragraph Malcolm X says, "Anyone who has read a great deal can imagine the new world that opened." What does he mean?
4. What do the following words mean in the context of the writing? *Articulate, hustler, functional* (para. 2); *emulate* (para. 4); *tablets* (para. 5); *riffling* (para. 6); *painstaking, ragged* (para. 7); *immensely* (para. 9); *succeeding* (para. 10); *inevitable* (para. 11).

Your Turn: Responding to the Subject

a. Malcolm X records in great detail the process he followed as he educated himself. What process have you followed as you learned to do something? For this assignment, write an essay in which you explain the process you have developed to do one of the following: study for an examination; write an essay, term paper, letter, or extensive e-mail; or master a software program or computer game.

b. Have you ever observed someone working to learn something as an adult that many people learn as a child? Some examples would be ice- or in-line-skating, tying shoes, riding a bike, solving a math problem, and swimming. For this assignment, explain the process you witnessed.

Other Possibilities for Using Process

Here are additional subjects that could be developed into papers featuring process. If you choose one of these topics, remember to develop it fully and provide plenty of supporting details to guide your reader through the steps.

- How to pack a suitcase efficiently
- How tsunamis occur
- How to scan and e-mail a photo or document
- How to perform a simple magic trick
- How you made a serious mistake at work
- How to transfer bank funds electronically
- How you learned to make a complex move in a sport, chess, video game, and so on
- How to interview effectively for a job
- How to perform a simple experiment
- How a serious accident you witnessed or were involved in occurred
- How to serve in tennis or volleyball
- How the human liver functions
- How thunderstorms occur
- How to stretch before exercise
- How fossils were created

Writing at Work

PROCESS

MASSACHUSETTS DRIVER'S MANUAL
Parking

Whether it is used to explain how something occurs, how someone accomplished something, or how to do something, process is a mode that appears frequently in real-world writing. Newspaper and magazine articles about natural phenomena, manuals for computers, government documents such as tax forms, and directions for use of products are just a few examples of ways that process helps writers communicate. The following excerpt, which appears in the Massachusetts Registry of Motor Vehicles Driver's Manual, *relies almost exclusively on process. This piece, entitled "Parking," is designed to help prospective drivers master a simple, yet important part of effectively operating an automobile.*

Stopping and parking your motor vehicle is regulated to ensure safety and a smooth traffic flow. You should practice parking maneuvers and know the laws that govern parking.

Here are some rules about stopping and parking:

- You must not create a traffic hazard while parking or while your vehicle is stopped.
- You must always make sure that you leave at least a 12-foot wide, unobstructed roadway for traffic to pass in either direction.
- When you leave your vehicle unattended, state law requires you to stop the motor, set the brake, make sure the ignition is locked, remove your ignition key, and lock the door.
- When you pull away from the curb, you must wait for vehicles in the travel lane to pass, signal your intention to pull out, and move slowly into traffic.

Parallel Parking

1. Choose a space on the roadside that is long enough for your vehicle. Make sure parking is legal.
2. Pull up alongside the vehicle in front of the space, leaving about 2 or 3 feet between your vehicle and the parked one. Position your vehicle so that your rear bumper or front seats align with the rear bumper or front seats respectively of the other vehicle.
3. Look behind you both ways to see if your path is clear of pedestrians and other traffic.
4. Slowly back up and turn the steering wheel all the way toward the curb. Rest your foot lightly on the brake. Look directly out your rear window. Do not use your mirrors.
5. When your front passes the parked vehicle's rear bumper, turn your steering the opposite way and continue backing up. Do not hit the vehicle behind you.
6. When you are back far enough, straighten your wheels and pull forward. Make sure you keep enough space in front of and behind you so that other vehicles can get out.

Parking on Hills

Always set your parking brake and leave your vehicle in gear when parking on a hill. In case the brake fails while your vehicle is parked, you must turn your front wheels in the proper direction to prevent it from rolling downhill.

- **No Curb**—Turn your wheels inward, toward the edge of the road.
- **Uphill Against a Curb**—Turn your wheels outward, toward the travel lane.

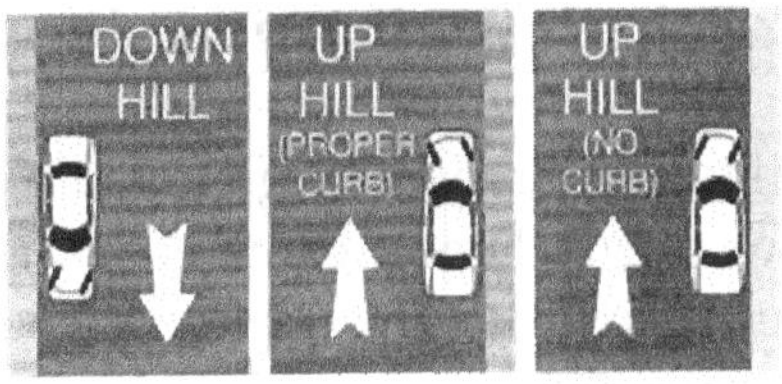

- **Downhill Against a Curb**—Turn your wheels inward,toward the curb.

Focusing on the Message and Aim

Answer each of the following questions in a brief paragraph, referring specifically to the passage you've just read.

1. The piece is intended to help someone master a common but necessary part of driving. How does the writer adjust the material so that it effectively addresses its intended audience, the inexperienced driver-in-training?
2. Before the steps of the process of parking are presented, a series of guidelines, in a bulleted list, appears. What is the relationship between these two sections, and how does the list of guidelines influence the overall effectiveness of the piece?
3. The illustrations included with the text are fairly simple. Are they sufficient, or would additional and more elaborate illustrations make the piece more effective? Why or why not?

Applying the Principles

a. Although these instructions are prepared for anyone learning to drive, the vast majority of the people who would use the instructions are about 16 years old. What additional kinds of details or approaches would be especially effective for this particular audience? Using your own experience, make a list of suggestions for addressing people this age.

b. Imagine you have been commissioned to write another section of the *Massachusetts Driver's Manual.* Choose some other aspect of driving, for example, passing, bringing a car out of a skid, or entering a highway, and using the excerpt on parking as a model, write a new section.

Practical Application: Process

As you are working toward your degree, you have the opportunity to intern with your town's largest commercial bank. The officers of the bank are so impressed with the quality of your work that the director of human resources offers you a position when you finish school. Three days after graduation, you begin work in the customer relations division.

After a two-week orientation, you attend your first weekly staff meeting. The subject under discussion is the use—or lack of use—of the automatic teller machines (ATMs) in the downtown branch. Because customers aren't taking advantage of the ATMs, they often face long lines to meet with tellers for such basic banking services as deposits and withdrawals, leading to numerous complaints.

The problem appears to be a matter of demographics. A survey conducted in response to the complaints indicates that the average age of patrons of this branch is 68, an older group that has limited experience with and therefore less confidence in anything computerized, especially when it concerns their hard-earned money. The bank's goal, then, is to find a way to make using the ATMs less intimidating.

After some discussion, one of the vice presidents suggests sending a one-page mailer to all patrons that explains in simple, clear terms how to use an ATM and the advantages patrons gain with the ATM in terms of saving time and gaining flexibility in scheduling. The vice president looks around the table, recognizes you from your work during your internship, and assigns you the task of preparing the one-page mailer, emphasizing the importance of maintaining an upbeat and encouraging tone. As you begin your work, he supplies a guideline, a set of instructions he has received about on-line registration for college courses, to be an example of approach and format.

eSelect Registration at Taylor College

Introduction

Welcome to eSelect, Taylor College's on-line registration system. For years, registering for classes at Taylor meant actually coming to campus and waiting in long lines as staffers from the Registrar's Office filled out your schedule by hand, the paper and pencil method. But all that changed a few years ago with the advent of eSelect. Now registering for classes is a simple matter of a few clicks of your computer mouse.

The Steps Involved

The process itself couldn't be easier. During the last month, you had the opportunity to visit the campus advisement center and confer with an academic adviser and to identify prospective courses for next semester. At the conclusion of that session, you received a personal identification number (PIN), which is needed to complete your registration. All you need now is access to a computer.

1. Before accessing the College's homepage, list your Social Security or student identification number and the PIN provided by your adviser on a piece of paper. On the same paper, write the titles and numbers of the courses you wish to take, for example, *ENG 101: College English.*
2. Go to the College's homepage and click on **Spring Registration.** When the page appears, enter your Social Security number and your PIN in the appropriate fields and then click **Continue.**
3. When the master list of available courses for the spring semester appears, identify the specific section of each course you wish to take. Each course section carries a five-digit course registration number (CRN), for example, *75673.* Next to each course name and number you have listed on your paper, write the CRNs as well as the days and time each course meets. A typical notation will look like this:

   ENG 101: College English 10 a.m. M, W, F 75673.
4. Double-check your proposed schedule to make sure that no time conflicts exist. eSelect will automatically reject any courses with conflicting times.
5. When you have completed your selection of course sections, click **Register Now.** When the registration page appears, fill in the appropriate fields (**Course number** *ENG 101,* **Course Title** *College English,* **CRN** *75673*) for each course. Click **Continue.** A grid showing your entire schedule will appear on the screen.
6. Check your schedule for errors. If you need to make changes, click **Return**, which will take you back to the previous page to make any corrections. If your schedule is correct, click **Complete**. In a moment, a message indicating that your registration is complete will appear. A copy of your schedule will automatically print out.
7. Click **Log Off** to exit eSelect.

That's all there is to it. For most students, the entire process takes less than five minutes.

Final Words

We at Taylor College's Registrar's Office want to know what you think. If there are ways you think we could improve the eSelect system, stop by or contact us (Register@TaylorC.edu or 1-800-555-2534). Thanks and good luck with your courses.

9

Definition

The Technique

Writing successfully on any subject depends greatly on whether your reader understands what you mean. For this reason alone, you will find *definition* invaluable in your writing. If you were writing an essay about the strength of a family grieving over the loss of a child, the definition of strength would be important. By *strength,* do you mean a stoic denial of emotions, a willingness to seek counseling, the courage to break down in public and show emotions, or something else entirely? Clearly, the effectiveness of your essay would depend on how well you communicated the meaning of strength to your reader.

To take full advantage of definition when you write, you should make sure to

- recognize the elements of an effective definition;
- use formal, limited, and extended definition;
- consider denotation, connotation, and etymology; and
- explore negation.

The Elements of an Effective Definition

A dictionary is the logical place to begin for any writer dealing with definition. Dictionary entries generally follow a simple formula: A word is presented, placed in its appropriate class, and then differentiated from other items in the same classification. It's a formula that is designed to ensure clarity.

With many words, ensuring clarity is relatively simple because they are concrete—as their dictionary definitions indicate, they have identifiable physical characteristics. *Abstract* words, however, which name ideas, concepts, and situations that are intangible or lack consistent characteristics, represent more of a problem. When you are writing about an abstract subject, your reader needs plenty of context and examples to understand the complete meaning of its elements and characteristics.

In these cases, the secret to clear definitions is to use appropriate concrete words and specific examples as support. For instance, you might define a term like *fear* by delineating what happens physically when one experiences fear as well and by giving examples of events or situations that trigger fear. You might define a term like *fair use* by spelling out particular contextual limitations: You may make copies for your own personal use but not for anyone else, whether you charge a fee or not.

William Lutz clearly understood these principles when he wrote this passage from "Weasel Words," which defines the abstract term *new:*

> What makes a product "new"? Some products have been around for a long time, yet every once in a while you discover that they are being advertised as "new." Well, an advertiser can call a product new if there has been "a material functional change" in the product. What is "a material functional change," you ask? Good question. In fact, it's such a good question it's being asked all the time. It's up to the manufacturer to prove that the product has undergone such a change. And if the manufacturer isn't challenged on the change, then there's no one to stop it. Moreover, the change does not have to be an improvement in the product. One manufacturer added artificial lemon scent to a cleaning product and called it "new and improved," even though the product did not clean any better than without the lemon scent. The manufacturer defended the used of the word "new" on the grounds that the artificial scent changed the chemical formula of the product and therefore constituted "a material functional change."

Formal, Limited, and Extended Definition

Definition appears in a variety of forms, including

- **formal definition**—an item placed in a class and then distinguished from other things in that class

Example: An assault is a criminal act that involves an attempted physical attack or threat to injure another.

- **limited definition**—a sentence or two offering a precise, focused explanation
  Example: An optimist is a person who sees the good even in the worst situations. You name the problem—unemployment, lost credit cards, missing computer files. An optimist believes that this problem is merely a character-developing challenge and that things will always work out. They always do.
- **extended definition**—a fully developed explanation, complete with multiple examples
  Example: When some people think of physical humor, they immediately thing of slapstick humor. The appeal of this type of humor, which involves such violent actions as hitting, punching, slapping, slipping, and falling, is difficult to justify. Hit your own thumb as you work on some project, and you might bleed, swear, or pass out. Watch a comic actor hit his thumb with a hammer, however, and you'll probably laugh. Everyone knows that a person could slip on a banana peel and be seriously hurt, maybe even die, yet people still break up with laughter over an actor slipping and falling.

When definition plays a supporting role in an essay, you may find limited or formal definitions sufficient to make your case. In other cases, however, a particular assignment will call for a more thorough explanation of some term or concept. With these assignments, an extended definition is the proper choice.

Extended definitions incorporate key elements of context—details that answer the question, "In what situations or circumstances does this definition apply?"—as well as concrete examples that demonstrate what would or would not count as or fit in a certain concept.

Think of a term such as *charisma,* for instance. If you relied on a limited definition of *charisma,* explaining it as a quality possessed by those who are able to attract the admiration and devotion of many others, you wouldn't paint a clear enough picture of the word for your reader. You'd be better off providing an extended definition discussing the ways that people have been affected by specific charismatic individuals. Such a definition would do a far better job of illustrating the power wielded by famous (or infamous) religious and political leaders; actors and musicians; media personalities; and so forth.

Consider the following passage from *Special Kids Need Special Parents,* a parenting guidebook. It contains an extended definition of the concept "successful parents," refined over a number of sentences, as well as concrete examples illustrating the characteristics of successful parents. In addition, it provides an appropriate context, making it clear that this particular definition of "successful parents" is specific to the circumstances of special needs intervention:

> Successful parents of special needs children focus on the fact that people labeled "disabled" are not "unable." They concentrate on their child's strengths instead of weaknesses. They are there for the child, but they are also able to separate. They seek help and intervention from the beginning. Often, it's the early interventions that start them on the right course. And, they learn to communicate to get what they need. Perhaps from that parental attitude some children labeled "disabled" grow to be the most abled.

DENOTATION, CONNOTATION, AND ETYMOLOGY

Preparing an effective definition also means taking into account the literal meaning of the word—*denotation*—and the additional subjective meanings the word suggests or implies—*connotation.* The denotation of the word *clever,* for example, is "to be mentally quick and capable," but it connotes or suggests different meanings depending on how it is used. When you say a child is clever, for instance, you are generally making a positive statement. But when you say a criminal is clever, you are implying something negative, a statement about the individual's ability to manipulate or take advantage of others. In order to communicate your point to your reader, you must consider the shades of meaning in each term and concept you define.

You may also occasionally find a word's origin and historical development—its *etymology*—useful. The etymology of a word is generally available in any collegiate dictionary, although an unabridged dictionary such as *Oxford English Dictionary* (*OED*) is the best place to find extensive etymological information. If you've ever wondered, for example, whether the world is slanted against left-handed people, consider the etymology of two words, *gauche* and *adroit. Gauche* is defined as "lacking tact or social graces." It comes from a French word, *gauche,* which means *left. Adroit* is defined as "deft and skillful," and it, too, is derived from a French word, *droit,* which means *right.* What is gained by an examination of the etymology of these two words is the implication that left-handed people are somehow awkward or unrefined whereas right-handed people are capable and proficient.

Consider this brief passage from Barbara Lawrence's "Dirty Words Can Harm You," which draws on etymology to show that a common profanity—the F-word—means far more than most people realize when they hear or use it:

> The best known of the tabooed sexual verbs, for example, comes from the German *ficken,* meaning "to strike"; combined, according to Partridge's etymological dictionary *Origins,* with the Latin sexual verb *futuere;* associated in turn with the Latin *fustis,* "a staff or cudgel"; the Celtic *buc,* "a point, hence to pierce"; the Irish *bot,* "the male member"; the Latin *battuere,* "to beat"; the Gaelic *batair,* "a cudgeller"; the Early Irish *bualaim,* "I strike"; and so forth. It is one of what etymologists sometimes call "the sadistic group of words for the man's part in copulation."

NEGATION

Sometimes the best way to define something is to explain what it isn't, a technique called *definition by negation.* This technique—illustrating the way a subject differs from another, often more familiar, subject—often proves to be an effective way to communicate the meaning of a complex subject to your reader. When you write that "intelligence isn't merely the knowledge of a great volume of facts," for instance, you also suggest that being intelligent involves not only knowing the facts but also recognizing the significance of and connections among these facts.

Take a look at the example below, from *The Second Fifty Years,* a collection of informational materials designed for senior citizens and their families. This definition of a nursing home begins by examining what nursing homes are not, making what they are—centers for rehabilitation, support, and so on—easier for the audience to understand:

> A nursing home is not like a hospital. Many people, especially after recent hospitalizations, think of the nursing home as an extension of hospital care. They expect the same kind of intensive care they received in the hospital. A nursing home is different. First, it is a home with nursing care available as needed, 24 hours a day, 7 days a week.

The goals of the nursing home are to:

- Rehabilitate the resident to maximum potential and enable him or her to return to independent living arrangements if possible;
- Maintain that maximum rehabilitation as long as possible within the realities of age and disease;
- Delay deterioration in physical and emotional well-being; and
- Support the resident and family, physically and emotionally, when health declines to the point of death.

CHECKLIST FOR USING DEFINITION

---

1. Have the elements of definition been considered to ensure that the material is **complete**, **clear**, and **precise?**
2. Has some combination of **formal**, **limited**, and **extended definition** been included?
3. Do the elements in the definition answer **the needs of the audience?**
4. Have **denotation**, **connotation**, or **etymology** been employed to help develop the definition?
5. Has definition through **negation** been used when appropriate?

AN ANNOTATED EXAMPLE

ELLEN GOODMAN
The Workaholic

In the United States, the legend goes, work hard and you will succeed. But some people step far beyond merely working hard and lose themselves in the process. These individuals are the workaholics. In this piece Ellen Goodman, nationally syndicated Boston Globe *columnist, defines the term* workaholic *by discussing the life—and death—of Phil, the ultimate company man. Widely recognized for her insightful writing, Goodman, Associate Editor of the* Boston Globe, *whose columns regularly appear in the* Washington Post *and other newspapers across the United States, was awarded the Pulitzer Prize for commentary in 1980. Goodman, who began her career in 1963 as a researcher and reporter for* Newsweek, *has seen her work collected in several volumes, including* At Large *(1981),* Keeping in Touch *(1985),* Making Sense *(1989), and* Value Judgments *(1993). She is also coauthor (with Patricia O'Brien) of* I Know Just What You Mean: The Power of Friendship in Women's Lives *(2000).*

Why is it that Phil never sees where his attitude and lifestyle are taking him?

The opening paragraphs identify the characteristics that typify a workaholic.

1 He worked himself to death finally and precisely at 3 a.m. Sunday morning.

2 The obituary didn't say that, of course. It said that he died of a coronary thrombosis—I think that was it—but everyone of his friends and acquaintances knew it instantly. He was a perfect Type A, a workaholic, a classic, they said to each other and shook their heads—and thought for five or ten minutes about the way they lived.

His background and status are part of the definition of workaholic.

3 This man who worked himself to death finally and precisely at 3 a.m. Sunday morning—on his day off—was 51 years old and he was a vice-president. He was, however, one of the six vice-presidents, and one of the three who might conceivably—if the president died or retired soon enough—have moved to the top spot. Phil knew that.

Goodman includes additional parts of the definition.

4 He worked six days a week, five of them until 8 or 9 at night, during a time when his own company had begun the four-day week for everyone but the executives. He worked like the Important People. He had no outside "extracurricular interests," unless, of course, you think about a monthly golf game that way. To Phil, it was work. He always ate egg-salad sandwiches at his desk. He was, of course, overweight, by 20 or 25 pounds. He thought it was okay though, because he didn't smoke.

Note the irony.

5 On Saturdays, Phil wore a sports jacket to the office instead of a suit, because it was the weekend.

He had a lot of people working for him, maybe 60, and most of them liked him most of the time. Three of them will be seriously considered for his job. The obituary didn't mention that. 6

She shifts to others affected—this is also a part of the extended definition.

But it did list his "survivors" quite accurately. He is survived by his wife, Helen, 48, a good woman of no particular marketable skills, who worked in an office before marrying and mothering. 7

She had, according to her daughter, given up trying to compete with his work years ago, when the children were small. A company friend said, "I know how much you will miss him." And she answered, "I already have." 8

"Missing him all these years," she must have given up part of herself which had cared too much for the man. She would be "well taken care of." 9

She includes other consequences—part of the definition.

His eldest of the "dearly beloved" children is a hard-working executive in a manufacturing firm down South. In the day and a half before the funeral, he went around the neighborhood researching his father, asking the neighbors what he was like. They were embarrassed. 10

Others in the family are affected by Phil's workaholism.

His second child was a girl, who is 24 and newly married. She lives near her mother and they are close, but whenever she was alone with her father, in a car driving somewhere, they had nothing to say to each other. 11

12

The youngest is 20, a boy, a high-school graduate who has spent the last couple of years, like a lot of his friends, doing enough odd jobs to stay in grass and food. He was the one who tried to grab at his father, and tried to mean enough to him to keep the man at home.

He was his father's favorite. Over the last two years, Phil stayed up nights worrying about the boy. 13

The boy once said, "My father and I only board here." 14

At the funeral, the 60-year-old company 15
president told the 48-year-old widow that the 51-year-old deceased had meant much to the company and would be missed and would be hard to replace. The widow didn't look him in the eye. She was afraid he would read her bitterness and, after all, she would need him to straighten out the finances—the stock options and all that.

She includes additional ramifications of Phil's workaholism.

Phil was overweight and nervous and 16
worked too hard. If he wasn't at the office, he was worried about it. Phil was a Type A, a heart-attack natural. You could have picked him out in a minute from a lineup.

She repeats these words from the first paragraph to signal the conclusion and the moral of the story.

So when he finally worked himself to 17
death, at precisely 3 a.m. Sunday morning, no one was really surprised.

By 5 p.m. the afternoon of the funeral, the 18
company president had begun, discreetly of course, with care and taste, to make inquiries about his replacement. One of three men. He asked around: "Who's been working the hardest?"

Your Turn: Responding to the Subject

a. In many ways, Goodman has supplied the portrait of the perfect worker, a man so devoted to the company that he dies on his own time. For this assignment, choose a subject—for instance, a politician, coach, public servant, or parent—and provide an extended definition of its ideal.

b. Following Goodman's lead, focus on the hazards associated with being the perfect example of anything.

JOE ROGERS

Yellow Skies, Blue Trees

Most sighted people take many things about vision for granted. Chief among these things is that when we look at the world around us, the colors we see around us match their names and the expectations that people in general have—the blue of the ocean, the green of the grass, the orange of, well, oranges. But as anyone who has taken a basic art course or who has simply closely examined places and things knows, any color includes a whole range of shades. Still, when the majority of people look at the yellow of a daffodil or the red of a Valentine heart, they perceive the same basic hue. Yet for a sizable minority, by some counts as many as 12 percent among males of European descent, the pink of a rose or the purple of an eggplant is quite different from what the majority sees. In the following essay, which originally appeared as a "My Turn" piece in Newsweek, *journalist Joe Rogers offers a extended definition of colorblindness that takes his reader into a world that is far from colorless.*

In a world full of vibrant colors, what does it mean to be colorblind?

A fellow fourth grader broke the news to me after she saw my effort on a class assignment involving scissors and construction paper. "You cut out a purple bluebird," she said. There was no reproach in her voice, just a certain puzzlement. Her observation opened my eyes—not that my eyes particularly help—to the fact that I am colorblind. In the 36 years since, I've been trying to understand what that means. I'm still not sure I do. 1

My research hasn't been overly scientific. I know colorblindness is almost always a genetic condition, affecting males far more often than females. It has to do with color receptors, called cones, in the retina. There's some question as to whether the problem exists in the cones themselves, or the brain's ability to process the signals the cones send. 2

That debate I leave to others. I'm more concerned with the practical effects, such as: how can I tell when the hamburgers I'm grilling are done? Some of my past dinner guests can attest to the difficulty I've had making that determination. 3

On the positive side, there's a certain conversational value in the condition. When I confess my colorblindness (it often has a way of coming up), people at first assume my world resembles a Matthew Brady 4 photograph or a 1930s movie, pre-Ted Turner. I explain to them the failing of the word itself. Total colorblindness is exceedingly rare. People who suffer from it usually have a host of other problems as well, including extreme sensitivity to light and poor visual acuity. Those of us with a simple color-vision deficiency face much more mundane problems: If I wear this shirt with these pants, will people stare? Or, worse, laugh?

5 Early on, I learned the hazards of shopping alone for clothes, when I bought a blue shirt that turned out to be—yes—purple. Even dressing myself is hazardous. I've mistaken green shirts for gray, brown pants for green. And I'm hopeless with ties. I never wear one unless it's been cleared for use by someone I trust.

6 Fortunately, some clothing makers include the color of their garments on price tags. Unfortunately, those colors tend to be listed in terms such as raisin, sesame, citron, salmon, shrimp, celery, saffron, wheat and maize. It doesn't help to tell me my clothes are the color of a fruit, grain, seasoning or water creature when I don't know what color any of them is, either.

7 Because the most common form of colorblindness involves distinguishing red and green, people logically assume it involves only those two hues. That is the type I have, but the problem is not as simple as it sounds. Sometimes I can tell red from green. Sometimes I can't. It depends on how intense the colors are, how much light is available, how far away I am from the objects in question.

8 I can always tell a red traffic signal from a green one, for instance. I can't tell a lone red signal from a yellow one. At night, from a distance, I can't tell a green signal from the glow of a street light. My confusion can make for some adventurous driving.

9 Other nonassertive colors can be troublesome, too. When I bought my house a few years back, I assumed the livingroom walls were some variation of a neutral white tone. A visitor told me they were, in fact, quite pink—that I was more or less living inside a bottle of PeptoBismol. I called a painter who recommended something he called eggshell. I took his advice.

10 That sort of thing is a source of great amusement for my color-visioned friends. When they learn my world is not completely black and white, they get a kick out of pointing to various items and asking what color I think they are. When I say I don't know, they almost invariably ask: "Well, what color does it look like?"

11 It's hard to explain that the color they see simply isn't on my list of options. They seem to prefer to think that I see all the right colors but in the wrong places. That life for me, and those similarly afflicted, is a psychedelic planet of yellow skies, blue trees and orange oceans. I admit, I sometimes wonder myself whether other people see a completely different world.

Usually my problem is of little consequence. Like not knowing whether I've picked up a spearmint or cinnamon gum ball until I put it into my mouth. Or having to ask a store clerk what, precisely, is meant by a tag that says a jacket is "bark." 12

Of course, my career options have been limited by my condition. Fashion designer or interior decorator were never on the list. And in the case of war, where it might be of real importance to differentiate the people in green uniforms from those in brown or gray, I would not be your man. 13

There have been certain drawbacks in my job as newspaper reporter. When it comes to painting a picture in words, my palette is limited. There are no comparative allusions to sunsets in my work, no evocations of azure or magenta. No one has ever described my writing as colorful. 14

At least two purported cures exist. One involves a red-orange contact lens, worn only on one eye. A Japanese clinic claims results with treatments involving electrodes at specific points—a sort of electric acupuncture. I haven't personally investigated either, partly because I'm not sure my brain could handle a world without color confusion. Besides, I wonder how much real need there is to be able to perceive jute or ocher. 15

Over the years I've considered petitioning the federal government to include colorblindness among the legally recognized disabilities, but I suspect we lack collective political clout. I've also made some passing effort to form an association—a League for the Color-Vision Impaired, say. Unlike left-handers, however, we seem disinclined to rally round our deviation from the norm. Thus there's no ready source of information about how many presidents, or military heroes, or rock singers have been colorblind. 16

Based on the law of averages, though, there must have been some. We are everywhere, trying to cope, trying to blend in. Usually we succeed. Until someone spots our purple bluebirds. Then the jig is up. 17

Understanding the Significance

1. How did Rogers first come to understand that he was colorblind?
2. What is the biggest misconception most people have about colorblindness?

3. What problem does Rogers note about efforts by some clothing manufacturers to identify the color of their garments?
4. Even though possible cures or corrections for colorblindness exist, why hasn't Rogers sought them out?

Discovering the Writer's Purpose

1. Why do you think Rogers didn't focus more on scientific or medical information about colorblindness? Do you agree with his approach? Why or why not?
2. Most of Rogers's examples concern mundane matters—mismatched clothes, shopping issues, decorating concerns, and so on. By concentrating on these kinds of examples, what is Rogers suggesting about being colorblind?
3. In the tenth paragraph, Rogers discusses the typical questions that his noncolorblind friends ask. What point do you think Rogers is making about those of us who are, in his words, color-visioned?
4. In his final two paragraphs, Rogers suggests and then discards the idea of political action to bring attention to colorblindness. In doing so, what point is he reemphasizing about being colorblind?

Examining the Writer's Method

1. In the second paragraph, Rogers offers a limited definition of colorblindness. How does this brief definition help move the extended definition forward?
2. In both the fourth and seventh paragraphs, Rogers includes negation. How does this use of negation help him develop his definition?
3. In your view, which of Rogers's many examples of colorblindness does the best job of developing or supporting his extended definition of colorblindness? What about this example makes it stand out?
4. How do the final two paragraphs serve as an effective conclusion for Rogers's essay?

Considering Style and Language

1. How would you describe the tone of Rogers's essay? How does this tone help Rogers explain the nature of colorblindness?
2. From your reading, how do you think Rogers feels about being colorblind? What in his essay leads you to this conclusion?
3. In several spots in his essay, Rogers includes the names of some exotic shades and hues. Why do you think he included these names rather than explain them as variations of more basic and easily recognized colors—red, blue, yellow, etc.? Do you agree with his choice? Explain your reasoning.
4. What do the following words mean in the context of the writing? *Reproach, puzzlement* (para. 1); *genetic, receptor, retina* (para. 2); *attest* (para. 3); *acuity, mundane* (para. 4); *intense* (para. 7); *adventurous* (para. 8); *nonassertive, troublesome, variation, neutral* (para. 9); *invariably* (para. 10); *option, afflicted, psychedelic* (para. 11); *consequence* (para. 12); *differentiate* (para. 13); *palette, allusion, evocation* (para. 14); *purported* (para. 15); *clout, disinclined, rally, deviation* (para. 16).

Your Turn: Responding to the Subject

a. As a colorblind person Rogers is different from the majority of people, an outsider of sorts. But what does it actually mean to be an outsider, someone who is beyond some part of the mainstream? In Rogers' case, it is being colorblind in a world of color-sighted people. For others, it is being left-handed, having a musical, artistic, or athletic gift, being overly sensitive, having a great or poor memory, and so on. For this assignment, consider an element of your own combination of talents and characteristics—or the combination in someone you know—that indicates outsider status. Then write an essay in which you spell out what it means to be different from most people.

b. In many ways, Rogers's essay concerns perception and sensitivity. For this assignment, choose one of these terms and write an essay in which you turn to definition to explain this general, abstract term in full detail.

ROGER ROSENBLATT

The Man in the Water

When Air Florida's Flight 90 hit a bridge and crashed into the Potomac River on January 14, 1982, shortly after takeoff from Washington National Airport, television cameras brought the aftermath of the tragedy right into the living rooms of America. Writer Roger Rosenblatt, whose work has appeared in Time, Life, *and the* Washington Post, *was one of the millions of television witnesses who watched as victims struggled to survive in the icy waters and rescuers risked their own lives to try to save them. In this essay, which appeared in* Time *shortly after the crash, Rosenblatt discusses the behavior and fate of one of the victims, a man who chose to help others rather than to save himself. Through this focus, Rosenblatt, who has also served as literary editor for the* New Republic, *director of education for the National Endowment for the Humanities, author of several books, including* The Man in the Water *(1994) and most recently* Rules for Aging: Resist Normal Impulses, Live Longer, Attain Perfection *(2000), and essayist and commentator for* Newshour with Jim Lehrer, *provides a moving definition of heroism.*

Amid the actions of many people who acted heroically, what makes this man in the water so special?

As disasters go, this one was terrible, but not unique, certainly not among the worst on the roster of U.S. air crashes. There was the unusual element of the bridge, of course, and the fact that the plane clipped it at a moment of high traffic, one routine thus intersecting another and disrupting both. Then, too, there was the location of the event. Washington, the city of form and regulations, turned chaotic, deregulated, by a blast of real winter and a single slap of metal on metal. The jets from Washington National Airport that normally swoop around the presidential monuments like rushed gulls are, for the moment, emblemized by the one that fell; so there is that detail. And there was the aesthetic clash as well—blue-and-green Air Florida, the name a flying garden, sunk down among gray chunks in a black river. All that was worth noticing, to be sure. Still, there was nothing very special in any of it, except death, which, while always special, does not necessarily bring millions to tears or to attention. Why, then, the shock here? 1

Perhaps because the nation saw in this disaster something more than a mechanical failure. Perhaps because people saw in it no failure at all, but rather something successful about their makeup. Here, after all, were two forms of nature in collision: the elements and human character. Last Wednesday, the elements, indifferent as ever, brought down Flight 90. And on that same afternoon, human nature—groping and flailing in mysteries of its own—rose to the occasion. 2

Of the four acknowledged heroes of the event, three are able to account for their behavior. Donald Usher and Eugene Windsor, a park police helicopter team, risked their lives every time they clipped the skids into the water to pick up survivors. On television, side by side in bright blue jumpsuits, they described their courage as all in the line of duty. Lenny Skutnik, a 28-year-old employee of the Congressional Budget Office, said: "It's something I never thought I would do"—referring to his jumping into the water to drag an injured woman to shore. Skutnik added that "somebody had to go in the water," delivering every hero's line that is no less admirable for its repetitions. In fact, nobody had to go into the water. That somebody actually did so is part of the reason this particular tragedy sticks in the mind. 3

But the person most responsible for the emotional impact of the disaster is the one known at first simply as "the man in the water." (Balding, probably in his 50s, an extravagant mustache.) He was seen clinging with five other survivors to the tail section of the airplane. This man was described by Usher and Windsor as appearing alert and in control. Every time they lowered a lifeline and flotation ring to him, he passed it on to another of the passengers. "In a mass casualty, you'll find people like him," said Windsor. "But I've never seen one with that commitment." When the helicopter came back for him, the man had gone under. His selflessness was one reason the story held national attention, his anonymity another. The fact that he went unidentified invested him with a universal character. For a while he was Everyman, and thus proof (as if one needed it) that no man is ordinary. 4

Still, he could never have imagined such a capacity in himself. Only minutes before his character was tested, he was sitting in the ordinary plane among the ordinary passengers, dutifully listening to the stewardess telling him to fasten his seat belt and saying something about the "no smoking sign." So our man relaxed with the others, some of whom would owe their lives to him. Perhaps he started to read, or to doze, or to regret some harsh remark made in the office that morning. Then suddenly he knew that the trip would not be ordinary. Like every other person on that flight, he was desperate to live, which makes his final act so stunning. 5

For at some moment in the water he must have realized that he would not live if he continued to hand over the rope and ring to others. He had to know it, no matter how gradual the effect of the cold. In his judgment he had no choice. When the helicopter took off with what was to be the last survivor, he watched everything in the world move away from him, and he deliberately let it happen. 6

Yet there was something else about the man that kept our thoughts on him, and which keeps our thoughts on him still. He was there, in the essential, classic circumstance. Man in nature. The man in the water. For its part, nature cared nothing about the five passengers. Our man, on the other hand, cared totally. So the timeless battle commenced in the Potomac. For as long as that man could last, they went at each other, nature and man; the one making no distinctions of good and evil, acting on no principles, offering no lifelines; the other acting wholly on distinctions, principles and, one supposes, on faith. 7

Since it was he who lost the fight, we ought to come again to the conclusion that people are powerless in the world. In reality, we believe the reverse, and it takes the act of the man in the water to remind us of our true feelings in this matter. It is not to say that everyone would have acted as he did, or as Usher, Windsor and Skutnik. Yet whatever moved these men to challenge death on behalf of their fellows is not peculiar to them. Everyone feels the possibility in himself. That is the abiding wonder of the story. That is why we would not let go of it. If the man in the water gave a lifeline to the people gasping for survival, he was likewise giving a lifeline to those who observed him. 8

The odd thing is that we do not even really believe that the man in the water lost his fight. "Everything in Nature contains all the powers of Nature," said Emerson. Exactly. So the man in the water had his own natural powers. He could not make ice storms, or freeze the water until it froze the blood. But he could hand life over to a stranger, and that is a power of nature too. The man in the water pitted himself against an implacable, impersonal enemy; he fought it with charity; and he held it to a standoff. He was the best we can do. 9

Understanding the Significance

1. The people that Rosenblatt identifies—Donald Usher, Eugene Windsor, Lenny Skutnik, and the man in the water—are all heroes. In paragraph 3, he says the first three can "account for

their behavior." What does he mean by that statement? Does that fact make their actions somehow less heroic?

2. Certainly most people would agree that the man in the water acted heroically. But isn't there a fine line between heroism and self-destruction? As Rosenblatt points out in paragraph 6, "at some moment in the water he must have realized that he would not live if he continued to hand over the rope and ring to others." Why do you think he ultimately refused to save himself?
3. At the end of paragraph 8, Rosenblatt states that "if the man in the water gave a lifeline to the people gasping for survival, he was likewise giving a lifeline to those who observed him." What does Rosenblatt mean? Explain.
4. In the final paragraph, Rosenblatt makes this statement: "The odd thing is that we do not even really believe that the man in the water lost his fight." The man in the water perishes, so what do you think Rosenblatt means? Do you agree with his reasoning? Why or why not?

Discovering the Writer's Purpose

1. In his introduction to this essay, Rosenblatt provides a number of striking details. In your judgment, which phrase or image does the most to bring the scene to life?
2. In paragraph 2, Rosenblatt suggests that people didn't see the crash as a failure but as an event that showed "something successful" in our makeup. What element of the human character is he talking about? In what way did the actions of people after the crash, especially the man in the water, display this successful aspect?
3. Part of Rosenblatt's definition, as he notes in paragraph 8, is that "everyone feels the possibility in himself" to perform heroically. Do you agree? Why or why not?
4. In the final paragraph, what is Rosenblatt saying about the relationship between man and nature?

Examining the Writer's Method

1. Rosenblatt doesn't establish his main focus until paragraph 4, when he first mentions the man in the water. Do you feel his essay would have been more effective if he had indicated this focus in the opening paragraph? Explain.

2. In paragraph 4, Rosenblatt notes that one thing that makes this situation unique is that the hero was anonymous. How might Rosenblatt's definition have been different if he knew the name of the man in the water?
3. In paragraph 5, Rosenblatt suggests what the man in the water might have been thinking and experiencing before the crash. How does this material tie into Rosenblatt's definition of heroism?
4. If you were going to reduce Rosenblatt's extended definition of heroism (as illustrated by the story of the man in the water) to a limited definition, what characteristics or elements would you include in that definition?

Considering Style and Language

1. Some readers might point out that in his opening paragraph Rosenblatt seems almost to undercut this tragedy. Why do you think he chose to discuss it in this way?
2. In paragraph 7, Rosenblatt sums up the struggle of the man in the water as "the essential, classic circumstance. Man in nature." What point does he make through this comparison?
3. From paragraph 5 on, Rosenblatt uses the first-person plural (*we, our,* and *us*) as he discusses the man in the water. What point is Rosenblatt making by using the plural rather than the singular?
4. What do the following words mean in the context of the writing? *Chaotic, aesthetic, clash* (para. 1); *indifferent, groping, flailing* (para. 2); *extravagant, commitment, selflessness, invested, universal* (para. 4); *capacity, dutifully* (para. 5); *classic* (para. 7); *abiding* (para. 8); *pitted, implacable* (para. 9).

Your Turn: Responding to the Subject

a. The concrete actions of the man in the water enable Rosenblatt to define the abstract concept of heroism. For this assignment, choose another abstract concept, such as charity, fear, apathy, and so on, and use the actions of some person or persons to define the term.
b. The crash of Air Florida's Flight 90 certainly qualifies as a tragedy, but why exactly? In other words, what constitutes a tragedy? For this assignment, define tragedy.

ANNA QUINDLEN

Homeless

A 1974 graduate of Barnard College, Anna Quindlen joined the New York Times *in 1977 as a general assignment reporter. Following stints writing the* Times' *"About New York" and "Hers" columns and serving as the deputy metropolitan editor, Quindlen took a brief sabbatical from journalism to concentrate on raising her family and to work on her fiction. Her first novel,* Object Lessons, *was published in 1991; her most recent,* Black and Blue, *was published in 1998. In 1986, she returned to the* New York Times, *this time to write columns entitled "Life in the 30's," a collection of which were published in 1987 under the title of* Living Out Loud. *In 1990, she moved to the op-ed page of the* New York Times, *writing a column entitled "Public and Private" that covered a wide variety of topics, including social issues, politics, and abortion for which she was awarded the Pulitzer Prize for commentary in 1992. A collection of "Public and Private" pieces was published in 1993 under the title* Thinking Out Loud. *More recently, Quindlen has written a biweekly column for* Newsweek, *where she serves as a contributing editor. Her most recent books include* How Reading Changed My Life *(1998) and* A Short Guide to a Happy Life *(2000). In this essay, from* Living Out Loud, *Quindlen focuses on the issue of homelessness, examining what this apparently simple term actually means.*

Is homelessness more than merely being without a place to live?

Her name was Ann, and we met in the Port Authority Bus Terminal several Januarys ago. I was doing a story on homeless people. She said I was wasting my time talking to her; she was just passing through, although she'd been passing through for more than two weeks. To prove to me that this was true, she rummaged through a tote bag and a manila envelope and finally unfolded a sheet of typing paper and brought out her photographs. 1

They were not pictures of family, or friends, or even a dog or cat, its eyes brown-red in the flashbulb's light. They were pictures of a house. It was like a thousand houses in a hundred towns, not suburb, not city, but somewhere in between, with aluminum siding and a chain-link fence, a narrow driveway running up to a one-car garage and a patch of backyard. The house was yellow. I looked on the back for a date or a name, but neither was there. There was no need for discussion. I knew what she was trying to tell me, for it was something I 2 had often felt. She was not adrift, alone, anonymous, although her bags and her raincoat with the grime shadowing its creases had made me believe she was. She had a house, or at least once upon a time had had one. Inside were curtains, a couch, a stove, potholders. You are where you live. She was somebody.

I've never been very good at looking at the big picture, taking the global view, and I've always been a person with an overactive sense of place, the legacy of an Irish grandfather. So it is natural that the thing that seems most wrong with the world to me right now is that there are so many people with no homes. I'm not simply talking about shelter from the elements, or three square meals a day or a mailing address to which the welfare people can send the check—although I know that all these are important for survival. I'm talking about a home, about precisely those kinds of feelings that have wound up in cross-stitch and French knots on samplers over the years. 3

Home is where the heart is. There's no place like it. I love my home with a ferocity totally out of proportion to its appearance or location. I love dumb things about it: the hot-water heater, the plastic rack you drain dishes in, the roof over my head, which occasionally leaks. And yet it is precisely those dumb things that make it what it is—a place of certainty, stability, predictability, privacy, for me and for my family. It is where I live. What more can you say about a place than that? That is everything. 4

Yet it is something that we have been edging away from gradually during my lifetime and the lifetimes of my parents and grandparents. There was a time when where you lived often was where you worked and where you grew the food you ate and even where you were buried. When that era passed, where you lived at least was where your parents had lived and where you would live with your children when you became enfeebled. Then, suddenly where you lived was where you lived for three years, until you could move on to something else and something else again. 5

And so we have come to something else again, to children who do not understand what it means to go to their rooms because they have never had a room, to men and women whose fantasy is a wall they can paint a color of their own choosing, to old people reduced to sitting on molded plastic chairs, their skin blue-white in the lights of a bus station, who pull pictures of houses out of their bags. Homes have stopped being homes. Now they are real estate. 6

People find it curious that those without homes would rather sleep sitting up on benches or huddled in doorways than go to shelters. Certainly some prefer to do so because they are emotionally ill, because they have been locked in before and they are damned if they will be locked in again. Others are afraid of the violence and trouble 7 they may find there. But some seem to want something that is not available in shelters, and they will not compromise, not for a cot, or oatmeal, or a shower with special soap that kills the bugs. "One room," a woman with a baby who was sleeping on her sister's floor, once told me, "painted blue." That was the crux of it; not size or location, but pride of ownership. Painted blue.

This is a difficult problem, and some wise and compassionate 8
people are working hard at it. But in the main I think we work around it, just as we walk around it when it is lying on the sidewalk or sitting in the bus terminal—the problem, that is. It has been customary to take people's pain and lessen our own participation in it by turning it into an issue, not a collection of human beings. We turn an adjective into a noun: the poor, not poor people; the homeless, not Ann or the man who lives in the box or the woman who sleeps on the subway grate.

Sometimes I think we would be better off if we forgot about the 9
broad strokes and concentrated on the details. Here is a woman without a bureau. There is a man with no mirror, no wall to hang it on. They are not the homeless. They are people who have no homes. No drawer that holds the spoons. No window to look out upon the world. My God. That is everything.

Understanding the Significance

1. In the first two paragraphs, Quindlen introduces the reader to Ann. What does Ann do to demonstrate to Quindlen that she is not homeless?
2. From the description Quindlen provides, what kind of life do you think Ann had once enjoyed?
3. According to Quindlen, why do some people prefer living on the street instead of living in a shelter?
4. As Quindlen sees it, what is the difference between someone who is homeless and someone who has no home?

Discovering the Writer's Purpose

1. In the opening paragraph, Quindlen notes that Ann keeps her photographs wrapped in a sheet of typing paper. What point is Quindlen trying to make by mentioning this detail?

2. Quindlen states that she has "an overactive sense of place" (paragraph 3). What do you think she means?
3. In paragraph 8, Quindlen states that to keep ourselves from becoming too involved in the problems of others we "turn an adjective into a noun." What point is she making?
4. Quindlen uses the brief sentence "That is everything" twice, once in paragraph 4 and again in paragraph 9. In your view, does the sentence have the same meaning each time? Explain.

Examining the Writer's Method

1. In the introduction, Quindlen makes it a point to identify the homeless woman by name. Why do you think she chooses to discuss the woman in this way?
2. In your view, where in her essay does Quindlen provide the most thorough definition of homelessness?
3. What does Quindlen mean in the sixth paragraph when she discusses a home versus real estate?
4. How does the concluding paragraph help Quindlen reiterate her point about the homeless?

Considering Style and Language

1. Quindlen uses negation in the third paragraph as a way to expand her definition of homelessness. Why do you think she chooses to state what homelessness isn't rather than to concentrate on what homelessness is?
2. Quindlen makes it a point in paragraph 7 to say that one homeless woman with a baby had once told her that what she wanted was a single room, "painted blue." What is the significance of the woman's aspiration? Why does Quindlen repeat the words?
3. In the concluding paragraph, Quindlen first uses some specific details ("a woman without a bureau," "a man with no mirror, no wall to hang it on") to reiterate what she feels is the difference between being homeless and lacking a home. But then, rather than ending her essay, she provides a few other specific details. Why does she structure the paragraph in this way? Why doesn't she provide all the specific details before emphasizing the distinction between the two states of existence?

4. What do the following words mean in the context of the writing? *Rummaged* (para. 1); *adrift, anonymous, grime* (para. 2); *legacy, cross-stitch, French knots, samplers* (para. 3); *ferocity, certainty, stability, predictability* (para. 4); *enfeebled* (para. 5); *huddled, crux* (para. 7); *bureau* (para. 9).

Your Turn: Responding to the Subject

a. Quindlen makes it abundantly clear in this essay that a home is far more than simple shelter from the elements. But what makes a home a home? For this assignment, examine in detail your view of the elements that constitute a home.
b. In the third paragraph, Quindlen notes that she has "never been good at looking at the big picture, taking the global view...." The big picture and the global view are both common expressions, but what do they mean? For this assignment, choose one of these terms and define it as you understand it.

Other Possibilities for Using Definition

Here are some additional subjects for a paper that features definition. Feel free to adapt these topics until you feel more comfortable with them. Then concentrate on explaining your main idea in detail and providing plenty of support in the form of specific details and examples.

- Faith
- A masterpiece of literature, music, or art
- Freedom
- Rationalization
- Success
- Beauty
- Conscience
- Sexual harassment
- Etiquette
- Humor
- An effective boss or supervisor
- A sports, music, dance, computer, or religious fanatic
- Academic dishonesty
- Respect
- Charisma

Writing at Work

DEFINITION

EARTH & SKY

Tonight's Sky

Clarity is one of the factors that is most required in the various documents we are exposed to on a daily basis. In many cases, definition is the writing technique that provides that clarity. In a computer manual, it's definition that explains what a disk cache *is. In an insurance policy, it's a definition that explains what a* deductible *is. And in a booklet published by a human resources office, it's definition that spells out what* personal leave *is. Definition plays a major role in the following passage, which is a web page excerpt from* Earth & Sky, *an award-winning radio report.* Earth & Sky *is heard daily on hundreds of commercial and public radio stations in the United States and Canada, across the South Pacific, and on international networks, presenting information about astronomy. In this broadcast, definition is used to explain the familiar constellation Orion.*

FRIDAY, OCTOBER 20, 2000—LOOKING EAST-SOUTHEAST AROUND MIDNIGHT. By midnight around now, the constellation Orion the Hunter can be seen starting its ascent into the southeastern sky. Orion is a mighty star figure. The most noticeable thing about the constellation is the Belt of Orion—a straight line of three medium-bright stars at the Hunter's mid-section. You'll also see a very bright star on either side of the Belt—somber red Betelgeuse on the left, in this picture—and blue-white Rigel on the right. Orion is striking by itself, but it's an important constellation at this time of year because it's the "radiant point" for an annual meteor shower. Since meteor showers are named for the constellations from which they appear to radiate, this shower is called the Orionids. The Orionids are predicted to peak tomorrow morning. Unfortunately, there's a bright moon up after midnight now—so the Orionids will be mostly a washout this year. Still, if you're up around midnight gaze southeastward for Orion the Hunter—always worth a look!

Tonight's Sky for Friday, October 20, 2000
Northern hemisphere

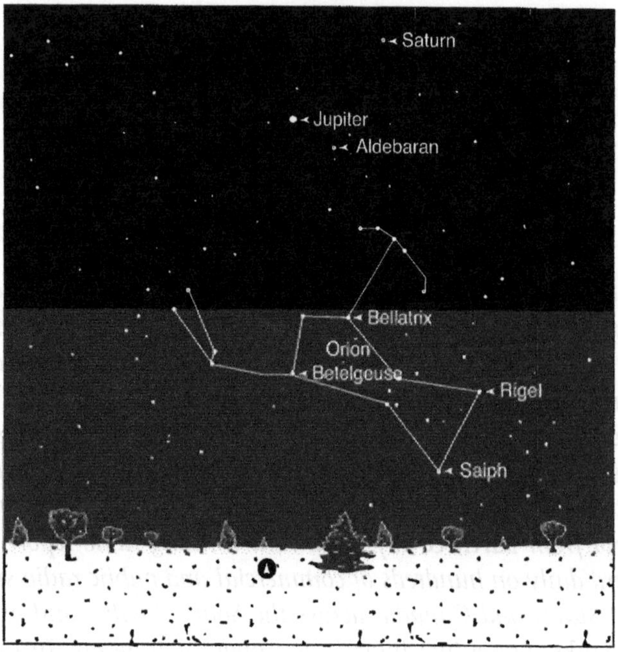

Images created using "Starry Night Deluxe" by Sienna Software.

Let us know what you think!

Focusing on the Message and Aim

Answer each of the following questions in a brief paragraph.

1. How does the definition of Orion help to explain the relationship between the constellation and the meteor shower that occurs each year around October 20?

2. In the definition, the constellation Orion is called "mighty," and the star Betelgeuse is described as "somber." What are the connotations of these words, and what part do these meanings play in the effectiveness of the piece?
3. In the fifth sentence, the term *radiant point* is used. On the basis of the information provided about the Orionids, how would you define *radiant point*?

Applying the Principles

a. Choose another term, element, or characteristic related to astronomy, geography, physics, or geology and, using this piece about Orion as a model, create a brief definition.
b. The constellation that is the subject of this piece is named for a character from Greek mythology. What is mythology? After researching the term, complete a one-page definition of the word, providing examples from at least three mythological systems.

Practical Application: Definition

"I like my job as administrative assistant to the chair of the Chamber of Commerce," you were just telling a friend the other day. "The best part is that I never know from one day to the next what I'll be asked to do." So you shouldn't really have been surprised when your boss approached you this afternoon, looking uncharacteristically flustered.

The problem, she explains, is tomorrow evening's annual Chamber banquet and the five-minute speech she is supposed to make about the award winner. Each year the selection committee chooses a theme and then selects the nominee whose qualities and actions match the theme. This year's theme is heroism, and the recipient is Miss Lucretia Salinger, a retired legal secretary in her late 70s who has devoted her energies to the cause of adult literacy. Three afternoons a week since her retirement 15 years ago, she has worked with adults who desperately want to learn to read and write, tutoring them one-on-one in a small room in the back of the public library.

Your boss knows how deserving Miss Salinger is of the award; so far she has not been able to express her admiration effectively, however, and she has four other tasks on her desk that must be done by the end of the day. "You had a course in speech in college—would you write it up for me, about three hundred words or so? And would you also list the main ideas in a rough outline to make it easier for me to keep things straight? Thanks!" After swallowing nervously, you agree. To make your job easier, she gives you a copy of the speech "Courage: A Hero in Our Midst"—with a brief outline—prepared by staffer Stephen M. Haugh on the theme of courage for last year's presentation. Use it to guide you in terms of approach and format as you prepare your speech and outline about Miss Salinger.

Courage: A Hero in Our Midst

Good evening, ladies and gentlemen, and welcome to our annual banquet. It's great to see such a big turnout, and I know we're all going to enjoy ourselves tonight.

As you know, the theme of this year's banquet is courage. We are so very proud to honor our nominee this year. In fact, this is not the only award he has received this month. Our guest of honor, Mr. John Slovack, recently was awarded one of our nation's top military honors—the Silver Star medal.

John Slovack grew up in this town. He has raised a fine family and is a respected member of the community. Like many of our young men, he enlisted in the army in the late 60s and served in Vietnam. Now, I knew that John saw plenty of action on the front lines and was wounded in battle himself. What I certainly did not know about was the exceptional courage and bravery that he exhibited in that terrible war.

During a fierce battle, according to his fellow soldiers, John's unit was pinned down by artillery fire and was in a very bad way. A few members of his squad had already been killed or wounded.

Well, apparently, that's when our John took matters into his own hands. Crawling on his belly, he worked his way around and behind the enemy fire and knocked out their stronghold single-handedly, probably saving the lives of his entire unit.

Now John should have received his Silver Star more than 25 years ago, but the paperwork somehow got lost. So that's why we're finally hearing about all this now. A group of his buddies petitioned Washington and got it all straightened out. Lord knows, we never heard a word about it from the man himself.

In addition to your courage, John, we ought to honor you for your modesty as well. Honestly, a war hero in our midst all these years, and we never knew. Well it's out now, John.

Now I know this little award of ours is nothing compared to the Silver Star, but we had to let you know just how proud we are of you.

Ladies and gentlemen, it is indeed our privilege and honor to award to John Slovack this humble award for courage above and beyond the call of duty.

I. Welcome
II. This year's theme: Courage; John Slovack—Silver Star
III. Slovack—local boy—Vietnam
IV. Fierce battle—pinned down
V. Bravery in action
VI. Should have received medal 25 years ago—finally straightened out
VII. A hero in our midst all these years
VIII. Our award versus Silver Star
IX. Our privilege and honor—humble award

10

Comparison and Contrast

The Technique

In writing, the analytical method used to examine similarities or differences is called *comparison and contrast,* with *comparison* referring to an examination of similarities and *contrast* referring to an examination of differences. You'll probably find that you use comparison and contrast frequently when you write, both in a supporting role and as the dominant mode in an essay.

Although you'll rely on comparison and contrast in a variety of writing situations, you'll find this mode especially helpful in the academic writing you'll be expected to complete. In a literature class, for instance, you might be asked to discuss the similarities of characters in a novel or the imagery in some poems. In a history class, you might be asked to examine one civilization or political system in relation to another. In a psychology class, you might be asked to note the differences among behavioral disorders. To gain the most from your use of comparison and contrast, regardless of your purpose, you need to

- establish a clear basis for comparison;
- make a thorough and specific presentation;
- use appropriate analogies as illustration; and
- provide an effective arrangement for the material.

A CLEAR BASIS FOR COMPARISON

Whenever you use comparison and contrast, you need to establish a clear basis for comparison. In other words, once you have your subjects, you need to decide whether you are going to examine the similarities, the differences, or both. Then you choose the aspects, characteristics, or elements of each subject you are going to present.

In some ways, the framework of comparison and contrast often lends itself most easily to considering *two* alternatives—for example, determining the relative advantages of public schooling versus home schooling or of buying a new fleet of trucks versus fixing a company's aging ones. Dealing with two subjects means fewer switches from subject to subject, reducing the opportunities for confusion on the part of the reader.

Once you've zeroed in on your subjects, you need to decide which elements to examine. For the essay about which of two laptop computers to purchase, you would identify several aspects that potential buyers would need to know, such as price, types and availability of bundled software, processor speed, and warranty. With a clear basis of comparison established, you're prepared to develop the essay, discussing each element in relation to each subject.

The following is a brief excerpt from "Listening to Khakis," Malcolm Gladwell's essay on Levi Strauss & Company's successful marketing strategy to sell Docker pants. As he refers to Professor Joan Meyers-Levy's research on this subject, Gladwell sets up his basis of comparison for his discussion of the different ways that women and men process information:

> This idea—men eliminate and women integrate—is called by Meyers-Levy the "selectivity hypothesis." Men are looking for a way to simplify the route to a conclusion, so they seize on the most obvious evidence and ignore the rest, while women, by contrast, try to process information comprehensively. So-called bandwidth research, for example, has consistently shown that if you ask a group of people to sort a series of objects or ideas into categories, the men will create fewer and larger categories than the women will. They use bigger mental bandwidths. Why? Because the bigger the bandwidth, the less time and attention you have to pay to each individual object.

A THOROUGH AND SPECIFIC PRESENTATION

As is true any time you write, when you craft an essay in which you compare or contrast subjects, you need to examine the subjects fully. Of course, no rule sets an automatic number of points of comparison you should establish, but common sense indicates that subjects striking you as similar or dissimilar do so because of more than one or two aspects. Therefore, as you work through the writing process, shoot for a basis of comparison that contains at least three points and then add any additional points that you develop as you write.

For example, imagine you were going to write a paper contrasting downhill skiing with cross-country skiing. Certainly, these two winter sports are different in terms of the expense involved and specialized equipment required. But these activities also differ in terms of terrain required (steep mountain slopes for downhill versus rolling terrain for cross-country); degree of danger involved (considerable danger in downhill, especially to legs because of speed and strain from sharp turns, versus minimal danger in cross-country); and amount of training involved (several hours of lessons and practice for downhill skiing versus a brief lesson and an hour or so of practice for cross-country skiing). A paper dealing with only the first two points of comparison would be inadequate; an essay that features these five points of comparison would clearly do a better job of showing that these two sports are indeed vastly different.

Take a look at the following example, from *101 Ways to Help Your Daughter Love Her Body,* which offers several characteristics associated with the typical heroine before and after the advent of movies:

> Our grandmothers had close extended families and stable communities filled with women of numerous body types. Of course, they also dreamed of romance and excitement, but those dreams were encouraged via literature and the radio. These images were more a product of the individual's imagination. As listeners and readers pictured a heroine, they adapted to a wide range of body types based on the women in their lives—tall, buxom, self-assured aunts; portly sisters with a bloom in their cheeks; a favorite teacher who was feather light.
>
> These images narrowed as Hollywood sought out a body type that would look good on the silver screen and eventually on television, media that make actors appear about fifteen pounds heavier than they really are. . . . The media now promote a look that can catch the eye to sell a product. With heights of five feet seven inches or taller and weights between 100 and 110 pounds, fashion models are about 23 percent slimmer than 75 percent of American women, who weigh, on average, about 143 pounds and are five feet four or shorter.

APPROPRIATE ANALOGIES AS ILLUSTRATION

One way to illustrate and explain your comparison and contrast is to include an occasional **analogy**, a comparison of two quite dissimilar things—for example, going on a scholarship or job interview and running a 5K road race. Because an analogy is a surprising or unexpected comparison, it can stimulate a reader's interest in and understanding of your subjects.

Consider the following analogy from a report by the Institute of Medicine concerning work in health care and work on an aircraft carrier. Chances are that most readers have never considered the kind of evaluation this analogy represents. But the passage clearly conveys the rationale for comparing health care systems with aircraft carriers—to specify *how* health care differs from manufacturing processes—so this analogy offers a useful insight on the dynamic and collaborative nature of health care:

> [Health care] is very different from a manufacturing process, mostly because of huge variability in patients and circumstances, the need to adapt processes quickly, the rapidly changing knowledge base, and the importance of highly trained professionals who must use expert judgment in dynamic settings. . . . The performance of crews and flight personnel on aircraft carriers provides an example that has features that are closer to those in health care environments than manufacturing. . . . On the flight deck, 100 to 200 people fuel, load munitions, and maintain aircraft that take off and are recovered at 48- to 60-second intervals. As in health care, it is not possible in such dynamic settings to anticipate and write out a rule for every circumstance.

AN EFFECTIVE ARRANGEMENT

How you present the material constituting an essay is always important because an effective arrangement makes it easier for your reader to follow your line of reasoning. In writing that features comparison and contrast, organization is especially important because the focus is on an examination of more than one subject.

For an essay comparing or contrasting two subjects, you have three possible methods of arrangement: the *block method,* the *alternating method,* and the *mixed method.* Imagine, for example, that you were writing about two bosses for whom you've worked, and you had established this basis of comparison: knowledge of the job, leadership, patience with workers, and basic fairness.

With the block method, you would first discuss—paragraph by paragraph—these qualities for Boss One and then the same criteria in the same order for Boss Two. With the alternating method, you would first discuss knowledge of the job for Boss One and then for Boss Two. Next, you would discuss leadership for Boss One and then for Boss Two, and so on. Brief outlines for these two methods would look like this:

Block Method	*Alternating Method*
Boss One	**Knowledge of Job**
Knowledge of job	Boss One
Leadership	Boss Two
Patience with Workers	**Leadership**
Basic Fairness	Boss One
Boss Two	Boss Two
Knowledge of job	**Patience with Workers**
Leadership	Boss One
Patience with Workers	Boss Two
Basic Fairness	**Basic Fairness**
	Boss One
	Boss Two

The following paragraph from an astronomy textbook by Jay M. Pasachoff relies on the block pattern to discuss Earth and its nearest neighbor, Venus:

> Venus and the Earth are sister planets: their sizes, masses, and densities are about the same. But they are as different from each other as the wicked sisters were from Cinderella. The Earth is lush; it has oceans and rainstorms of water, an atmosphere containing oxygen, and creatures swimming in the sea, flying in the air, and walking on the ground. On the other hand, Venus is a hot, foreboding planet with temperatures constantly over 750 K° (900°F), a planet on which life seems unlikely to develop. Why is Venus like that? How did these harsh conditions come about? Can it happen to us here on Earth?

And the following paragraph from Aubrey Menen's "Dazzled in Disneyland" illustrates the alternating pattern in its discussion of Disneyland's Tom Sawyer's Island versus Pinocchio's Village:

> There are two kinds of legends: with one sort we can get inside them; with the other we are always spectators. I suppose there can be no American male who has not, at some time in his life, found himself alone in the countryside and explored Tom Sawyer's Island, or fought Indians, or crept on his belly up to a paleface fort. But nobody, I think, at any age plays Water Rat and Toad, or goes into Mole's house, or plays Prince Charming or Cinderella (unless driven to it by sentimental elders). These stories are too complete to have room for the outsider. We would know what to say to Pinocchio if we met him, or the Three Ugly Sisters. But we do not imagine ourselves being these people. A lesser man than Disney would not realize this. But here Tom Sawyer's Island is big enough for children to play on; and Pinocchio's Village is so small there is not even room in its streets to put one's foot. Once again Disney shows himself a master of the use of proportion.

Of course with the mixed method, as the name suggests, you set up the information in some other way. In the essay contrasting your two bosses, using the block format to present the first three points and then switching to the alternating format for the final point enables you to emphasize how important it is that a supervisor consistently treat employees with basic fairness.

CHECKLIST FOR USING COMPARISON AND CONTRAST

---

1. Is the **basis for comparison and contrast** in the document **clearly established**, identifying what **elements** or **characteristics** will be **evaluated?**
2. Have you chosen **appropriate subjects** for analysis by comparison and contrast and identified the **focus of the analysis:** differences, similarities, or a combination?
3. Is the **presentation** of similarities or differences **thorough,** covering four or more aspects or features?
4. Do any **analogies** offer **stimulating illustrations** or **explanations** of the subjects, making it easy to understand the larger issue?
5. Are the similarities or differences **arranged explicitly** through the **block** or **alternating method** or an **effective combination** of the two?

AN ANNOTATED EXAMPLE

DEBORAH TANNEN

Conversation at Warp Speed

The cliché The Generation Gap refers to a very real divide between two different age groups. In its most common usage, Generation Gap points to the division between teenagers and their parents (and others of their parents' age groups) in terms of social issues, music, style of dress, and so on. But this particular Generation Gap isn't the only one. Numerous elements of modern society have created and fostered numerous generation gaps—divisions between groups holding opposing attitudes about or reactions to these elements. Change, an inevitable reality of life, especially of life at a 21st century pace, creates and fuels many of these gaps, as some people hold on to what was while others embrace what is or will soon be. In the following essay, linguist and writer Deborah Tannen relies on a clear basis of comparison and contrast and numerous specific examples—including some statistical details—to analyze the gap in the way that different groups of people talk today, both in person and on the screen.

Does the rapid speech of today's young people differ enough from that of their parents to impede communication?

She uses the opening paragraph to focus attention on her general subject: the speed of speech.

1 I have interrupted the brilliant young student in my graduate seminar, who is making an important contribution to the discussion. To justify my rude interjection, I add, "We have non-native speakers in the class. They may not be able to follow if you talk that fast."

She identifies what she is contrasting, the degree of rapidity of speech with which two different generations are comfortable.

2 But the truth is, I'm having trouble following her myself. I feel as if I'm hanging on by the skin of my earlobes, still trying to figure out the point she just made while she's already on to the next one—and the next, and the one after that. The student confesses, "My mother tells me the same thing. She goes. . . ." and demonstrates the mouth-noise her mother uses to re-create the impression made by her daughter's fast speech: Her tongue trills while

her throat emits a steady, high-pitched sound, like a tape recording of someone making motor sounds played back at Donald Duck speed. I'm relieved to learn that my student's mother feels as I do: that I'm running to catch up with someone who is widening the gap between us with every word.

This feeling comes over me not only when 3
I'm listening to some of my students, but also when I'm watching many popular forms of entertainment. The scenes in movie trailers flit by so fast I'm still trying to decipher and digest the single line (or half-line, or quarter-line) from one scene while the picture has zipped through three more. (I've clocked it: two seconds per scene.) And, as the executive producer of one television news magazine confirmed, segments on these shows are shorter now, with more frequent shot changes.

She uses comparison and contrast to discuss a difference between one of today's shows and shows of the past.

She uses comparison and contrast to highlight differences between her parents' generation and her own relative to the speed of speech in some of today's TV shows.

If it's tough for me, it's even tougher for 4
my father, a lifelong devotee of political talk shows. When I ask him what he thinks of Chris Matthews, he says he has no idea: Matthews talks too fast for him to understand. It's not as if TV producers don't know they might be losing the older generation, even as they court the younger one. Aaron Sorkin, creator and chief writer of *The West Wing*, says that each week he gets a call from his parents, saying "Great show. Tell them to talk slower." Apparently his parents don't know that their son and other producers are doing just the opposite: egging on the actors to talk faster.

She uses comparison and contrast to underscore the way things were for her parents' generation versus the way they are today.

This is one more way that the gap between 5
old and young is widening as fast as the frequently noted gap between rich and poor. My father is frustrated not only by fast-paced commentator talk but also by countless other ways that technology has made the world harder to navigate. When he makes a phone call to a business, he rarely encounters people he can ask to slow down, speak louder or explain what they said. Instead he gets menus

that fly by too fast, are too hard to hear and offer choices that don't apply to the purpose of his call.

It's easy to see why cost-conscious companies prefer automated phone systems to employees who require salaries, rest rooms and health insurance. But why would TV and film writers want to obscure the dialogue they worked so hard to create, making it harder for us to hear their words? 6

I've always assumed that it was a miscalculation, a misstep in the quest for ever snappier and more riveting shows. But it turns out that I'm the one who didn't understand: This is the result of a deliberate determination to speed up dialogue, comprehension be damned. 7

This thinking was explained by the producer of a popular TV show on the WB network, *Gilmore Girls,* which features a mother-daughter duo who are more like friends than like parent and child. The elder Gilmore, Lorelai, became a single mother while still in her teens; now she is in her early thirties and her daughter, Rory, is a teen. The creator, Amy Sherman-Palladino, told *The Wall Street Journal* recently that zippiness is the motivation for many aspects of *Gilmore Girls*: no close-ups (they slow things down); frequent shots of characters talking as they walk from place to place; and scenes shot over and over to shave a few seconds off the already dizzying pace. Screenwriters traditionally figure a page of dialogue to a minute on air; Sherman-Palladino figures 20 to 25 seconds a page. 8

She uses comparison and contrast to illustrate how a particular TV show differs from other shows.

Surely the fast-forward speech of *Gilmore Girls* helps the characters sound like hip teenagers, just as their jeans and midriff-baring blouses clinging skin-tightly to their teen-thin bodies help both "girls" look like teens. But network shows aimed at fully adult audiences, like the wildly popular *West Wing,* follow the same trend. Hollywood producers, according to *The Wall Street Journal* article, think that people seem smarter if they talk faster. 9

She uses comparison and contrast to show how two shows aimed at different audiences employ the same technique.

As a linguist, author and passionate lover of words, I'm a professional analyst of conversation; my life's work is deconstructing the dialogue of everyday life. So shouldn't I celebrate the news that TV shows have more dialogue? Yes, if the talk is there to communicate ideas. Yes, if it means that packing more talk into limited air time means that talk is receiving more emphasis, more pride-of-place, as I have always thought it should have in our understanding of relationships. But not if the dialogue flies by so fast that it cannot be fully processed or even, in many cases, literally comprehended. The general ideas may get through: I'm sure that fans of *Gilmore Girls* and *West Wing* can recount each show's plot and theme. But I suspect that their understanding is gleaned from the general march of scenes and the gist of dialogue—rather than from the subtle nuances of phrasing and the precise wording or sequence of ideas. 10

She uses comparison and contrast to demonstrate how younger audiences interpret what they see and hear on the TV screen in contrast to how audiences in the past interpreted them.

From this view, the speeding up of TV dialogue is more like life and less like art. Letting dialogue roll over you, rather than putting it in a frame that invites you to examine it closely, is not all that different from what we do in everyday conversation, where we might not process every word that passes our ears, or every image that flits by our line of vision. We get a sense of what's going on—or at least think we do. 11

We all choose our words, and our style of saying them, not only to communicate ideas but also—perhaps mostly—to convey the kind of person we are (or want to be). Teenagers talk the way they do (not only quickly, but also with intonation that makes their statements sound like questions and with generous sprinklings of "like") because they want to sound like their friends. That's why parents who tell their teen-age children not to say "like," to send their intonation down rather than up at sentence ends and to "Slow down!" are fighting a losing battle— 12

She uses comparison and contrast to illustrate teenagers' attitudes about speech versus their parents' attitudes.

though it's a battle most parents will win without a fight when their kids grow up.

She uses comparison and contrast to remind her reader that different generations react in different ways to the speed of speech they experience when they watch TV or other media.

I rarely have to tell my brilliant young student to slow down anymore. This may be because she's two years older or because she'll soon be applying for jobs and knows she'll need to sound more like a professor than a teenager. I have no doubt, though, that the entertainment media will continue the lip-trilling pace of dialogue designed to appeal to the younger, free-spending viewers—as well as the graying, balding and paunching older ones who want to feel that we're still capable of being cool. 13

Your Turn: Responding to the Subject

a. In her essay, Tannen focuses on the differing comfort levels experienced by teenagers and those a generation or two older when they experience the speed of speech in television and film productions. For this assignment, think of other ways that your generation differs from people your parents' or grandparents' age. Then, turning to comparison and contrast, write an essay that details these differences.

b. As Tannen notes in her essay, she is "a professional analyst of conversation," immersing herself not just in what people say but in how they say it. And how people say it—more specifically the different accents that characterize different areas or regions—is your topic. For this assignment, consider two different locales with which you are familiar, for instance, your home town and another city or town where you have lived or visited, two regions of the country (the Midwest and New England), two countries that have a common language (the U.S. and Australia, Portugal and Brazil), and so on. Then write an essay in which you explore the accents of the two areas.

KAY REDFIELD JAMISON

Speaking of Madness

A thesaurus, both the actual one and the virtual one on the computer screen, should occupy a prominent place on every writer's desktop. This invaluable tool, a compilation of synonyms, provides broad possibilities in terms of words that could be used in a document. The tricky thing about using a thesaurus is to keep in mind that synonyms are not perfect equivalents, a potential problem when your goal is precision. This is exactly the point that Kay Redfield Jamison raises about terms and expressions used to label mental illness in this excerpt from her book An Unquiet Mind: A Memoir of Moods and Madness. *After discussing differing attitudes relative to the way people describe mentally ill people, she narrows her focus to the substitution of bipolar disorder for manic-depressive illness. With this framework established, she uses comparison and contrast, with definition providing additional support, to emphasize that, in her view as someone managing this condition, the switch falls far short in accurately describing this condition.*

What does the language often used to describe mental illness say about the public's perception and understanding of mental health?

Not long before I left Los Angeles for Washington, I received the most vituperative and unpleasant letter that anyone has ever written me. It came not from a colleague or a patient, but from a woman who, having seen an announcement of a lecture I was to give, was outraged that I had used the word "madness" in the title of my talk. I was, she wrote, insensitive and crass and very clearly had no idea at all what it was like to suffer from something as awful as manic-depressive illness. I was just one more doctor who was climbing my way up the academic ranks by walking over the bodies of the mentally ill. I was shaken by the ferocity of the letter, resented it, but did end up thinking long and hard about the language of madness. 1

In the language that is used to discuss and describe mental illness, many different things—descriptiveness, banality, clinical precision, and stigma—intersect to create confusion, misunderstanding, and a gradual bleaching out of traditional words and phrases. It is no longer clear what place words such as "mad," "daft," "crazy," "cracked," or "certifiable" should have in a society increasingly sensitive to the feelings and rights of those who are mentally ill. Should, for example, ex- 2 pressive, often humorous, language—phrases such as "taking the fast trip to Squirrel City," being a "few apples short of a picnic," "off the wall," "around the bend," or "losing the bubble" (a British submariner's term for madness)—be held hostage to the fads and fashions of "correct" or "acceptable" language?

One of my friends, prior to being discharged from a psychiatric hospital after an acute manic episode, was forced to attend a kind of group therapy session designed as a consciousness-raising effort, one that encouraged the soon-to-be ex-patients not to use, or allow to be used in their presence, words such as "squirrel," "fruitcake," "nut," "wacko," "bat," or "loon." Using these words, it was felt, would "perpetuate a lack of self-esteem and self-stigmatization." My friend found the exercise patronizing and ridiculous. But was it? On the one hand, it was entirely laudable and professional, if rather excessively earnest, advice: the pain of hearing these words, in the wrong context or the wrong tone, is sharp; the memory of insensitivity and prejudice lasts for a long time. No doubt, too, allowing such language to go unchecked or uncorrected leads not only to personal pain, but contributes both directly and indirectly to discrimination in jobs, insurance, and society at large. 3

On the other hand, the assumption that rigidly rejecting words and phrases that have existed for centuries will have much impact on public attitudes is rather dubious. It gives an illusion of easy answers to impossibly difficult situations and ignores the powerful role of wit and irony as positive agents of self-notion and social change. Clearly there is a need for freedom, diversity, wit, and directness of language about abnormal mental states and behavior. Just as clearly, there is a profound need for a change in public perception about mental illness. The issue, of course, is one of context and emphasis. Science, for example, requires a highly precise language. Too frequently, the fears and misunderstandings of the public, the needs of science, the inanities of popularized psychology, and the goals of mental health advocacy get mixed together in a divisive confusion. 4

One of the best cases in point is the current confusion over the use of the increasingly popular term "bipolar disorder"—now firmly entrenched in the nomenclature of the Diagnostic and Statistical Manual (DSM-IV), the authoritative diagnostic system published by the American Psychiatric Association—instead of the historic term "manic-depressive illness." Although I always think of myself as a manic-depressive, my official DSM-IV diagnosis is "bipolar I disorder; recurrent; severe with psychotic features; full interepisode recovery" (one of the many DSM-IV diagnostic criteria I have "fulfilled" along the way, and a personal favorite, is an "excessive involvement in pleasurable activities"). Obviously, as a clinician and researcher, I strongly 5 believe that scientific and clinical studies, in order to be pursued with accuracy and reliability, must be based on the kind of precise language and explicit diagnostic criteria that make up the core of DSM-IV. No patient or family member is well served by elegant and expressive language if it is also imprecise and subjective. As a person and patient, however, I find the word "bipolar" strangely and powerfully offensive: it seems to me to obscure and minimize the illness it is supposed to represent. The description "manic-depressive," on the other hand, seems to capture both the nature and the seriousness of the disease I have, rather than attempting to paper over the reality of the condition.

Most clinicians and many patients feel that "bipolar disorder" is 6
less stigmatizing than "manic-depressive illness." Perhaps so, but perhaps not. Certainly, patients who have suffered from the illness should have the right to choose whichever term they feel more comfortable with. But two questions arise: Is the term "bipolar" really a medically accurate one, and does changing the name of a condition actually lead to a greater acceptance of it? The answer to the first question, which concerns accuracy, is that "bipolar" is accurate in the sense that it indicates an individual has suffered from both mania (or mild forms of mania) and depression, unlike those individuals who have suffered from depression alone. But splitting mood disorders into bipolar and unipolar categories presupposes a distinction between depression and manic-depressive illness—both clinically and etiologically—that is not always clear, nor supported by science. Likewise, it perpetuates the notion that depression exists rather tidily segregated on its own pole, while mania clusters off neatly and discreetly on another. This polarization of two clinical states flies in the face of everything that we know about the cauldronous, fluctuating nature of manic-depressive illness; it ignores the question of whether mania is, ultimately, simply an extreme form of depression; and it minimizes the importance of mixed manic-and-depressive states, conditions that are common, extremely important clinically, and lie at the heart of many of the critical theoretical issues underlying this particular disease.

But the question also arises whether, ultimately, the destigmatiza- 7
tion of mental illness comes about from merely a change in the language or, instead, from aggressive public education efforts; from successful treatments, such as lithium, the anticonvulsants, antidepressants, and antipsychotics; from treatments that are not only successful, but somehow also catch the imagination of the public and media (Prozac's influence on public opinion and knowledge about depression, for example); from discovery of the underlying genetic or other biological causes of mental illness; from brain-imaging techniques,

such as PET and MRI (magnetic resonance imaging) scans, that visually communicate the location and concrete existence of these disorders; from the development of blood tests that will ultimately give medical credibility to psychiatric diseases; or from legislative actions, such as the Americans with Disabilities Act, and the obtainment of parity with other medical conditions under whatever health-reform system is put into place. Attitudes about mental illness are changing, however glacially, and it is in large measure due to a combination of these things—successful treatment, advocacy, and legislation.

The major mental health advocacy groups are made up primarily 8
of patients, family members, and mental health professionals. They have been particularly effective in educating the public, the media, and the state and national governments. Although very different in styles and goals, these groups have provided direct support for tens of thousands of individual patients and their families; have raised the level of medical care in their communities by insisting upon competence and respect through, in effect, boycotting those psychiatrists and psychologists who do not provide both; and have agitated, badgered, and cajoled members of Congress (many of whom themselves suffer from mood disorders or have mental illness in their families) into increasing money for research, proposing parity for psychiatric illnesses, and passing legislation that bans job and insurance discrimination against the mentally ill. These groups—and the scientists and clinicians who make treatment possible—have made life easier for all of us who have psychiatric illnesses, whether we call ourselves mad or write letters of protest to those who do. Because of them, we now have the luxury of being able to debate the fine points of language about our own and the human condition.

Understanding the Significance

1. What complaint does the woman who writes to Jamison raise in the letter mentioned at the opening of this excerpt?
2. What was the rationale offered to Jamison's friend as she was being discharged from a psychiatric hospital concerning banishing from use commonly used colloquial expressions about mental illness?
3. What is her main objection about substituting *bipolar disorder* for *manic-depressive illness?*
4. According to Jamison, who has been most effective in raising public awareness and dispelling misconceptions about mental illness?

Discovering the Writer's Purpose

1. What do you think is Jamison's primary message about language used to describe mental illness? Do you think she successfully communicates it? Explain your reasoning.
2. Why does Jamison feel that restricting the kinds of "language of madness" that some people find demeaning or insensitive is probably not worth fighting about?
3. Through her detailed explanation of the various elements of the condition formerly called manic-depressive disorder, what point do you think she makes about this condition and mental illness in general?
4. How does Jamison's conclusion help to reinforce her main point?

Examining the Writer's Method

1. In your view, how does Jamison's introduction help to lay out her case concerning the public's understanding of and reaction to mental illness?
2. Jamison uses comparison and contrast to examine several different aspects of her subject of the language of madness. In doing so, does she rely more on the block method or the alternating method? How does this arrangement affect the impact and accessibility of the points she is making?
3. In the fifth paragraph, Jamison notes that she is "a clinician and researcher" and also "a person and patient". How does this particular use of comparison and contrast add to her presentation?
4. Jamison includes the definition for bipolar I disorder from the *Diagnostic and Statistical Manual*—the *DSM-IV*—the primary diagnostic lexicon employed by practitioners. In what other ways does definition support comparison and contrast and help Jamison make her case that manic-depressive illness is a more accurate title for her condition?

Considering Style and Language

1. Jamison opens this essay with a number of euphemisms—terms considered to be less objectionable and more socially acceptable

than the terms they replace—to describe being mentally ill. Since she admits that some people find these words offensive, why do you think she chose to include them?

2. Throughout this document, Jamison employs first-person point of view. In your view, how would the overall effectiveness of the piece have been changed if she had relied entirely on third-person point of view instead?
3. In the seventh paragraph, Jamison uses the word *glacially* to discuss how public attitudes about mental illness are changing. What is she suggesting about people when the subject is as profound and complex as mental illness?
4. What do the following words mean in the context of the writing? *Vituperative, crass, ranks, ferocity* (para. 1); *banality, stigma, bleaching out, expressive* (para. 2); *manic, perpetuate, patronizing, laudable, earnest, unchecked* (para. 3); *assumption, dubious, inanities, divisive* (para. 4); *entrenched, nomenclature, diagnostic, psychotic, elegant, obscure* (para. 5); *presupposes, clinically, etiologically, perpetuate, notion, tidily, segregated, clusters, discreetly, polarization, cauldronous, fluctuating* (para. 6); *parity* (para. 7); *badgered, cajoled* (para. 8).

Your Turn: Responding to the Subject

a. What makes a state of mind or behavior abnormal—or normal? For this assignment, address this question, using comparison and contrast to explain what marks the difference between a normal attitude, interest, belief, or action and an abnormal one.

b. Sometimes, what we mean to say and what another person hears are entirely different, leading to an unexpected outcome. For this assignment, consider a time when you experienced or witnessed this kind of interaction, and then turn to the power of comparison and contrast to detail exactly what was said and meant versus what the listener heard and understood.

STEPHEN BAYLEY

The Triumph of the Good Bad Book

Sometimes, knowing when something is good—truly good—isn't as simple and easy as one might think. For instance, what happens when others, presumably more expert in evaluating the subject under discussion hold a different opinion from yours? Is a thing good if you, yourself, believe it is, or only if others think it's good? These are the questions that Stephen Bayley addresses in this essay, which originally appeared in the Los Angeles Times. *Bayley, a British art and culture critic, is a contributing editor for* GQ *magazine. He is also the author of a number of books, including* Taste: The Secret Meaning of Things *and* A Dictionary of Idiocy: And Other Matters of Opinion.

Is critical opinion of a work an accurate way to distinguish between a great book and one that just doesn't make it—and why should it matter anyway?

With "The Da Vinci Code" in the dock here in Britain, the good bad book is in the news. It's a category that riles serious literary critics. 1

Reviewing Dan Brown's best-seller, the *Times of London* described it as "without doubt the silliest, most inaccurate, ill-informed, stereotype-driven, cloth-eared, cardboard-cutout-populated piece of pulp fiction." But 40 million or so buyers have been severely entertained by it—always something that troubles the highbrows. The very literary John Updike criticized the very popular Tom Wolfe as "entertainment not literature."

George Orwell wrote an article on good bad books just after the end of World War II. This oxymoronic category attracted the author of "Animal Farm" because he was both personally and professionally committed to slumming—either on the streets of Paris or in the great halls of literature. Orwell said "Uncle Tom's Cabin" would outlive Virginia Woolf. He found that you could be amused or excited by what the intellect despises. "By any test that can be devised," Orwell wrote, "Carlyle would be found to be a more intelligent man than Trollope. Yet Trollope has remained readable and Carlyle has not." 2

Good bad books are not the same as books that are merely bad. Good bad is more subtle. A good bad book is one that achieves a 3 surprisingly exhilarating effect despite flaws of style and construction, which disqualify it as (what Updike calls) "literature." Significantly, good bad books translate very well into film, perhaps suggesting that cinema is an intellectually and artistically undemanding medium. "The Guns of Navarone," "The Graduate" and "Jaws," for example, were feeble literature but made magnificent movies.

The good bad critical label can be traced to G. K. Chesterton, inspired by the extraordinary number of very bad books, ripe with imperial pomp, scintillating with sexually repressed jingoism, that were published in the Edwardian era. But boorish pulp can be enjoyable. Bad can be good. 4

Indeed, there may be something in our circuitry that wills confusion between these poles. Urban blacks appropriated bad to mean its opposite many years ago, and the joys of inversion were taken up at the dawn of punk by Malcolm McLaren, who said of his Sex Pistols and their epic crassness on stage: "They are so bad they are good." 5

Then there are bad good books—the ones written with high artistic purpose that fail. Ernest Hemingway, Graham Greene and, more recently, Bruce Chatwin or Salman Rushdie would be many people's candidates here. Very high levels of critical toxicity are recorded in peer-group assessments of bad good books. For example, is Greene good? Bad? Good bad? Or bad good? Possibly all those things. Author Anthony Powell said, "He was good at reportage, a lively journalist, able businessman, but the novels are vulgarized Conrad, to which tedious Roman Catholic propaganda is added, and the occasional efforts at humor dreadful." 6

Rivalry may be an issue in these judgments, as one great travel writer writing on another revealed. Jan Morris said of Chatwin: "Too much for me. Snobbism, equally camp and genuine; showy connoisseurship of a quirky kind; the deadly energy of a raconteur; the insensitivity of the tuft hunter; a gift for mimicry; sexual ambiguity of the Strength Through Joy kind." 7

If there is a relish in the high-minded over recording the failures of the competition, there is also a reluctance to accept the sometimes keen pleasures of the good bad book. Brown most certainly has all the clunking faults described by the Times' crotchety critic, but "The Da Vinci Code" is an infectious read. And if great literature is not always entertaining, there are great books and poems as cloth-eared as Brown's book. 8

Alberto Manguel, Jorge Luis Borges' amanuensis, explained how the writer used to treasure terrible lines from literature. One was a character in John Webster's "The Duchess of Malfi" who says, "We are merely the stars' tennis balls." Emily Bronte's "Wuthering Heights" contains this shocker: "I had no desire to aggravate his impatience, previous to inspecting his penetralium." 9

Bad, it turns out, can be better than good and is always better than bad good, but good bad is perhaps the best of all (certainly the most entertaining). "Beowulf" has many qualities, but it is not a page-turner to rival "The Da Vinci Code." This delicious confusion makes me feel, in Mark Twain's execrable expression, "as sweet and contented as an angel half-full of pie." By any test that can be devised, that's a really bad line. 10

Understanding the Significance

1. What criticisms did the London *Times* have concerning *The DaVinci Code,* the best-selling novel written by Dan Brown?
2. As Bayley explains it, why do good bad books often translate well into movies?
3. Bayley mentions several authors acclaimed for writing great literature who also wrote bad good books, including Ernest Hemingway and Salman Rushdie. What made their bad good books different from their other writings?
4. What does Bayley think of *The Da Vinci Code* in terms of its entertainment value?

Discovering the Writer's Purpose

1. What is Bayley saying about the interests of the public versus the opinions of critics by discussing *The DaVinci Code* in his opening paragraph?
2. By including in the third paragraph the example of literary giant George Orwell, what is Bayley suggesting about the appeal of good bad books?
3. Bayley mentions noted American author and literary critic John Updike twice, first in the second paragraph and then again in the fourth paragraph. In the second instance, however, he puts Updike's name in parentheses. In your view, what comment is he making by presenting Updike's name this way?
4. In the seventh and eighth paragraphs, Bayley includes critiques that some writers have offered about works by their peers. What do these examples add to his discussion of good bad books?

Examining the Writer's Method

1. Bayley includes a number of direct quotations in his essay. Why do you think Bayley chose this method rather than to paraphrase the passages? Do you agree with his strategy? Why or why not?
2. Throughout his essay, Bayley uses comparison and contrast to discuss good bad books versus other types of books. In your view, at what point in the essay is his use of comparison and contrast most effective? Explain your reasoning.
3. Bayley relies on the alternating method to arrange his discussion of good bad books. How would his essay have been different if he had instead used the block method to discuss good bad books all at once?
4. In what way does Bayley's conclusion reinforce his main point about good bad books?

Considering Style and Language

1. How would you describe the tone in Bayley's essay? What examples or details best support your point of view?
2. In the final two paragraphs, Bayley includes samples of terrible lines from works that are considered great literature. By including these examples, what is he indicating about the nature of great literature?
3. Bayley clearly considers the connotation of a number of the words he uses to discuss critics who dismiss good bad books without considering their potential impact. In your view, which word best conveys Bayley's attitude in this regard? Why do you feel it stands out from the others?
4. What do the following words mean in the context of the writing? *Riles* (para. 1); *stereotype, pulp fiction, highbrows* (para. 2); *oxymoronic, despise* (para. 3); *subtle, exhilarating, feeble* (para. 4); *ripe, imperial, pomp, scintillating, repressed, jingoism, Edwardian, boorish* (para. 5); *inversion, epic, crassness* (para. 6); *toxicity, vulgarized, propaganda* (para. 7); *camp, connoisseurship, raconteur, mimicry, ambiguity* (para. 8); *keen, crotchety, infectious* (para. 9); *amanuensis, aggravate, penetralium* (para. 10); *execrable, devised.*

Your Turn: Responding to the Subject

a. In the fourth paragraph, Bayley notes that good bad books are often the basis for great movies. Which is better—the book or the movie—often sparks debate. For this assignment, think of a book you've read, one for adults or one for children, that has been made into a movie you have also seen. If a film version exists for a book you've read but you haven't seen it, watch it. Then use comparison and contrast to explain which version is better and why.

b. Clearly, young people aren't choosing reading as a hobby in the same numbers that they did 30, 40, or 50 years ago, a trend that has serious implications for reading success in the classroom. For this assignment, write an essay for middle-school children in your city in which you lay out why reading can be as much fun—and far more valuable—than another activity popular with middle-school-age kids.

ELIZABETH WONG

To Be an All-American Girl

Few people would dispute that childhood can often be extremely difficult, especially when children don't feel that they fit in. In Elizabeth Wong's case, being forced to attend Chinese school reinforced for her how different she felt from the rest of the world. Wong is an award-winning playwright who worked as a staff writer for the 1990s ABC sitcom All-American Girl. *She also worked as a field producer for NXT-TV* Channel Two News, *as a reporter for the* San Diego Tribune *and the* Hartford Courant, *and as an editorial writer for the* Los Angeles Times. *In this essay, which originally appeared in the* Los Angeles Times *in 1989, Wong uses comparison and contrast to show how her personal world, the world of her family and culture symbolized by the enforced Chinese language lessons, differed from the world at large.*

What power does the mainstream have that causes some people to reject their heritage in order to join the majority?

It's still there, the Chinese school on Yale Street where my brother and I used to go. Despite the new coat of paint and the high wire fence, the school I knew 10 years ago remains remarkably, stoically the same. 1

Every day at 5 p.m., instead of playing with our fourth- and fifth-grade friends or sneaking out to the empty lot to hunt ghosts and animal bones, my brother and I had to go to Chinese school. No amount of kicking, screaming, or pleading could dissuade my mother, who was solidly determined to have us learn the language of our heritage. 2

Forcibly, she walked us the seven long, hilly blocks from our home to school, depositing our defiant tearful faces before the stern principal. My only memory of him is that he swayed on his heels like a palm tree, and he always clasped his impatient twitching hands behind his back. I recognized him as a repressed maniacal child killer, and knew if we ever saw his hands we'd be in big trouble. 3

We all sat in little chairs in an empty auditorium. The room smelled like Chinese medicine, an imported faraway mustiness. Like ancient mothballs or dirty closets. I hated that smell. I favored crisp new scents. Like the soft French perfume that my American teacher wore in public school. 4

5 There was a stage far to the right, flanked by an American flag and the flag of the Nationalist Republic of China, which was also red, white and blue but not as pretty.

6 Although the emphasis at the school was mainly language—speaking, reading, writing—the lessons always began with an exercise in politeness. With the entrance of the teacher, the best student would tap a bell and everyone would get up, kowtow, and chant, "Sing san ho," the phonetic for "How are you, teacher?"

7 Being ten years old, I had better things to learn than ideographs copied painstakingly in lines that ran right to left from the tip of a moc but, a real ink pen that had to be held in an awkward way if blotches were to be avoided. After all, I could do the multiplication tables, name the satellites of Mars, and write reports on "Little Women" and "Black Beauty." Nancy Drew, my favorite book heroine, never spoke Chinese.

8 The language was a source of embarrassment. More times than not, I had tried to disassociate myself from the nagging loud voice that followed me wherever I wandered in the nearby American supermarket outside Chinatown. The voice belonged to my grandmother, a fragile woman in her seventies who could outshout the best of the street vendors. Her humor was raunchy, her Chinese rhythmless, patternless. It was quick, it was loud, it was unbeautiful. It was not like the quiet, lilting romance of French or the gentle refinement of the American South. Chinese sounded pedestrian. Public.

9 In Chinatown, the comings and goings of hundreds of Chinese on their daily tasks sounded chaotic and frenzied. I did not want to be thought of as mad, as talking gibberish. When I spoke English, people nodded at me, smiled sweetly, said encouraging words. Even the people in my culture would cluck and say that I'd do well in life. "My, doesn't she move her lips fast," they would say, meaning that I'd be able to keep up with the world outside Chinatown.

10 My brother was even more fanatical than I about speaking English. He was especially hard on my mother, criticizing her, often cruelly, for her pidgin speech—smatterings of Chinese scattered like chop suey in her conversation. "It's not 'What it is,' Mom," he'd say in exasperation. "It's 'What is it, what is it, what is it!'" Sometimes Mom might leave out an occasional "the" or "a," or perhaps a verb of being. He would stop her in midsentence: "Say it again, Mom. Say it right." When he tripped over his own tongue, he'd blame it on her: "See, Mom, it's all your fault. You set a bad example."

11 What infuriated my mother most was when my brother cornered her on her consonants, especially "r." My father had played a cruel joke on Mom by assigning her an American name that her tongue wouldn't allow her to say. No matter how hard she tried, "Ruth" always ended up "Luth" or "Roof."

After two years of writing with a moc but and reciting words with multiples of meanings, I finally was granted a cultural divorce. I was permitted to stop Chinese school. 12

I thought of myself as multicultural. I preferred tacos to egg rolls; I enjoyed Cinco de Mayo more than Chinese New Year. 13

At last, I was one of you; I wasn't one of them. 14

Sadly, I still am. 15

Understanding the Significance

1. Why were Wong and her brother unable to play with their classmates in the late afternoon?
2. What was the first lesson Wong and her brother faced each day at the Chinese school?
3. Why was Wong distressed by the presence of her grandmother in the supermarket outside of Chinatown?
4. Why was the American name that Wong's father had chosen for Wong's mother "a cruel joke"?

Discovering the Writer's Purpose

1. What point is Wong making in paragraph 2 when she refers to hunting for ghosts and animal bones?
2. In paragraph 3, Wong refers to the principal as "a repressed maniacal child killer." Why do you think she describes him in this way?
3. What might account for the fear Wong expresses in paragraph 9 that she would be thought of as mad?
4. Wong carefully details the way she felt about her mother's speech and the ways her brother would make life difficult for their mother. Why does Wong include these details?

Examining the Writer's Method

1. In the introduction, Wong suggests that, despite some changes, the school is "remarkably, stoically the same." How does this description help to prepare the reader for the body that follows?

2. Wong employs comparison and contrast to examine the two worlds she lives in. Which paragraph do you think contains the most effective use of comparison and contrast? Explain.
3. In paragraph 8, Wong focuses her attention on her grandmother. How does her childhood desire "to disassociate myself" from her grandmother help to embody her overall dissatisfaction with her life and her culture as she understood them then?
4. The last few paragraphs serve as Wong's conclusion. Why does she choose to end her paper with a single, brief sentence?

Considering Style and Language

1. Paragraph 2 contains several effective modifiers to describe the attitudes about and reactions of Wong, her brother, and her mother to attending the Chinese school. Which of those modifiers do you think is most effective? Why?
2. In both paragraph 7 and paragraph 12, Wong discusses the writing she was required to do in the Chinese school. She makes a special point in both cases to call the instrument she used by its Chinese name, moc but, rather than simply to call it a pen. Why do you think she makes this choice? How does it affect her essay?
3. What does Wong mean in paragraph 12 by "cultural divorce"?
4. What do the following words mean in the context of the writing? *Stoically* (para. 1); *dissuade; heritage* (para. 2); *forcibly, defiant, repressed, maniacal* (para. 3); *kowtow* (para. 6); *ideographs, painstakingly* (para. 7); *disassociate, fragile, raunchy, lilting, refinement, pedestrian* (para. 8); *chaotic, gibberish* (para. 9); *fanatical, pidgin, smatterings, exasperation* (para. 10).

Your Turn: Responding to the Subject

a. In the next to the last sentence, Wong states, "At last, I was one of you; I wasn't one of them," which clearly indicates her desire to be part of the majority rather than part of a minority. For this assignment, focus on what it means to be an outsider in terms of class, ethnicity, religion, physical appearance, race, or educational level. How does life for someone out of the majority, out of the mainstream, differ from the life of someone in the majority?

b. In many ways, Wong's essay concerns the world as she wishes it were versus the world as it actually is. For this assignment, consider your own childhood and then use comparison and contrast to help you answer this question: Did the life you lived at the time match the life you wanted to live?

Other Possibilities for Using Comparison and Contrast

Here are some additional subjects from which you might develop a paper focusing on comparison and contrast. As always, adapt the topic as you write your paper. For instance, if you feel the two subjects that are ordinarily seen as different are actually quite similar, feel free to follow that line of reasoning.

- Two electronic game systems
- Two teaching methods you have experienced
- Two physical activities or methods of exercise
- Two vacation spots
- The way you reacted to a situation in the past and the way you would react now
- Two professional athletes, musicians, or politicians
- The typical family today versus the typical family twenty-five years ago
- Public versus private schools or colleges
- Two teachers, dates, partners, or siblings
- Advertisements for two brands of the same kind of product
- Two different types of investments
- Two cultures
- Love versus an infatuation
- Two jobs you've held
- Two writers of horror, satire, romance, intrigue, or mystery novels

Writing at Work

COMPARISON AND CONTRAST

RONALD J. RAPAPORT, MD

Dexa Scan Report

Because examining alternatives plays such a large role in people's lives, comparison and contrast appears frequently in real-world documents. A newspaper or magazine analysis of new cars, a position paper examining the platforms of presidential candidates, and a research report concerning competing Internet companies are just a few examples of this writing technique. Comparison and contrast also plays a central role in the following document, which presents the results of a Dexa scan, a sophisticated medical test that is primarily used to measure bone density. This test is a prime weapon in the fight against osteoporosis, the debilitating disease that causes a loss of bone mass, often leading to constant pain and generally increasing disability for elderly persons as a result of repeated bone fractures. This document details the positive changes a patient has experienced since the last examination.

Focusing on the Message and Aim

Answer each of the following questions in a brief paragraph, referring specifically to the passage on the next page.

1. At various points in the piece, the writer refers to *standard deviation, T-score,* and *Z-score,* all respected statistical measures of the degree to which individual scores vary from the average. By referring to such accepted standards of analysis, what point is the writer making about these findings?
2. How would you paraphrase the message that the writer uses comparison and contrast to make in the second full paragraph, and how does the use of comparison and contrast help the reader to explain the patient's current condition?
3. Clearly this is a piece that is written from one expert to another. How would this piece be different if the writer had chosen to

Southcoast Hospitals Group
Charlton Site
Fall River, MA
D E X A S C A N R E P O R T

Name: JAMES, WILLIAM J.
Location: C-WHE **Sex:** M
Adm/Svc Date: 07/25/08
Medical Rec #: CM1104
Account #: CZ1309
Date of Birth: 12/01/53
Age: 54
Discharge Date:

JOB #: 40541

The Dexa scan was performed on 07/25/08 on a Hologic QDR 4500 W.

The average T-score of the lumbar vertebrae (L1-L4) was -0.65 standard deviations, which is 93 percent of peak bone. The T-score of the total hip was +0.11 standard deviations or 101 percent of peak bone.

This patient has had two prior scans dated 02/11/97 and 07/27/98. During this time, there has been an overall increase in the bone mineral density of the lumbar spine of 5.3 percent with 3.6 percent occurring during our last determination. The total hip has had an increase since our last determination of 3.4 percent, this too being significant.

The T-score compares patients' bone mass to normal peak bone density. This is the value which helps us determine whether treatment is necessary.

The Z-score compares patients' bone mineral density to others in their age group. This may be of interest, but it is not usually used to assess the need of therapy.

CONCLUSION: This patient has a normal bone mineral density. I would repeat his scan as clinically indicated.

Ronald J. Rapoport, M. D.

Ronald J. Rapoport, M.D.

Dictated: 07/26/08
Trans: 07/26/08 1346 Initials: DAA
Report Number: 427-11
CC: Ronald J. Rapoport, M.D.
Marc Andre Theroux, M.D.

prepare the message directly for the patient rather than for another physician?

Applying the Principles

a. How does osteoporosis differ from osteoarthritis? Do some research in print or electronic sources and then develop a 200- to 300-word explanation, suitable for distribution at the local community health center, of the similarities and differences between the two conditions.
b. This report is clearly different from other pieces in this chapter. Choose one of the other essays and prepare a one-page examination of the two documents in which you discuss the differences.

Practical Application: Comparison and Contrast

Just as you are about to save the document you have been working on for the last half-hour, your computer screen goes blank. At the same moment, you hear the angry exclamations of your supervisor and the other computer operator at the end of the room. Your blank screen and their screams can mean only one thing: The office computer system has crashed again, the third time in the last two weeks.

In many ways, it's no wonder the system keeps going down. The components are over five years old, ancient by computer standards. For the last year, you and your coworker have been urging your supervisor to replace the system. He has been resistant, citing the expense involved. Your argument has been that he should be considering the cost to the business in terms of loss or delayed work every time the system crashes, an expense that is sure to increase as the system ages further and breaks down more often.

This last crash has convinced your supervisor to change his mind. As a result, you have a new assignment. Right now, the company can absorb a $10,000 expenditure, and that translates to five complete computer systems at $2,000 each. Your job is to check the large national electronics retailers, computer magazines, mail-order houses, the Internet, and so on, and identify the two best brands available for $2,000 or less per complete unit—computer, printer-scanners, flat-screen monitors, and extended service warranties. Once you finish this research, prepare a one- to two-page memorandum outlining the characteristics and capabilities of the two best systems to help him decide which system to buy. To assist you in terms of approach and format he gives you a copy of the following memo, prepared by your coworker,

Alline Lelis, that examines two additional options for workers to communicate with each other, text messaging and instant messaging.

IBC
1133 Westchester Avenue
White Plains, New York

Memorandum

To: All employees in the accounting department
From: Alline Lelis, Group Experience Leader *AL*
Date: October 27, 2005
Re: Innovative ways of communication

Excuses such as "I couldn't reach you" and "I just can't get a hold of you" these days are obsolete. We are living the era of fast and easy communication. Telephones, faxes, pagers, e-mails, and cell phones are examples of common paths to communicate. Cell phones and e-mails have been taken to the next step, however, through text messaging and instant messaging, both of which have the potential to improve company communication.

A text message is a written cell phone message. When received on the device, the message can be read on the screen. It can be answered by using the phone's number pad. Number 1 consists of commonly used symbols in grammar, such as a comma and period, and numbers 2 through 9 are letters of the alphabet. When writing a text message, suppose you want to type "Yes." First you press 9 three times to reach "y," then press "3" two times and "7" four times to finish the word. Text messaging is simple, fast, and easy to use. It can be used to send short messages and reminders.

Text messaging is convenient but not free. Charges vary from 5 to 10 cents a text message, sent or received. Cell phone carriers offer plans for text messages. An example is Verizon Wireless. For 10 dollars a month a subscriber can have 1,000 text messages. Not everyone needs such a high number of text messages, so this carrier also offers different plans to meet different needs, including special programs for corporations.

Instant messaging is another innovative way to communicate. It is a system for real-time text messaging on the Internet. Programs such as AOL Instant Messenger and MSN Messenger allow people to talk back and forth by sending typed messages. A person can sign up for an account, and add people that have the same type of account to a list. From that list, the account holder can see who is available for conversation at the time. If a friend is available, that person just has to open an instant messaging box and talk away. An account holder chooses a screen name; a name represents that person on-line and is used by those responding. Instant messaging is free and fast, but it requires a computer, connected to the Internet, with an instant messaging program installed.

Both text and instant messaging users use a common language when communicating these ways. Words are shortened to make the typing easier and faster. Abbreviations and acronyms are often used. Some words can be replaced by a single letter, such as "you" by "u," and common sentences, such as "I don't know" to "Idk" or "I dunno." After one is familiar with text and instant messaging these will come naturally.

Through text messaging and instant messaging, communicating has been made easier, faster and more convenient. Both are simple and easy to use, so adding these innovations to our overall communications strategy makes great sense. Now that you are acquainted with these pathways of communication, go ahead and use them to make your work here more efficient and effective.

11

Cause and Effect

The Technique

Appreciating the full significance of a subject involves recognizing what has led up to it and what has resulted or may result from it. When you write, the technique that enables you to handle such subjects, to establish what led to an event, condition, or situation, or what resulted from it, is known as *cause and effect. Cause* refers to what led to something, and *effect* refers to what resulted from it. A writing examining the work of civil rights leaders Malcolm X and Martin Luther King, Jr., might point out the effects that their personal sacrifices and ultimate deaths had on the struggle for equality. It might also include background information explaining what caused each of the two to become so deeply involved in the struggle for equal rights for all people. In addition to serving as a supporting mode, cause and effect is often called upon to be the dominant mode in an essay. A paper examining the possible reasons for the rise in crimes such as carjacking would be an example. Regardless of the subject, to use cause and effect properly you must make sure to

- distinguish between direct and related causes and effects;
- acknowledge multiple cause-and-effect situations;
- choose an appropriate focus; and
- provide an effective arrangement of the material.

DIRECT AND RELATED CAUSES AND EFFECTS

All events and situations have both direct and related causes and effects, and it's important to distinguish between them to avoid overstating the relationships between what has led up to something and what has occurred as a result. Consider what happened to the U.S. Midwest during the 1930s, a phenomenon that became known as the "Dust Bowl." After several years of drought, the topsoil became so parched that it literally turned to dust and blew away.

Clearly, the *direct* cause of this disaster was the weather. But *related* causes included the farmers' ignorance about such farming techniques as proper crop rotation, fertilization, and irrigation, and the marketplace demands, which encouraged farmers to grow the same crops year after year, even though doing so would eventually strip the soil of its vitality. The direct effect of the calamity was widespread crop failure. Two related effects were the permanent displacement of thousands of farming families, whose heavily mortgaged farms were taken by the banks, and an increase in the population of migrant workers in agriculturally rich California.

Regardless of the subject, you can avoid overstating your case by using qualifying language—words such as *might be, seems, appears, rarely, often, sometimes, maybe, perhaps, probably,* and *seldom.* By using these kinds of words, you will avoid making a claim that can't be supported.

In this brief excerpt from *Tuesdays with Morrie: An Old Man, a Young Man, and Life's Greatest Lesson,* writer Mitch Albom spells out the direct effects of the amyotrophic lateral sclerosis (ALS), commonly called Lou Gehrig's disease, that is destroying Professor Morrie Schwartz's entire neurological system:

> ALS is like a lit candle: it melts your nerves and leaves your body a pile of wax. Often, it begins with the legs and works its way up. You lose control of your thigh muscles, so that you cannot support yourself standing. You lose control of your trunk muscles, so that you cannot sit up straight. By the end, if you are still alive, you are breathing through a tube in a hole in your throat, while your soul, perfectly awake, is imprisoned inside a limp husk, perhaps able to blink, or cluck a tongue, like something from a science fiction movie, the man frozen inside his own flesh. This takes no more than five years from the day you contract the disease.

Incidentally, one potential hazard when using cause and effect is confusing actual cause-and-effect relationships with *coincidence,* a sequence of events that, while accidental, appear to have been arranged or planned. This error in logic is referred to as *post hoc,* short for *post hoc, ergo prompter hoc,* a Latin phrase meaning "after this, therefore because of this."

A famous example of this kind of error appears in Robert Ablesome's *Statistics as Principled Argument.* On the Monday nine months after the fateful Monday when the massive 1965 New England blackout occurred, a reporter noted that a higher-than-average number of births had occurred. His speculation was that the loss of electricity led to increased sexual activity, resulting in a boom in the baby business. What is the truth behind this fallacy? Physicians tend to schedule planned births early in the week, so *all* Mondays and Tuesdays have more births than any other weekdays. In any case, relatively few women give birth exactly nine months to the day of conception anyway. The blackout-births connection was probably just a random relationship without any cause—it was just a coincidence.

It's also important to distinguish between *correlative* events—that is, episodes that occur at about the same time—and actual cause-and effect situations. Imagine that a year-long study of high-school students shows a decline in college board scores statewide, and another study of the same population of students shows a decline in the use of alcohol and illegal drugs over the same period of time. Surely no reasonable person would suggest that a reduction in the use of alcohol and drugs results in lower test scores. The two findings are simply matters of correlation, not cause and effect.

MULTIPLE CAUSE-AND-EFFECT SITUATIONS

Most situations and conditions have multiple causes and multiple effects. Once you have determined that you are dealing with a legitimate causal relationship, you need to present the relationship in its **full complexity**. A single cause may have more than one effect, and one effect may have several causes. For example, the single action of one character in a drama may affect the behavior of everyone else involved. Perhaps a business decides to lease, rather than purchase, a photocopying machine. An investigation into the cause leading to this decision would reveal more than one factor, including cost, frequency of repair, and quality of print.

In the following example from *The Packing Book*, a guide to effective packing while traveling, multiple causes (anxiety and, perhaps, the need to be a fashion plate) lead to one effect: overpacking. The passage also identifies overpacking itself as a cause of multiple effects—being overburdened, waiting in line, and so on—thus illustrating another aspect of cause and effect reasoning: The effect of one cause often becomes the cause of a subsequent effect:

> Welcome to Overpackers Anonymous! If you've ever experienced that sinking feeling while staring at your bed on the night before departure, clothes piled high and an open suitcase on the floor, this is the book for you. Perhaps you suffer from "just-in-case" syndrome, convinced you have to take every piece of clothing you own on a two-week trip. Do you feel compelled to pack a different fashion garment for morning, noon and night?
>
> We all know the consequences—being weighed down by luggage, dependent on others to help, waiting in endless lines, constantly managing "inventory." And for what? Most people don't use half of what they bring and swear that next time will be different.

AN APPROPRIATE FOCUS

The organizational strategy of cause and effect has enormous value to you as a writer because of its power to untangle the web of relationships inherent in complex subjects. Although the causes and effects of situations, conditions, and events are clearly related, the exact focus—on both cause and effect, primarily cause, or primarily effect—will of course depend on the scope of your writing task, your aim, and the needs of your audience.

Sometimes, you'll find an examination of both cause and effect necessary in order to help your reader toward a full understanding of the significance of your subject.

Historian Garry Wills deals with both causes and effects in this excerpt from "The Words That Remade America: Lincoln at Gettysburg," as he discusses changes that appeared in Lincoln's writing style during his political career:

> It would be wrong to think that Lincoln moved toward the plain style of the Gettysburg Address just by writing shorter, simpler sentences. Actually, that address ends with a very long sentence—eighty-two words, almost a third of the whole talk's length. So

does the Second Inaugural Address, Lincoln's second most famous piece of eloquence: its final sentence runs to seventy-five words. Because of his early experiments, Lincoln's prose acquired a flexibility of structure, a rhythmic pacing, a variation in length of words and phrases and clauses and sentences, that make his sentences move "naturally," for all their density and scope.

In some documents, however, you will focus primarily on cause. In other cases, you'll need to concentrate exclusively on cause. In this brief passage from his essay dealing with the medical amputation of a finger, "Losing Touch," A. John Roche does exactly this, focusing on what led to the need for the amputation:

> It had started about 25 years before, when, working for a gardener one summer, I cut the end of my finger with an electric hedge trimmer. The finger healed, but a piece of it was missing; a scar ran from the first knuckle up under the fingernail, and because some of the nerves were damaged, the pad of my finger didn't have much feeling.

And some situations will call for a focus on effect alone. In this excerpt from his article "The Warming of the World," for example, scientist and writer Carl Sagan deals with effect—in this case, what would happen should the sun cease to shine on our planet:

> It is warm down here on Earth because the Sun shines. If the Sun were somehow turned off, the Earth would rapidly cool. The oceans would freeze, eventually the atmosphere itself would condense out and our planet would be covered everywhere by snowbanks of solid oxygen and nitrogen 10 meters (about 30 feet) high. Only the tiny trickle of heat from the Earth's interior and the faint starlight would save our world from a temperature of absolute zero.

AN EFFECTIVE ARRANGEMENT

In order to present all cause-and-effect relationships as clearly and convincingly as possible, you must select an **effective arrangement**. Although you have a variety of options to draw on, you'll find *chronological order* and *emphatic order* particularly useful.

With chronological order, you present events in the order they occur in time, emphasizing how causes lead to particular effects. For an essay that discusses causes or consequences occurring over a period of time, such as the gradual and cumulative effects of acid rain, chronological order would be the logical choice.

As the following brief excerpt from *Crime Science: Methods of Forensic Detection* demonstrates, chronological order is ideal for a scientific analysis of processes that can't be witnessed by usual means or that occur more quickly than human perception can take in. In this case, chronological order explains the ordinary physics of an extraordinary phenomenon and thus helps illuminate the answer to this mystery: How can a shot from a .38 caliber gun cause an entrance wound smaller than .38 inches in diameter?

> We conducted experiments at length using deer skulls and a duplicate .38 revolver. Eventually one of us succeeded in producing a keyhole defect that measured only .287 across. In a subsequent article in *Identification News* and in a chapter in a book, we gave this possible explanation for a "keyhole" defect being smaller than the bullet that produced it: "as it strikes the bone tangentially, the bullet's rounded nose creates the initial small hole, and a triangular portion of bone is knocked free (or shattered into fragments) ahead of it. As the main portion of the bullet passes through the now semi-circular opening, it now forces open the 'jaws' of the same, thus allowing the larger bullet to pass on through."

Emphatic order, on the other hand, presents events in the order of their relative importance. Most useful in writing situations involving multiple causes and/or effects—for example, a paper for a public health course discussing obesity in the young or a legislative proposal to require yearly license requalification for all drivers over age 70—emphatic order introduces less important factors first and saves the strongest examples for last.

This section from *Standardized Minds: The High Price of America's Testing Culture and What We Can Do to Change It* discusses the multiple causes of the widespread use of standardized testing in the United States, with strong examples building to even stronger ones, resulting in a convincing position:

> First, Americans are obsessed with mental measurement to a degree that is rare in other countries. In contrast to what Europeans call "American tests," the examinations for college or university admission in other industrial countries are typically essay tests, in which students demonstrate knowledge of various subjects they've learned in the classroom. These tests are not unlike what

American educators call performance assessment. Compared to other countries, Americans appear to be far more obsessed with IQ, the notion that intelligence—most often defined narrowly as logical-analytical ability—is both inborn and representable as a single numerical score. . . .

What's more, standardized tests serve the perceived economic interests of colleges and universities, particularly their need for prestige, which is often the main asset they have to market to potential "customers." Pick up any of the numerous commercially published guides to colleges, universities, and graduate schools: High among the factors the guides use to rate institutions are average standardized test scores of students admitted. In a sense, Harvard would not be Harvard if those math or verbal SAT scores averaging 750 or so didn't leap from the page at readers of the *U.S. News and World Report*. . . .

Perhaps most responsible for the grip that mental testing holds on America is that it is a highly effective means of social control, predominately serving the interests of the nation's elite. Most would agree that, in a democracy, merit is a good basis for deciding who gets ahead. The rub is how you define merit. We have settled on a system that defines merit in large part as the potential to achieve according to test results. It turns out that the lion's share of the "potential" in our society goes to those with well-to-do, highly educated parents.

CHECKLIST FOR USING CAUSE AND EFFECT

---

1. Has a distinction been drawn between direct and related causes and effects, and has **qualifying language** (*might be, seems, appears, could, may*) been used in appropriate spots?
2. Is the document free from errors such as **mistaking a coincidence** or **correlative relationship** for an **actual causal relationship?**
3. Are **all causal relationships** explored in **full complexity**—that is, with attention given to possible **multiple causes** and **effects** and the ways they can affect each other?
4. Is the **focus**—on **both cause and effect**, on **cause alone**, or on **effect alone—suitable** for the **aim** and **scope** of the document and the **needs of the audience?**
5. Does the **method of arrangement** help make the cause-and-effect relationships clear to the audience?

AN ANNOTATED EXAMPLE

KEN WEBER

The Varying Wonders of Waves

Sometimes, the forces of nature seem to exert an irresistible draw on us. We seem compelled to look, whether the scene is a majestic mountain, a flowing river, a field of bright wildflowers, or a desolate expanse of desert. That's the point that Ken Weber is making with this essay about another force of nature, ocean waves. Weber, a long-time copy editor with The Providence Journal, *writes a popular feature on nature and the outdoors, which appears weekly in the Saturday edition. In this writing, Weber employs cause and effect to examine the allure of these endless movements of the sea.*

How are we affected by the natural phenomena that occur around us?

He uses his opening sentences to suggest general reactions to waves.

He lists some of the effects waves have on people.

They can soothe, they can inspire. They also can intimidate, and they can destroy. Few things in the natural world are as changeable as ocean waves. Gentle as a lullaby one day, wild and deadly another. Maybe that's why few things have captured the imagination of human beings as much, or for as long, as waves. They are mesmerizing. 1

People who venture onto the seas have to deal with waves directly, of course, and they may have a different perspective—although certainly as much respect—and destructive waves such as those spawned by hurricanes are another matter altogether. But most of us relish the endless variety of waves. When they're small and sedate, we walk in them and sit beside them and listen to their soft sloshing. A calm sea calms us. When waves are bigger, we play in them and delight in their sounds and admire their might. Energized waves energize us. And when they are very big, very loud, we are spellbound. 2

I remember, when an ocean storm was spinning around off the Carolina coast, going 3

He uses cause and effect to illustrate how weather in one area can affect another area hundreds of miles away.

down to Beavertail Park on Jamestown [RI] to check on the waves. A big storm even that far away causes a major effect up here—just ask any surfer—and I wanted to see the swells crash onto the rocks at Beavertail. The park's position at the head of Narragansett Bay makes it a perfect place to see waves that have been traveling through hundreds of miles of ocean. Storm scenes at Beavertail are always wonderful, in the original meaning of the word, filled with wonder, and what I saw that day lived up to expectations. Wave after wave surged forward, the walls of water startingly green in the sunshine. They charged close to shore, then rolled into the magnificent curls topped with gleaming white that surfers love. But the curls aren't only for surfers; they are among the most exquisite scenes in nature . . . beauty and power and grace and fleeting impermanence. Most are gone very quickly, the waves exploding on contact with the rocks. Amid the thunderous crash of water, white spray shoots upward. There is a distinctive hiss as the water drains back toward the sea. Then the next wave breaks.

He suggests that the beauty of waves is one reason why people are drawn to watch them.

As spectacular as the waves were, I became just as intrigued by the reaction of the people gathered there. A few remained in cars but most were like me, watching from a short distance out on the rough mass of rock that has been taking batterings like this from the ocean for ages. The people were simply looking. Not jabbering about the glorious curls, not exulting over the crashing or spraying, not even chatting. They watched, in virtual silence, almost reverence. When I mentioned this to a gray-haired man, he said, "Sure . . . waves are hypnotic." While answering, he never took his eyes off the water. 4

He focuses on the effects these waves have on people.

What is it about waves? Why are even people who rarely go swimming or boating, let alone surfing, so enchanted by them? What is endlessly alluring about moving water? Why do we love waves? 5

He turns his attention to the reasons people are drawn to waves.

He offers possible reasons why people like to watch waves.

Answers might be hard to put into words. Perhaps it's because the waves are constantly changing—no two are alike, no two days are the same—and maybe it's because waves have these enormous, illogical strengths. They can rise to 100 feet out on the ocean. They can toss the largest ships. They can travel for thousands of miles. Nothing can stop them. Yet, just as they can be forces of incredible destruction, they can be forces of incredible beauty, too. What is prettier than whitecaps rolling beneath shimmering sunshine? Or gentle surf reflecting a golden sunset? Or green curls with frothy white heads slamming into rocks? We like the sounds of the sea, too, the mighty crashes and the easy splashes. We like its dependability; the waves themselves may change but we know there will be waves every day. We know we can count on the sea. And maybe we like waves because they seem so alive, so . . . well, human. We even give the sea human emotions, calling it angry or calm, seething or tranquil. *6*

He presents motives for people to watch waves and the results of doing so.

There are some people who walk along the beaches every day. They say they go to exercise, to think, to recharge their batteries, the emotional and spiritual as well as the mental and physical. They know the waves when they're high and wild and when they are so slight they're barely noticeable. Ask them which they prefer and I think most would have a tough time deciding. I remember one woman saying she loved the big swells because she found them relaxing. When I asked what she liked about the tiny waves she laughed and said, "They're relaxing, too." Most people might find big waves exciting and small ones soothing, but maybe it would be the other way around. Or the words might be comforting, or inspiring, or maybe even hypnotic. *7*

Whatever it may be, many of us have a strong relationship with waves, just as our ancestors and their ancestors did. Even those *8*

He uses his conclusion to link our fascination with waves to our historical connection to the sea.

who have spent generations far from the sea feel the pull once they are back at the shores. It's as inevitable as the tide: when the waves roll in, we want to be close by. We want to watch them and listen to them and admire them. This fascination is not always easy to put into words, but it doesn't have to be explained. It's down deep inside, and it feels right. That's all that matters.

Your Turn: Responding to the Subject

a. In this essay, Weber focuses on the effects that ocean waves have on people observing them. For this assignment, consider another natural phenomenon or occurrence that you have witnessed in the company of other people—perhaps a sunrise or sunset, a meteor shower, a serious thunderstorm, or a heavy rainfall—and discuss the effects it produced on those observing it.

b. In his concluding paragraph, Weber makes the following observation: "Whatever it may be, many of us have a strong relationship with waves, just as our ancestors and their ancestors did. Even those who have spent generations far from the sea feel the pull once they are back at the shore." Weber's point is that there seems to be certain patterns that attract people, patterns that people follow without necessarily being aware of them. For this assignment, think of patterns of action, behavior, reasoning, or other habits that some people repeat from generation to generation without seeming to notice or make any efforts to change. Then use cause and effect to discuss why people act in this fashion or what happens when they do.

STANLEY ARONSON

The Sweet, Fresh Smell of Morning

Sadly, many of us are far more concerned than we should be about what others think of us. The brand of clothing to wear, the neighborhood in which to live, the type of car to buy: What happens if we make the wrong choice—what will people think? Our fears can be far more severe with things over which we have precious little control, however—things like skin texture, baldness, blushing—that others may judge as socially inferior or offensive. But how did these things come to be judged as socially unacceptable in the first place? What are the causes? This is the question that Stanley Aronson, dean emeritus of the Brown University School of Medicine, addresses about one such social no-no: bad breath. In this essay, he uses cause and effect, outlined in thorough detail, to explain how bad breath was transformed from a simple condition to a horrible social offense.

How was it possible to convince people that a naturally occurring, harmless phenomenon was something that called for immediate and regular intervention and treatment?

In a tormented world burdened with all manner of human affliction, it is bizarre, if not outrageous, to go out of one's way to create a new disease. Were this to happen today, it might properly be construed as an act of bioterrorism. In fact, such a happening did take place in 1921; it was the brainchild not of some malevolent enemy, but of a paid publicist. 1

1921 was a year of renewed hope, progress and recovery. American troops had recently returned from this nation's first major conflict conducted on European soil. And the American people, both civilian and military, were recuperating from a devastating influenza pandemic that had killed more people than the trench warfare of the recently concluded Great War. Warren Harding from Ohio was president and this nation was soberly functioning with a constitutional amendment prohibiting the manufacture and sale of alcoholic beverages. The peacetime economy, no longer based upon armaments, was seeking alternative products and newly innovative ways of using previously established products. The American economy, increasingly, relied upon advertising as its medium for converting skeptics to consumers. 2

The pharmacies of the 1920s provided many products for mouth care. Over a score of toothpastes were available, differing only in the 3 composition of their flavoring agent. And in a saturated market, there was little, beyond rank hyperbole, that these oral-hygiene products could possibly offer to the public. Unless, of course, a new threat to human health could be identified—or devised.

One of these oral-hygiene companies offered an astringent mouthwash to supplement the twice-daily use of toothbrushing. It was called Listerine to exploit the 19th century accomplishments of the great British surgeon Lord Joseph Lister, who had revolutionized surgery by converting the operating room into an aseptic chamber, thereby reducing postoperative mortality caused by infection. 4

The original formulation for Listerine was devised by Dr. J. J. Lawrence in the early 1880s and was then sold to the Lambert Drug Co. of St. Louis. Other companies eventually duplicated the formula, and by 1921 Listerine was no longer unique. Its makers then asked the obvious question: Since all mouthwashes were essentially of the same composition, what claim might be made in behalf of Listerine to make it again indispensable to the general public? And in some smoke-filled room, a group of eager young publicists sought an answer. 5

All of the mouthwashes extolled the bacteria-killing attributes of their product. But the public, in the absence of some immediate threat to themselves, continued to remain indifferent. However, if some palpable hazard could be ascribed to these oral bacteria, it was argued, the public passivity might abate. 6

It was known that oral bacteria somehow caused bad breath. But bad breath was not life-threatening nor had medicine listed it as a definable disease. The first step, then, was to provide bad breath with the aura of clinical disease. And thus, in 1921, was created a new hybrid word, halitosis (from the Latin, *halitus*, meaning breath) and the Greek suffix *-osis* (meaning an excess of, or disease of). The accusation was then spelled out: If you have bad breath you suffer from a defined social disease called halitosis and you are therefore at grave risk of being isolated by a public offended by fetid breath. 7

A great advertising campaign was then initiated, carrying whispered hints of job loss, marital discord and social quarantine unless one's bad breath was instantly neutralized. The full extent of this campaign can still be measured over eight decades later. 8

Offensive breath did not originate in the Roaring Twenties. Physicians, particularly those examining the mouth, were certainly aware of it; it is likely that even the breaths of ancient cave dwellers were less than aesthetic; but given their more compelling problems, they probably didn't get terribly excited about it. 9

If, then, bad breath accompanied man through the millennia, what the admen of 1921 had intentionally created was not a new disease, but rather a profound fear of the possibility of bad breath, a social condition now called halitophobia. 10

Once halitosis had been ingrained in the public consciousness as a major social lapse (comparable in stature, perhaps, to embezzlement) it then easily aroused latent fears and defensive behaviors such as talking with a hand covering one's mouth or avoiding close contact with other persons. 11

The specter of halitosis was made somewhat more complex by two opposing realities: First, that in truth halitosis was quite common (an estimated 31 percent of Americans are identified by spouses or close friends as having offensive breath); and second, that dental research has now clearly identified its causes and cures. 12

Bad breath may be a sign of certain systemic diseases such as diabetes; or it may be generated by smoking or by ingesting substances such as garlic. But in the overwhelming majority of instances halitosis is caused by colonies of bacteria, on the back of the tongue, metabolizing sulfur-containing proteins originating in post-nasal secretions or in saliva-yielding aromatic organic substances. These oral bacteria, usually anaerobic, proliferate in the small crypts on the back of the tongue. Offensive breath may then be reduced by bacteriocidal lavage or by regularly brushing the back of one's tongue. 13

Our credulous children, learning the fundamentals of life from 30-second television advertisements, have come to believe that moral failings such as premature baldness, body odor, dandruff and bad breath are major impediments to social acceptance and the good life. But those who have created unrest by bluntly disclosing these human shortcomings are not without compassion. They also offer solutions. And providentially these solutions are readily available as over-the-counter products in our neighborhood pharmacies. 14

Last year, Americans invested almost $4 billion on oral-hygiene products alone, a sum exceeding the national budgets of some Third World nations. 15

Halitosis yields readily to simple interventions, but the cure of obsessive halitophobia, on the other hand, will require a more substantial tolerance of one's body image, receding hairline and even one's occasional bad breath. 16

Understanding the Significance

1. In 1921, what changes were occurring in the economy of the United States?
2. What is the origin of the brand name Listerine?

3. How did the newly created word *halitosis* contribute to the idea that bad breath was a terrible social failing?
4. In his final three paragraphs, what is Aronson saying about the relationship between advertising and social attitudes?

Discovering the Writer's Purpose

1. In your view, what is Aronson's primary intent in this essay? What aspects of the document lead you to this conclusion?
2. Aronson offers a brief overview of life in America in 1921. In what way does this background help the reader understand how simple bad breath could be elevated to such a worrisome matter?
3. With his discussion of the way bad breath was elevated from a naturally occurring condition to a social disease, what point is Aronson making about advertising and marketing in general?
4. In what way does Aronson's conclusion help to reinforce his main point in the essay?

Examining the Writer's Method

1. For the most part, Aronson's article focuses on both causes and effects. In what ways would the effectiveness of his article have been altered had he chosen to focus on causes *only* or on effects *only*?
2. How does Aronson's approach to cause and effect arouse and maintain the interest of his readers in bad breath's improbable journey from a simple fact of living to a condition that could ruin one's life?
3. Aronson waits until nearly the end of the article—paragraph 13—to explain in specific terms the likely biological or medical causes of bad breath. Why do you think he saved this information for the end of the document rather than present it at the beginning? Do you agree with his strategy? Explain your reasoning.
4. Why do you think Aronson chose to include the amount of money Americans annually spend on oral-hygiene products in paragraph 15? Do you agree with his strategy? Why or why not?

Considering Style and Language

1. How would you describe the tone of Aronson's article? How does it help Aronson make his point about the effects of advertising on social attitudes?
2. In your view, what is Aronson's attitude toward the advertising firms that created the idea that bad breath is a serious social issue? What phrasing, details, and examples in the text convey this idea to you?
3. At a few points, especially concerning the medical aspects of bad breath and the etymology of the word to describe it, Aronson's language becomes more formal and technical. Why do you think Aronson made the decision to make this shift in language? Do you agree with his choice? Explain your reasoning.
4. What do the following words mean in the context of the writing? *Tormented, affliction, construed, malevolent* (para. 1); *pandemic, soberly, medium, skeptic* (para. 2); *score, agent, saturated, rank, hyperbole* (para. 3); *astringent, aseptic* (para. 4); *attribute, palpable, ascribed, passivity* (para. 6); *aura, hybrid, fetid* (para. 7); *discord, quarantine* (para. 8); *aesthetic* (para. 9); *millennia, profound* (para. 10); *ingrained, latent* (para. 11); *specter* (para. 12); *systemic, ingesting, metabolizing, organic, anaerobic, proliferate, crypt, lavage* (para. 13); *credulous, mortal, impediment, providentially* (para. 14); *yield* (para. 16).

Your Turn: Responding to the Subject

a. Aronson is certainly correct about how easily people can be convinced that baldness, sweaty palms, dandruff, body odors, and so on are "moral failures" or somehow the result of some action on our part or on our families' part. But what are the true causes and effects of a common physical characteristic or condition? For this assignment, select one of the conditions above or choose another, do some research, and then use cause and effect to explain the truth behind the myths or old wives' tales.

b. When was the last time you felt genuinely embarrassed? For this assignment, use cause and effect to examine why this particular incident had such an impact and how you behaved or reacted or reasoned as a result. Or you might consider what caused the embarrassing incident or the ways this incident has influenced your thinking or behavior.

NICOLE KRYSTAL

"Tutoring" Rich Kids Cost Me My Dreams

It may indeed be true that money can't buy happiness, but that may be the only thing it can't buy. Just about anything else is available if the interested people have enough cash. That includes hiring someone else to do things that they are legally or morally responsible to do themselves. And at the other end of the equation, some people are willing to do just about anything in their thirst for the money that these ethically challenged rich folks are so willing to spend to evade personal responsibility. Nicole Krystal learned all this firsthand when she signed up to become a tutor to affluent high school and college kids. As Krystal explains in the following essay, a "My Turn" piece in Newsweek, *she quickly discovered the truth: Everyone involved—the kids, their parents, her boss—expected her not to tutor these clients but to do their work for them.*

What happens when a person agrees to serve the needs of people who abuse the power that money can provide?

For three years, I was an academic prostitute. I ruined the curve for the honest and ensured that the wealthiest, and often stupidest, students earned the highest marks. I was a professional paper-writer. 1

It all started when I quit my journalism job in order to pursue my dream of being a singer-songwriter. I snagged a job tutoring inner-city foster children, but it didn't pay the bills. One day, I found a TUTORS WANTED flier on the UCLA campus. A small tutoring agency that serviced affluent families hired me. 2

"Just sit at her computer and type for her," my boss advised me with my first client, a private-high-school student. But as I typed her name at the top right corner of the screen, she slithered onto her bed to watch "Are You Hot?" I asked her what she remembered about Huxley's Brave New World. 3

"She's a slut," my client said with a sigh, referring either to the character of Lenina or the woman on TV. After a handful of three-word responses like that, I realized she didn't care. I was hired to do the thinking. The parents knew it. So did my boss. 4

Welcome to the world of professional paper-writing, the dirty secret of the tutoring business. It's facilitated by avaricious agencies, 5 perpetuated by accountability-free parents and made possible by self-loathing nerds like me. For three-hour workdays, the ability to sleep in and the opportunity to get paid to learn, I tackled subjects like Dostoevsky while spoiled jerks smoked pot, took naps, surfed the Internet and had sex. Though some offered me chateaubriand and the occasional illicit drug, most treated me like the help. I put up with it because I feared working in an office for $12 an hour again.

Six months into the job, my boss sent me on a problem-solving mission for $10 more per hour than I was already making. He had earned C's and D's on papers for Evan (not his real name), a USC freshman my boss described as a "typical surfer retard." Evan's parents had hired "tutors" to compose their son's papers since he was 12 because he "wasn't going to be a writer anyway." They were furious. 6

In Evan's penthouse, surfers carved across the screen of his 51-inch television, next to a poster of "Scarface." The former clothes model handed me his assignment: to describe utopia. "I couldn't ask for a better life. I mean, ——— was my soccer coach," Evan said, naming a famous studio head. 7

Despite living in utopia, during the session Evan purchased an ounce of weed and a bag of Xanax. His WASPY girlfriend washed down a pill with some Smart Water and offered me one. I declined. Evan sent me home with his $3,000 PowerBook to write his paper because he was "too busy" to work. Before I left, his girlfriend hired me to write her paper on "Do the Right Thing." I drove home at midnight, once again missing my chance to hit the music scene and battle my stage fright. 8

No matter. After I scored an A on Evan's paper, he promised to pass my demo on to a legendary music producer—a family friend. He also promised a few leftover pairs of designer jeans. He never mentioned either again, and I knew I'd been played. The only help Evan offered came in the form of new clients, such as his roommate, who had one-night stands with strippers and said things like "Why should I care about some little black girl?" in regard to Toni Morrison novels. 9

When my streak of A's ended after I scored a B-minus on Evan's paper about clanship in "My Big Fat Greek Wedding," I never heard from him again. His teenage sibling, for whom I composed countless high-school English papers, revealed that Evan had replaced me with a classmate. 10

That summer break, my boss referred me to a junior at a private Christian university who couldn't spell "college." Come fall, the kid leased my brain three hours a day, five days a week. Depressed, I lounged around in my bathrobe until he finished class, then waded through rush-hour traffic to demoralize myself. One day, my Ford 11

Bronco lost all power on the freeway and I could have died. I hadn't played a gig for seven months. I could barely pay my bills because I refused to take on more paper-writing clients.

Last spring, two months shy of my client's graduation date, I snapped while staring at a term-paper assignment on Margaret Thatcher. "I can't do this anymore," I mumbled. I had completed nearly two years of college for him. He replaced me with a teacher about to earn his Ph. D. who charged $15 less per hour than I did. 12

Despite my intellect, I handed over my self-respect to rich losers. I allowed myself to be blinded by privilege and the hope that some of it would rub off on me and help my flailing music career. Ultimately, trading my morals for money cost me the confidence I needed to turn my dreams into reality. Unemployment was a small price to pay to restore my fractured dignity. 13

Understanding the Significance

1. What led Krystal to become involved in the professional paper-writing industry?
2. What about her experiènce with her first client helps Krystal discover the true nature of her position?
3. Besides her paycheck, what motivated her to keep writing for the client named Evan?
4. When she finally quits the business, what does her last client do?

Discovering the Writer's Purpose

1. Krystal opens the third paragraph with the following words from her supervisor: "Just sit at her computer and type for her." Since this instruction contrasts dramatically with the work she actually ends up doing, what is she suggesting about this business?
2. What impression do you think Krystal is trying to create through the descriptions of the various students for whom she worked?
3. What does the episode concerning Evan indicate about how this work affected her reasoning process?
4. By describing her physical and emotional state while working for her final client, what is Krystal indicating about the effects of doing someone else's work?

Examining the Writer's Method

1. Why do you think Krystal decided to open her essay by identifying herself as "an academic prostitute"? Do you agree with her strategy? Explain your reasoning.
2. In your view, does Krystal concentrate more on cause or on effect in her essay? Would the effectiveness of the essay have been altered if the focus had been the opposite? Why or why not?
3. How would you describe the order that Krystal employs to present her examples? Do you agree with this arrangement or would you have rearranged the order of one or more of the episodes?
4. In what ways does the conclusion reinforce Krystal's main point about this business?

Considering Style and Language

1. In the second paragraph, Krystal notes that she found the advertisement for tutors on the campus of UCLA. Why do you think she included this detail?
2. Does Krystal's explanation of her job make it appealing or appalling? What words and phrases lead you to this conclusion?
3. What does this essay make you think of Krystal? What in her presentation creates this impression?
4. What do the following words mean in the context of the writing? *Snagged* (para. 2); *serviced, affluent* (para. 2); *slithered* (para. 3); *facilitated, avaricious, perpetuated, self-loathing, illicit* (para. 5); *utopia* (para. 7); *clanship* (para. 10); *demoralize* (para. 11); *flailing* (para. 13).

Your Turn: Responding to the Subject

a. Regardless of how the people at every level of the professional paper-writing business rationalize it, what they are doing is cheating. Yet the fact that professional paper writing exists is evidence that cheating is both widespread and widely tolerated. But why? For this assignment, identify some aspect of cheating and then, using cause and effect, consider motivations and consequences associated with this behavior.

b. In the sixth paragraph, Krystal refers to people like herself as "self-loathing nerds." What events or experiences can lead a person to develop such a negative self-image? And how does holding such a view affect a person's day-to-day experiences? For this assignment, consider your own self-image or the self-image of someone you know, and then explore the origins or impacts associated with it.

ANNIE DILLARD

Hitting Pay Dirt

Annie Dillard has experienced success as a writer in a number of areas, including poetry, fiction, nonfiction, and autobiography. The author of several books, including The Writing Life, The Living, *and, most recently,* For the Time Being, *she was awarded the Pulitzer Prize in 1975 for her nonfiction narrative,* Pilgrim at Tinker Creek, *which deals with her yearlong exploration of the wonders of her own backyard. She is also widely known as an essayist; her writings have appeared in a number of publications, including* Harper's, American Heritage, The Atlantic Monthly, *and The* New York Times Magazine. *This passage comes from her 1987 memoir,* An American Childhood. *In it, Dillard relies on cause and effect to show how the fulfillment of a child's simple quest to see a microscopic creature ultimately came to take on far more significance.*

How do you know that you have reached a new stage and become your own person separate from your family?

After I read *The Field Book of Ponds and Streams* several times, I longed for a microscope. Everybody needed a microscope. Detectives used microscopes, both for the FBI and at Scotland Yard. Although usually I had to save my tiny allowance for things I wanted, that year for Christmas my parents gave me a microscope kit. 1

In a dark basement corner, on a white enamel table, I set up the microscope kit. I supplied a chair, a lamp, a batch of jars, a candle, and a pile of library books. The microscope kit supplied a blunt black three-speed microscope, a booklet, a scalpel, a dropper, an ingenious device for cutting thin segments of fragile tissue, a pile of clean slides and cover slips, and a dandy array of corked test tubes. 2

One of the test tubes contained "hay infusion." Hay infusion was a wee brown chip of grass blade. You added water to it, and after a week it became a jungle in a drop, full of one-celled animals. This did not work for me. All I saw in the microscope after a week was a wet chip of dried grass, much enlarged. 3

Another test tube contained "diatomaceous earth." This was, I believed, an actual pinch of the white cliffs of Dover. On my palm it was an airy, friable chalk. The booklet said it was composed of the siliceous bodies of diatoms—one-celled creatures that lived in, as it were, small glass jewelry boxes with fitted lids. Diatoms, I read, come 4 in a variety of transparent geometrical shapes. Broken and dead and dug out of geological deposits, they made chalk and a fine abrasive used in silver polish and toothpaste. What I saw in the microscope must have been the fine abrasive—grit enlarged. It was years before I saw a recognizable, whole diatom. The kit's diatomaceous earth was a bust.

All that winter I played with the microscope. I prepared slides from things at hand, as the books suggested. I looked at the transparent membrane inside an onion's skin and saw the cell. I looked at a section of cork and saw the cells, and at scrapings from the inside of my cheek, ditto. I looked at my blood and saw not much; I looked at my urine and saw a long iridescent crystal, for the drop had dried. 5

All this was very well, but I wanted to see the wildlife I had read about. I wanted especially to see the famous amoeba, who had eluded me. He was supposed to live in the hay infusion, but I hadn't found him there. He lived outside in warm ponds and streams, too, but I lived in Pittsburgh, and it had been a cold winter. 6

Finally late that spring I saw an amoeba. The week before, I had gathered puddle water from Frick Park; it had been festering in a jar in the basement. This June night after dinner I figured I had waited long enough. In the basement at my microscope table I spread a scummy drop of Frick Park puddle water on a slide, peeked in, and lo, there was the famous amoeba. He was as blobby and grainy as his picture; I would have known him anywhere. 7

Before I had watched him at all, I ran upstairs. My parents were still at table, drinking coffee. They, too, could see the famous amoeba. I told them, bursting, that he was all set up, that they should hurry before his water dried. It was the chance of a lifetime. 8

Father had stretched out his long legs and was tilting back in his chair. Mother sat with her knees crossed, in blue slacks, smoking a Chesterfield. The dessert dishes were still on the table. My sisters were nowhere in evidence. It was a warm evening; the big dining-room windows gave onto blooming rhododendrons. 9

Mother regarded me warmly. She gave me to understand that she was glad I had found what I had been looking for, but that she and Father were happy to sit with their coffee, and would not be coming down. 10

She did not say, but I understood at once, that they had their pursuits (coffee?) and I had mine. She did not say, but I began to understand then, that you do what you do out of your private passion for the thing itself. 11

I had essentially been handed my own life. In subsequent years my parents would praise my drawings and poems, and supply me with books, art supplies, and sports equipment, and listen to my 12 troubles and enthusiasms, and supervise my hours, and discuss and inform, but they would not get involved with my detective work, nor hear about my reading, nor inquire about my homework or term papers or exams, nor visit the salamanders I caught, nor listen to me play the piano, nor attend my field hockey games, nor fuss over my insect collection with me, or my poetry collection or stamp collection or rock collection. My days and nights were my own to plan and fill.

When I left the dining room that evening and started down the dark basement stairs, I had a life. I sat down to my wonderful amoeba, and there he was, rolling his grains more slowly now, extending an arc of his edge for a foot and drawing himself along by that foot, and absorbing it again and rolling on. I gave him some more pond water. 13

I had hit pay dirt. For all I knew, there were paramecia, too, in that pond water, or daphniae, or stentors, or any of the many creatures I had read about and never seen: volvox, the spherical algal colony; euglena with its one red eye; the elusive, glassy diatom; hydra, rotifers, water bears, worms. Anything was possible. The sky was the limit. 14

Understanding the Significance

1. What is the result when Dillard examines the specimens supplied with the microscope?
2. During her first winter with her microscope, how does Dillard occupy herself?
3. What creature did Dillard most want to see under the lens of her microscope?
4. What happens when Dillard asks her parents to look through the microscope at her discovery?

Discovering the Writer's Purpose

1. In her opening paragraph, Dillard notes what professions rely on microscopes. Why does she include these details?
2. In paragraphs 3 and 4, Dillard details how she initially failed to see what she was hoping to see, but in paragraph 5, she points out that, despite her failures, she continued to work with her microscope. What point is she making?

3. When Dillard finally achieves what she had been working toward, she rushes to tell her parents and to invite them to look through her microscope. When they politely decline, Dillard is neither angry nor disappointed. In your view, why does Dillard react this way?
4. From the time she received her microscope, most of Dillard's efforts are devoted to seeing "the famous amoeba." What does this tiny creature represent to Dillard?

Examining the Writer's Method

1. How does Dillard use her introduction to indicate her focus on cause and effect?
2. In her essay, Dillard uses both direct and related cause and effect. What is the direct effect of her finally seeing the microscopic creature that had so eluded her? What was the related effect?
3. Although Dillard's paper focuses more on effect than cause, there are instances of cause. Choose one example of cause and explain why you believe it is especially effective.
4. How does Dillard's final sentence sum up the significance of her essay?

Considering Style and Language

1. Throughout the piece, Dillard chooses to use scientific terms, rather than substitute more general terms. Why do you think she makes this choice? How does it affect her essay?
2. The second sentence in paragraph 12 is quite long. In your view, why does she present the information in a single sentence rather than to create two or three smaller sentences?
3. Dillard opens her concluding paragraph with this sentence: "I had hit pay dirt." What does Dillard mean by this expression?
4. What do the following words mean in the context of the writing? *Blunt, scalpel, ingenious, fragile, array* (para. 2); *infusion* (para. 3); *friable, siliceous, geometrical, geological, bust* (para. 4); *iridescent* (para. 5); *amoeba* (para. 6); *festering* (para. 7); *pursuits* (para. 11); *arc* (para. 13); *spherical, colony; elusive* (para. 14).

Your Turn: Responding to the Subject

a. In the beginning of paragraph 12, Dillard notes that after her parents politely declined her request to look through her microscope, she knew that she "had a life," in other words, that she wasn't just an extension of her parents but that she was her own person. What event marked this shift in attitude for you or for someone you know? For this assignment, specify the event and then explain what led to its occurrence or what happened as a result.

b. In many ways, Dillard's essay is about a very basic human characteristic: curiosity. Consider the nature of curiosity, and then use cause and effect to explore what makes people so curious or what kinds of things can happen as a result of curiosity.

Other Possibilities for Using Cause and Effect

The following list contains a number of topics that could be developed into essays employing cause and effect. Remember: how you approach the topic is up to you. Feel free to focus on causes, on effects, or on both causes and effects.

- The breakup of a relationship
- A famous historical event
- Negative attitudes about the media
- A flood, hurricane, tornado, or other natural disaster
- Strict or lenient upbringing
- Beliefs in urban legends
- The decline in the number of people choosing marriage
- Your choice of college or major
- Cheating in the college classroom
- Sudden prosperity or poverty
- Water or air pollution
- A vice like greed, jealousy, hypocrisy
- Popularity of plastic surgery
- Loss of consumer confidence in a product or company
- Gun violence in schools

DIXIE CUPS
Wacky Uses

Much real-world writing has as its purpose identifying what led to something or what happened as a result. In these documents, cause and effect fulfills this aim. A newspaper report concerning the source of gasoline odor in a community's drinking water relies on cause and effect. So does a letter from a charitable association detailing what a simple $25 donation would enable the group to do, as does a police report examining the shooting of an undercover police officer by a fellow officer. Cause and effect serves the same role in the following passage, taken from a web page entitled Wacky Uses (www.wackyuses.com), developed by Joey Green, author of several books dealing with unusual uses for common household products. In this piece, which originally appeared in his 1977 book Wash Your Hair with Whipped Cream, *Green uses cause and effect to trace the history and development of the familiar Dixie Cup.*

Dixie® Cups

- In 1908, Hugh Moore started the American Water Supply Company of New England to market a vending machine that for one penny would dispense a cool drink of water in an individual, clean, disposable paper cup.
- Moore soon realized that his sanitary cups had greater sales potential than his water, particularly when Dr. Samuel Crumbine, a health official in Dodge City, Kansas, began crusading for a law to ban the public tin dipper. Lacking the capital to manufacture

enough paper cups to abolish the tin dipper, Moore and his associate Lawrence Luellen traveled to New York City with a few handmade samples and eventually hooked up with an investment banker who invested $200,000 in the venture, incorporated as the Public Cup Vendor Company in 1909.

- In 1909, Kansas passed the first state law abolishing the public dipper, and Professor Alvin Davison of Lafayette College published a study reporting the germs of communicable diseases found on public dipping tins. As state after state outlawed public drinking tins, Hugh Moore and his associates created a paper cup dispenser to be distributed for free to businesses and schools who would buy the paper cups. By 1910, the company changed its name to the Individual Drinking Cup Company, only to change it again in 1912 to Health Kups and yet again in 1919 to Dixie Cups.
- Inventor Hugh Moore's paper cup factory was located next door to the Dixie Doll Company in the same downtown loft building. The word Dixie printed on the company's door reminded Moore of the story he had heard as a boy about "dixies," the ten dollar bank notes printed with the French word dix in big letters across the face of the bill by a New Orleans bank renowned for its strong currency in the early 1800s. The "dixies," Moore decided, had the qualities he wanted people to associate with his paper cups, and with permission from his neighbor, he used the name for his cups.
- In 1923, Dixie Cups produced a two-and-a-half ounce Dixie Cup for ice cream, giving the ice cream industry a way to sell individual servings of ice cream and compete with bottled soft drinks and candy bars.
- Etymologists believe that the sobriquet for the southern United States, Dixie Land, originated on the Mississippi River before the Civil War by riverboat men for whom a dixie was a New Orleans bank note printed with the word dix, French for "ten."
- The Dixie Cups, a popular singing trio comprised of sisters Nadine, Marta, and Lucile LeCupsa, sang the 1964 hit song, "Chapel of Love."
- While playing telephone operator Ernestine on Saturday Night Live, Lily Tomlin said, "Next time you complain about your phone service, why don't you try using two Dixie Cups with a string?"

"Dixie" is a registered trademark of James River Corporation.

Focusing on the Message and Aim

Answer each of the following questions in a brief paragraph, referring specifically to the passage you've just read.

1. Green includes both cause and effect in this piece. Is the focus in the piece more on cause or on effect? What examples best support your view?
2. In presenting this extensive background and history about the Dixie Cup, what is Green suggesting about the hundreds of common household products that we see and use on a daily basis?
3. In your view, which of the examples is most important in the development of the Dixie Cup and which is the least significant? Why?

Applying the Principles

a. As Green explains it, the fear of contagious diseases was one of the primary causes leading to the development of the Dixie Cup. Do some research on a particular communicable disease from the past or the present, and then use cause and effect to write a one-page explanation of the societal response to the health crisis that resulted.
b. In the fourth section, Green explains that the name "Dixie" was chosen in large part because cup inventor Hugh Moore had remembered hearing about a particular paper currency that bore the French word *dix*. Paper currency still dominates in the modern United States monetary system, but the paper money we use today hasn't always looked like it does now. Choose a particular denomination ($1, $5, $10, $20, $50, or $100), and, after doing some research, write a 200- to 300-word explanation of the background of the particular bill, including reasons that the currency no longer has the same appearance.

Practical Application: Cause and Effect

Your internship with the Maplewood Neighborhood Association has taught you a lot about what can be done when people decide on a goal and work together to achieve it. You've also gained plenty of practical experience, too, as you have assisted the director with everything from setting the schedule for volunteers and workers to preparing the annual budget.

At yesterday's staff meeting, your director distributed an article about a federal grant program designed to help support small businesses and nonprofit organizations. The program provides financial awards to worthy projects in response to brief proposals (two pages maximum) that outline how the project will lead to concrete improvements.

This grant program is exactly what the Maplewood Neighborhood Association has been looking for. The group has long wanted to revamp the small playground at the center of the neighborhood, puling out the swings, slide, and jungle gym, putting down a safer, rubberized surface, and installing safer, more modern equipment. In addition, the group would like to resurface the basketball court, replace the hoops and install new backboards, and plant trees around the perimeter of the playground. The playground is regularly used by residents of all ages, so these improvements would have an immediate and positive effect on the entire neighborhood.

Your director has asked you to prepare a proposal that outlines the benefits that a refurbished playground would have. To guide you in terms of approach and form, she has provided Ian Alamilla's proposal to make the Living Reef Dive Center operate more efficiently.

Alternating Dive Personnel on Boats

Introduction

The Living Reef Dive Center currently has three boats, each boat with a captain, a divemaster, and a helper. In the high dive season, the divemasters are out doing three to four dives a day, for two weeks at a time. This workload not only pushes divemasters to their limit, but it also jeopardizes their health and the safety of their divers. If one of the divers accidentally goes deeper than the planned depth, the divemasters are not supposed to return again to assist that diver because their bodies are already saturated with nitrogen.

The problem here is that divemasters will usually disregard their own safety to help a diver who has descended too deep, facing serious injury because they have already pushed their own safety to the maximum. This not only creates a serious problem for the divemasters but also for the paying clients who expect that they are in good hands. This is why I'm proposing a new system that will help avoid a catastrophic incident involving employees or guests that ultimately would leave us with huge financial liabilities.

Proposed Solution and Steps for Change

My solution to this problem is to require that all boat captains become divemasters. This way we can limit the divemasters' exposure to excess nitrogen absorption that can cause Decompression Sickness (DCS). We will accomplish this goal by having the Living Reef Dive Center finance the necessary training that will be needed to get the boat captains up to divemaster level.

The training will take place over four months during the slow season. The boat captains who are currently working will get the first chance to upgrade to divemaster. The ones who don't wish to become divemasters will be allowed to work only as helpers and assistant captains on the boats. We will then find experienced boat captains who want to take advantage of this opportunity and train them. We want to stick with experienced boat captains because, while it's easy to train a divemaster, it's not that easy to train a boat captain. Becoming a good boat captain takes years of hands-on experience. Once the captains are trained, they will be compensated for their work as both divemasters and as boat captains.

Benefits of the Proposal

If we implement this change, the Living Reef Dive Center will get the benefit of having two divemasters on board each boat. One will work as the boat captain and the other as the divemaster. At the end of each week they will switch roles in order to avoid oversaturation of nitrogen and ultimately, DCS.

If a diver goes too deep, the first divemaster will be able to redirect that diver to safety. Then when divemaster and diver surface, the second divemaster can go down on the remaining dives for the day. These measures will guarantee the safety of everyone involved and also ensure guest satisfaction.

An additional benefit of this plan concerns situations when clearing ears becomes impossible for a divemaster. When this happens, serious ear injuries can occur. If this case, one divemaster can resurface and be replaced by the other who will continue with the dive before the guests even know what happened. This will reinforce the image of the Living Reef Dive Center as a highly professional organization.

Conclusion

By implementing these changes at the Living Reef Dive Center, we will not only guarantee the safety of our divemasters and guests but also put the business on a higher level than our competitors. The business will be even more efficient in its operations. The dive shop should see more business and more revenue just by making these changes. For all these reasons, I propose that our boat captains also become divemasters.

12

Division and Classification

The Technique

Writing often entails dealing with complex subjects that must be broken down or somehow simplified in order to communicate them clearly to a reader. With these subjects you will frequently rely on *division and classification.* For example, division and classification would be useful in a paper detailing the headaches involved in protesting a speeding ticket. *Division* would enable you to show the enormous bureaucracy in the judicial system. *Classification* would allow you to illustrate the various types of people who spend their days in the courthouse, from the uniformed court officers to the conservatively dressed attorneys to the agitated defendants.

In addition to using division and classification to support other modes, you will also face writing tasks that call for a use of division and classification as the dominant writing technique. An example of this would be an assignment concerning the types of business opportunities available for today's entrepreneur willing to invest a great deal of time but only a moderate amount of money. Regardless of whether you use division and classification to support other modes or as the main technique in an essay, you need to

- establish a logical method of analysis;
- maintain a clear and consistent presentation;
- use distinct and complete elements of analysis; and
- provide an effective arrangement for the elements of the analysis.

A LOGICAL METHOD OF ANALYSIS

When you focus on division and classification, effectively structuring the analysis means establishing a logical method of analysis so that your reader is able to view the concept piece by piece. As a result, the whole concept becomes easier to understand.

One subject can of course be presented in a variety of ways. If your intent is to explain the workings of a local hospital, for example, you might divide the topic on the basis of the hospital's role as a full health care center, discussing its emergency department, its inpatient treatment area, its diagnostic testing center, and its rehabilitation clinic. But you might also divide the hospital on the basis of its role as a business, focusing on its administrative division, customer-service area, treasurer's department, fund-raising center, and other functions.

You have the same variety of approaches available when you classify. If you were writing about the various sports in which high-school and college athletes can participate, you could classify these sports on the basis of the potential for injury involved, with football, hockey, and basketball ranking as high-risk sports; gymnastics, softball, and baseball as moderate-risk sports; and track and cross-country, tennis, golf, and swimming as low-risk sports. But you could also arrange the sports on the basis of how popular they are with student athletes, or how expensive they are to operate, and so forth.

In this brief excerpt from his book *Here Is New York,* esteemed essayist E. B. White explicitly lays out a logical rationale of division and classification to discuss the ways New York City is viewed by those who come into contact with it:

> There are roughly three New Yorks. There is, first, the New York of the man or woman who was born here, who takes the city for granted and accepts its size and its turbulence as natural and inevitable. Second, there is the New York of the commuter—the city that is devoured by locusts each day and spat out each night. Third, there is the New York of the person who was born somewhere else and came to New York in the quest of something. Of these three trembling cities the greatest is the last—the city of final destination. It is this third city that accounts for New York's high-strung disposition, its poetical deportment, its dedication to the arts, and its incomparable achievements.

A CLEAR AND CONSISTENT PRESENTATION

With division and classification writing, you also must ensure that your method of division and classification is *clear* and *consistent.* A method is clear when your reader can easily identify the elements of division and classification, and it is consistent when you provide the same general degree of coverage for each category or class. A critical paper about child abuse would be clear if it specified a focus on particular types—for example, *physical abuse, emotional abuse, verbal abuse*, and *sexual abuse*. It would be consistent if you provided a similar degree of attention and detail to each type.

Consider the clear and consistent method in this excerpt from a book entitled *Nice Job! The Guide to Cool, Odd, Risky, and Gruesome Ways to Make a Living*, which explains the options available to those interested in a career as a rodeo clown. The passage clearly classifies all rodeo clowns into three categories—the clown, the barrel man, and the bullfighter—on the basis of different job responsibilities. Furthermore, not only are the duties and relative risks of each duty described for every category listed, so are the types of details, which are virtually the same. Thus, not only is the categorization of rodeo clowns clear, that categorization is also consistently described.

> Roughly three types of rodeo performers fall under the umbrella term *rodeo clown*, although they blur around the edges. The first type is perhaps the most recognizable, the clown. In addition to running around the ring distracting a bull from a fallen rider, the clown is responsible for entertaining the crowd between stunts and does this by donning a standard clown uniform while making jokes and performing tumbling routines. This is the least risky part of the job, yet it requires comic timing and charisma, which do not typically come into play when working with the animals. The second type of rodeo clown is known as a barrel man because he sits inside a barrel and pops up to taunt the bull. The barrel is a protective barrier between you and the bull, but it is still a risky place to be. The third type is the bullfighter, who must draw the bull after it has tossed the rider, allowing the rider to get to safety—this involves more bull-handling than either a clown or a barrel man must do.

DISTINCT AND COMPLETE ELEMENTS OF ANALYSIS

When you use division and classification in your academic and workplace writing, make sure to provide **distinct** and **complete** segments or categories. *Distinct* means clearly different, with little or no blending or overlapping. *Complete* means encompassing all data, with all information in an appropriate section or group. Should you find exceptions or overlap of categories, be sure to acknowledge them to the reader, as the passage above does when it acknowledges a "blur around the edges" in the three types of rodeo clowns.

Consider the following passage from *The UFO Experience*, which discusses unidentified flying object (UFO) experiences known collectively as *close encounters*. The excerpt explicitly identifies the criteria for each category and carefully places all close encounters into one—and only one—category, thus supporting the writer's aim:

> *Close Encounters of the First Kind*: This category is the simple close encounter, in which the reported UFO is seen at close range, but there is no interaction with the environment (other than trauma on the part of the observer).
>
> *Close Encounters of the Second Kind*: These are similar to the First Kind except that physical effects on both animate and inanimate materials are noted. Vegetation is often reported as having been pressed down, burned, or scorched; tree branches are reported broken; animals are frightened, sometimes to the extent of physically injuring themselves in their fright. Inanimate objects, most often vehicles, are reported as becoming momentarily disabled, their engines killed, radios stopped, and headlights dimmed and extinguished. . . .
>
> *Close Encounters of the Third Kind*: In these cases the presence of "occupants" in or about the UFO is reported.

AN EFFECTIVE ARRANGEMENT

Once you have established your method of division and classification, you must choose an arrangement for its presentation to your reader. You must decide which category to introduce first, and last—and, most important, *why*. The order you choose should best serve the *purpose* of your document. For example, if you ultimately need your reader to understand the physical layout of an object or place, then you may want to use a system of *spatial* order—that is, order based on the physical location or subjects relative to other subjects.

In this excerpt from *How We Die*, spatial order helps the reader envision the geography of the human heart. The passage first describes the heart as a whole: a valentine-shaped unit of four chambers. Then it follows the heart front to back, and, finally, transversely—left to right—ultimately producing a three-dimensional image in the reader's mind:

As every child knows, the heart is shaped very much like a valentine. It is made almost entirely of muscle, called myocardium, wrapped around a large central space that is subdivided into four chambers. A vertical front-to-back wall of tissue, called the septum, separates the large space into right and left portions, and a transverse sheet at right angles to the septum divides each of these portions into upper and lower parts, making four in all.

If your purpose involves making your reader understand a process or series of events, use *linear order* or *chronological order*—that is, an order that focuses on time. The following selection on polygraph testing from HowStuffWorks.com employs chronological order to present the components of a polygraph test as they occur in time:

A polygraph exam is a long process that can be divided up into several stages. Here's how a typical exam might work:

Pretest—This consists of an interview between the examiner and examinee, where the two individuals get to learn about each other. This may last about one hour. At this point, the examiner gets the examinee's side of the story concerning the events under investigation. While the subject is sitting there answering questions, the examiner also profiles the examinee. The examiner wants to see how the subject responds to questions and processes information.

Design questions—The examiner designs questions that are specific to the issue under investigation and reviews these questions with the subject.

In-test—The actual exam is given. The examiner asks 10 or 11 questions, only three or four of which are relevant to the issue or crime being investigated. The other questions are control questions. A control question is a very general question, such as "Have you ever stolen anything in your life?"—a type of question that is so broad that almost no one can honestly respond with a "no." If the person answers "no," the examiner can get an idea of the reaction that the examinee demonstrates when being deceptive.

Finally, if your document intends to persuade or inform, *emphatic order* often ranks as the ideal strategy. This method of arrangement involves a movement from strong to stronger to even stronger, saving the most strongest point for last. In this brief excerpt from his book *I Can Sell You Anything*, Carl Wrighter presents several categories of words that advertisers often use, saving the most misleading type of these "weasel words" for last:

A *weasel word* is a word that's used to imply a meaning that cannot be truthfully stated. Some weasels imply meanings that are not the same as their actual definition, such as "help," "like," or "fortified." They can act as qualifiers and/or comparatives. Other weasels, such as "taste" and "flavor," have no definite meanings, and are simply subjective opinions offered by a manufacturer. A weasel of omission is one that implies a claim so strongly that it forces you to supply the bogus fact. Adjectives are weasels used to convey feelings and emotions to a greater extent than the product itself.

Ultimately, the most effective order of presentation is the one that best leads the audience in the direction you want them to go, showcasing your own objectives, conclusions, and recommendations.

CHECKLIST FOR USING DIVISION AND CLASSIFICATION

1. Has a **logical method of analysis** for division and classification been established?
2. Has a **clear** and **consistent method of division and classification** been followed, with **readily identified elements** that are discussed to a **comparable degree?**
3. Have the categories of the division and classification been presented as **distinct** from each other?
4. Does the information fit into one of the categories, with a **minimum of overlap** or **blending,** to ensure a **complete** discussion?
5. Have the **elements of the classification** been **arranged effectively** to reflect the aim of the document?

AN ANNOTATED EXAMPLE

DAVID BODANIS

What's in Your Toothpaste

Consider the many things you ingest or are exposed to every day. Do you know what ingredients make up all these items? Even something as apparently basic as drinking water isn't necessarily what people think. Tap water, for instance, generally contains any number of chemicals, some naturally occurring and some added to disinfect the water and make it safe for drinking. And the alternative that many people choose—pure bottled water—is sometimes anything but pure; in one 1999 study, one-third of the bottled water examined contained some level of contamination. So it should probably come as no surprise that a lot more goes into another common regularly used item—toothpaste—than most of us want to know. In the following excerpt from The Secret House, *David Bodanis employs division and classification, with a focus on division, to make the point that toothpaste, like many other products we use every day, is composed of both very ordinary and very strange elements.*

Should we really be surprised that the common, ordinary things we use every day are actually anything but common and ordinary?

Bodanis identifies the logical rationale for his document as the division and classification.

1 Into the bathroom goes our male resident, and after the most pressing need is satisfied it's time to brush the teeth. The tube of toothpaste is squeezed, its pinched metal seams are splayed, pressure waves are generated inside, and the paste begins to flow. But what's in this toothpaste, so carefully being extruded out?

He identifies the first distinct element *of his division of toothpaste: water.*

2 Water mostly, 30 to 45 percent in most brands: ordinary, everyday simple tap water. It's there because people like to have a big gob of toothpaste to spread on the brush, and water is the cheapest stuff there is when it comes to making big gobs. Dripping a bit from the tap onto your brush would cost virtually nothing; whipped in with the rest of the toothpaste the manufacturers can sell it at a neat and accountant-pleasing $2 per pound equivalent. Toothpaste manufacture is a very lucrative occupation.

He identifies the second distinct element of his division: chalk. Note the thorough, balanced coverage, designed to call attention to the ingredients that are likely to surprise his audience.

3 Second to water in quantity is chalk: exactly the same material that schoolteachers use to write on blackboards. It is collected from the crushed remains of long-dead ocean creatures. In the Cretaceous seas chalk particles served as part of the wickedly sharp outer skeleton that these creatures had to wrap around themselves to keep from getting chomped by all the slightly larger other ocean

creatures they met. Their massed graves are our present chalk deposits.

The individual chalk particles—the size of the smallest mud particles in your garden—have kept their toughness over the aeons, and now on the toothbrush they'll need it. The enamel outer coating of the tooth they'll have to face is the hardest substance in the body—tougher than skull, or bone, or nail. Only the chalk particles in toothpaste can successfully grind into the teeth during brushing, ripping off the surface layers like an abrading wheel grinding down a boulder in a quarry. 4

The craters, slashes, and channels that the chalk tears into the teeth will also remove a certain amount of build-up yellow in the carnage, and it is for that polishing function that it's there. A certain amount of unduly enlarged extra-abrasive chalk fragments tear such cavernous pits into the teeth that future decay bacteria will be able to bunker down there and thrive; the quality control people find it almost impossible to screen out these errant super-chalk pieces, and government regulations allow them to stay in. 5

Bodanis identifies the third distinct element in his division: titanium dioxide, a substance used in white wall paint. Note the movement from a surprising ingredient to a more surprising ingredient, indicating the use of emphatic order.

In case even the gouging doesn't get all the yellow off, another substance is worked into the toothpaste cream. This is titanium dioxide. It comes in tiny spheres, and it's the stuff bobbing around in white wall paint to make it come out white. Splashed around onto your teeth during the brushing it coats much of the yellow that remains. Being water soluble it leaks off in the next few hours and is swallowed, but at least for the quick glance up in the mirror after finishing it will make the user think his teeth are truly white. Some manufacturers add optical whitening dyes—the stuff more commonly found in washing machine bleach—to make extra sure that that glance in the mirror shows reassuring white. 6

These ingredients alone would not make a very attractive concoction. They would stick in the tube like a sloppy white plastic lump, 7

Bodanis reviews the elements of division as a means of transition to the rest of the elements of division.

hard to squeeze out as well as revolting to the touch. Few consumers would savor rubbing in a mixture of water, ground-up blackboard chalk, and the whitener from latex paint first thing in the morning. To get around that finicky distaste the manufacturers have mixed in a host of other goodies.

He indicates the next three elements of division of toothpaste—glycerine glycol, a form of which is used in antifreeze; a seaweed extract; and paraffin oil—in a movement in keeping with the emphatic order.

To keep the glop from drying out, a mix- 8
ture including glycerine glycol—related to the most common car antifreeze ingredient—is whipped in with the chalk and water, and to give that concoction a bit of substance (all we really have so far is wet colored chalk) a large helping is added of gummy molecules from the seaweed *Chondrus crispus.* This seaweed ooze spreads in among the chalk, paint, and antifreeze, then stretches itself in all directions to hold the whole mass together. A bit of paraffin oil (the fuel that flickers in camping lamps) is pumped in with it to help the moss ooze keep the whole substance smooth.

Bodanis again summarizes ingredients as a means of transition into the remaining elements of division.

With the glycol, ooze, and paraffin we're 9
almost there. Only two major chemicals are left to make the refreshing, cleansing substance we know as toothpaste. The ingredients so far are fine for cleaning, but they wouldn't make much of the satisfying foam we have come to expect in the morning brushing.

He indicates the next element of division: detergent.

To remedy that every toothpaste on the 10
market has a big dollop of detergent added too. You've seen the suds detergent will make in a washing machine. The same substance added here will duplicate that inside the mouth. It's not particularly necessary, but it sells.

He subdivides further, noting additional ingredients added to improve the taste of the concoction: peppermint oil, menthol crystals, and artificial sweeteners.

The only problem is that by itself this in- 11
gredient tastes, well, too like detergent. It's horribly bitter and harsh. The chalk put in toothpaste is pretty foul-tasting too for that matter. It's to get around that gustatory discomfort that the manufacturers put in the ingredient they tout perhaps the most of all. This is the flavoring, and it has to be strong. Double rectified peppermint oil is used—a fla-

Bodanis presents a thorough explanation of the final element of division: formaldehyde. Saving this most surprising ingredient for last preserves emphatic order.

Bodanis uses his conclusion to review the list of surprising ingredients that make up toothpaste, noting that brushing your teeth with the primary ingredient—water—is often as effective as using this strange combination of components.

vorer so powerful that chemists know better than to sniff it in the raw state in the laboratory. Menthol crystals and saccharin or other sugar simulators are added to complete the camouflage operation.

Is that it? Chalk, water, paint, seaweed, antifreeze, paraffin oil, detergent, and peppermint? Not quite. A mix like that would be irresistible to the hundreds of thousands of individual bacteria lying on the surface of even an immaculately cleaned bathroom sink. They would get in, float in the water bubbles, ingest the ooze and paraffin, maybe even spray out enzymes to break down the chalk. The result would be an uninviting mess. The way manufacturers avoid that final obstacle is by putting something in to kill the bacteria. Something good and strong is needed, something that will zap any accidentally intrudant bacteria into oblivion. And that something is formaldehyde—the disinfectant used in anatomy labs. 12

So it's chalk, water, paint, seaweed, antifreeze, paraffin oil, detergent, peppermint, formaldehyde, and fluoride (which can go some way towards preserving children's teeth)—that's the usual mixture raised to the mouth on the toothbrush for a fresh morning's clean. If it sounds too unfortunate, take heart. Studies show that thorough brushing with just plain water will often do as good a job. 13

Your Turn: Responding to the Subject

a. In this excerpt, Bodanis explains that the chalk particles in toothpaste are the remains of "wickedly sharp outer skeletons that these creatures had to wrap around themselves" to remain safe. They are not alone in this regard. Humans also work hard to protect themselves from danger, including threats to psychological and emotional well being, things like sadness, unpleasant situations, ideas or facts they don't want to hear, and so on. For this assignment, write an essay in which you explore at least four types or categories of behavior that people engage in to shield themselves from things they would rather avoid.

b. With many brands of toothpaste, when you buy the product, you have to remove the tube from a box. But since the tube itself securely holds the toothpaste, isn't the outside container just another instance of the enormous waste of natural resources and the damage to the environment inherent in some products or their packaging? For this assignment, use division and classification to identify four or more ways that some manufacturers are failing to protect our precious natural resources and keep our environment safe.

JONATHAN WALTERS

Throwing

Think of any of the ordinary things people do on a regular basis, and then think of how different people approach and perform the same task. That's essentially what sports enthusiast and writer Jonathan Walters does with this essay on the different ways people throw, which originally appeared in Sports Illustrated. *For his topic, Walters, who has also been a regular contributor on sports for* USA Weekend, *focuses on an action that is the fundamental element in a wide array of sports and other activities. He relies on division and classification to illustrate that while throwing may appear to be a simple act, it's one that many people perform many different ways for many different reasons.*

What elements of an action help to distinguish one method of performing it from another?

You've got tosses, flips, flings, slings, lobs, heaves, and Hail Marys. You can do it sidearm, underhand, overhand, and behind the back. When you try a tough one and hit it, it can be one of the sweetest feelings in the world—or one of the worst. 1

Throwing. Next to running it is probably the most natural athletic impulse we know. In a checkered career of chucking everything from dirt bombs to long bombs, I've come to know three basic types of tosses. 2

I unloaded a Type III one hot summer day at Crane's Beach in Ipswich, Mass. My father was 100 feet away, beyond two softly swept sand dunes, and moving. I heaved an ice cube. Threw it as hard as I could. The ends of my fingers hurt. My shoulder yelped. I watched with growing disbelief as it twirled and glinted toward its target, catching bits of the afternoon sun in its sweeping arc. It landed dead center on my father's hair-free pate. I escaped personal injury only because he couldn't believe I'd thrown it. 3

Type III throws, understand, are the most dangerous. You try them because you figure you haven't a chance in hell of making them. Not even a presidential motorcade is off limits. 4

My friend Paul recalls a Type III he let fly in his employer's parking lot. The sun was setting on one of those rare balmy February days in New England. A co-worker was pulling out of the lot, rolling open his sun roof as he went. Paul packed a snowball, subconsciously 5 calculated trajectory and force, and cranked it from about 40 yards away: "All I remember," he recalls, "is seeing the snowball explode all over the inside of this poor guy's windshield. It must have snuck in through about a six-inch opening."

The distinguishing and unfortunate feature of Type III throws is that you have no defense to offer for your action. True, you did mean to drop one through that sun roof, but you never figured you could do it. This is the feature that separates a Type III toss from a Type II. Type II's are merely mistakes; you aimed at one thing and hit another. Although Type II's can make for unpleasant surprises, when confronted with the evidence you can—weakly—claim you were aiming at something else. 6

Once my father and a friend were tossing a balled-up jacket around the Greyhound bus station in Bridgeport, Conn. Between them was a flashing neon greyhound, its front and back paws churning for a finish line it would never reach. With one particularly hard throw, my father clipped the hound's back legs. In a spray of sparks and a wisp of smoke, the animal was crippled. My father and his friend sprinted past it and onto the bus. But they'd been spotted. A frantic porter leaped on after them, saw them hunkered down in their seats a few rows back and, pointing at my father, began yelling, "You killed the greyhound! You killed the greyhound!" 7

"I never was a natural athlete," my father says. 8

The outcome of Type II throws doesn't have to be bad. Another friend of mine was sitting at his desk one morning when a fellow employee threw him a cherry tomato, expecting him to catch it. The amazing thing wasn't that she was 30 feet away when she threw it, but that my friend was on the other side of a five-foot-high partition, completely out of view. As if guided there by Mission Control in Houston, the little red orb landed neatly in the breast pocket of his shirt. 9

As dazzling as a good Type II can be, the most satisfying throws are Type I's. You want to make them, and you do. Hit your target with a Type I and you feel a surge of power and confidence that can turn your whole rotten week around. 10

A few years back, my friend Bill was teaching high school English in Madison, Va. Being the liberal sort, he allowed gum chewing in class, but no bubble blowing. One student in particular had been flouting the rule regularly—and loudly. "The kid was sitting in the center of the last row," Bill recalls. "I turned to write something on the blackboard and caught him out of the corner of my eye blowing another one—a big one. I picked up a piece of chalk, spun around and whipped it. Now, I can't throw. You know I can't throw. Well, the bubble just exploded all over this kid's face, and the class went bananas." 11

Although such Type I's may serve a valuable social purpose, the 12 most uplifting ones are undoubtedly those you unload just for fun. A high school buddy of mine was on the second floor of the Smith College library peeling an orange in lieu of studying applied mathematics. The woman he was with leaned over, asked him for a piece of peel and said, "Watch this." With a neat sidearm flip, she sent the skin spinning the width of the library's central atrium toward a wastebasket one floor below. Bingo. She hit it. "And an orange peel isn't that aerodynamic an object, either," my pal points out.

A throw like that is positively therapeutic. It elevates you. For a 13 second, you're Johnny Unitas, Cy Young, and John Havlicek rolled into one.

In the summer of 1972, I was working at a boatyard on a lake in 14 New Hampshire, and one day I was fantasizing about my Celtics. I had a three-quarter-inch bolt in my hand. There were two seconds left in Game 7 of the world championship. Overtime. The Celtics were trailing 102–101. I twisted past one Philadelphia defender and looked to the basket. I fired. The bolt rolled out of my hand with a neat backspin. It twirled away in a hypnotic arc. The buzzer sounded. With a sharp "clang" and an unequivocal "plop," the bolt ricocheted off the I-beam backboard and into the rusty blue Maxwell House coffee can 50 feet away. I did a five-second victory dance: hands held high, a little workboot shuffle thrown in. As a fellow worker looked on bemused—and slightly amazed—I spun on my heel and headed out to the dock to pump a little gas.

Understanding the Significance

1. As Walters explains it, what makes Type III throws so dangerous and so difficult to defend?
2. How does a Type II throw differ from a Type III toss?
3. What was particularly surprising about the Type II throw involving the cherry tomato?
4. According to Walters, what makes Type I throws so enjoyable?

Discovering the Writer's Purpose

1. Walters illustrates the three types of throws through a series of personal anecdotes. How do these anecdotes help him keep the classes distinct and complete?

2. Walters labels the first classification of tosses as Type III and then moves on to Type II and finally to Type I. Why do you think he labeled the classes in descending order rather than in ascending order (Type I to Type III)?
3. Walters uses a one-sentence paragraph in only one spot, paragraph 8. In your view, why does he set this sentence off without additional supporting sentences?
4. In paragraph 13, Walters refers to two legendary professional athletes from his youth, Baltimore Colts quarterback Johnny Unitas and Boston Celtics forward John Havlicek. What point is he making by invoking the names of these Hall of Fame athletes?

Examining the Writer's Method

1. In his opening paragraph, Walters offers a series of brief examples without identifying his specific focus. Why does he choose to offer a tease of the main point, which he then states at the end of paragraph 2?
2. For each type of throw, Walters provides two solid examples. Consider each grouping. In your view, does he present each pair of examples the same way, that is, a strong example followed by a stronger example, or does he do the opposite? Explain.
3. Walters provides three transitional paragraphs (4, 5, and 10). Which do you think is most effective and why?
4. The conclusion is the longest paragraph of the entire essay. In your view, why does he use such an elaborate example to conclude his writing?

Considering Style and Language

1. Walters uses direct quotation four times in his essay. Why do you think he decided to present what people actually said at these points rather than to paraphrase?
2. How would you describe the overall tone of this essay? Do you think his writing would have been as effective if he had approached the subject in another way?
3. Colloquial language is the term used to describe words characteristic of informal writing and conversation. In many of the paragraphs of this essay, Walters uses colloquial words, for instance

chucking (para. 2), *unloaded* and *yelped,* (para. 3), *drop one* (para. 6), and *whipped it* (para. 11). Do you agree with his decision to use these words, or should he have used more formal language? Explain.

4. What do the following words mean in the context of the writing? *Impulse* (para. 2); *arc* (para. 3); *balmy, trajectory* (para. 5); *distinguishing, confronted* (para. 6); *churning, spray, hunkered* (para. 7); *orb* (para. 9); *surge* (para. 10); *liberal, flouting* (para. 11); *undoubtedly, lieu, atrium, aerodynamic* (para. 12); *therapeutic, elevates* (para. 13); *hypnotic, arc, unequivocal, ricocheted, bemused* (para. 14).

Your Turn: Responding to the Subject

a. In this essay, Jonathan Walters takes the simple act of throwing and classifies the various ways people amuse themselves with it. For this assignment, consider other common activities that people perform (walking, singing, dancing, chewing), set up classes, and discuss them as Walters has.

b. Several of the examples in Walters's essay involve people throwing things when they were supposed to be doing work of some kind. For this assignment, classify the types of work-avoidance techniques you have seen people practice.

DIANE RIVA

Exposed Toes

Consider the old adage "clothes make the person," the implication being that what we wear defines us as people. In this essay, Diane Riva takes this old saying and narrows the focus a bit from clothes to just shoes. Riva describes herself this way: "I am a happily divorced, single parent with a fourteen-year-old daughter, Leah, who takes my breath away. I try to express the thoughts in my head through various forms: writing, painting, and working with metals." Currently working for a jewelry design firm, Riva draws on her varied work and personal experiences and in her essay puts a different twist on the familiar axiom. She suggests that the different shoes we wear in the different aspects of our lives—as children, as spouses, as parents, as workers, and so on—reflect different aspects of us.

What do the shoes you choose to wear at any time say about you at that moment?

The shoes scattered throughout the house belong to me. I will find a pair under the dining room table, a pair in the parlor, or one or two pairs in the kitchen, and even a few in my bedroom. In my childhood memories, I can still hear my mother asking me to pick up my wayward shoes. Some habits are hard to break, and leaving my shoes wherever my feet release them is one I am still trying to overcome. When I look at my shoes, I see endless memories. They are part of my personality, and if they could talk, what colorful tales they would tell. 1

I own three pairs of black sneakers; they are my proud work shoes, and we spend the most time together. There are times when my feet melt when I enter them. My work as a bartender has enabled my sneakers to taste Guinness Irish stout, fine Russian vodkas, assorted hot coffee drinks, or whatever else I am rushing around the bar to make. They are the constant recipients of the over-filled glass of alcohol. 2

My black, tattered sneakers with tiny knots in the shoelaces have heard hours of endless stories from lonely travelers stopping in the hotel lounge, guests pouring out tales of love, heartache, job stress, divorce, battles won, battles lost, and hundreds of irritating jokes. At the end of my shift, if we are fortunate and it has rained, I give the bottoms of my hard working sneakers a bath in a fresh puddle. It feels good to wash away work. When my feet arrive home, my sneakers are 3 usually slipped off and left in the parlor to slumber. This is where they will quietly remain until I torture them for another eight hours of work.

Along with my sneakers, I own a pair of boat shoes. The tops are a reddish brown, the same color as an Irish Setter, and the soles are made of rubber. I have had these shoes for over six years, and still they do not age as I do. When I occasionally wear my boat shoes, I don't like the way they look on my wide feet, but they feel so good. They know me the least but struggle to be in my world. I will probably have these shoes for the rest of my life. They are like memories of past boyfriends: hard to get rid of. 4

When I open my closet door, my dress shoes lie dead in dusty boxes. About every four months, I will remove a pair and struggle into them. When I wear these high-heeled shoes, it is usually for a wedding, a Christmas party, or a night on the town. When I add one or two inches to my height, I end up having this pretty feeling, and my legs have a tendency to like the way they look. The sound of a high-heeled shoe on a polished marble floor at a posh restaurant, I will admit, has a certain appeal to me. I gather it is my whole look, from the top of my perfectly set hair to the ends of my smothered toes, that gives me this feeling of attractiveness. 5

But how I look forward to removing these falsely overstated dress shoes and returning them to their dusty coffins. Funny how these shoes never lounge around the house; they are always returned to their boxes. I would not want to insult the everyday, comfortable shoe with the high society heel. 6

Among my most treasured shoes is a pair of sandals. They can be worn throughout all the seasons, with or without socks. My huaraches are from Tijuana, and on a hot day many years ago, I handpicked them myself from among many of their twins. The soles are made from black, recycled tires, and the upper portion consists of thick, tan leather strips that entwine to form an interesting open-toe design. They call my name constantly, but unfortunately, they are the most inappropriate shoe for all occasions. As I picked up my paycheck from work one cold November day, my boss commented on my unusual footwear for this time of year. He could not help but notice my well-worn extra-wide huaraches and my thick woolen socks, so he stated that it seemed an unsuitable time of year for sandals. I tried to explain the comfort zone of these broken-in shoes, but he just looked at me with confusion. I don't think that he could relate to the love-hate affair that women have with their shoes. I have had the pleasure of spoiling my feet with these huaraches for over eight years. Each spring they take a trip to the cobbler for their yearly checkup. I think the cobbler looks forward to this annual visit and admires the workmanship in these weary old sandals. 7

I must admit my shoes of choice were given to me by my parents, and I wear these constantly. Nothing has to be tied; they have no straps, no buckles, no leather between the toes, no heels. They are never too tight and always fit perfectly—my natural feet. Whenever possible, my feet are out of confinement, barefoot and happy. I love for my feet to touch and feel all the materials of life. They can be tickled, washed, counted, and colored. They hold all of my memories. They were on my honeymoon; they were at my daughter's birth; they feel spring and the ocean first; they have been bitten, cut, and bruised. I never have to look for them, they are always where I left them, and they never have to be put away. *8*

As I search throughout my house and pick up my wayward shoes before my mother arrives for a visit, I look down at the bundle of leather and laces in my arms, and days of my past shout out to me. I know why these shoes are scattered about. They are my memories, and I do not want to put them away. *9*

Understanding the Significance

1. In her essay, how does Riva justify leaving her shoes scattered around her home?
2. Why do you think Riva describes the boxes in which she stores her dress shoes as coffins?
3. As Riva explains it, what is the "love-hate affair" women have with shoes?
4. In her conclusion, she mentions that habits are hard to break. What evidence in this paragraph indicates that breaking bad habits is nevertheless possible?

Discovering the Writer's Purpose

1. A second look at this essay shows that it is much more than a discussion about shoes. What do you think Riva's real purpose is in relating the various stories?
2. From her explanation, what sense do you get about Riva's attitude toward her job?
3. In the fifth and sixth paragraphs, what impression do you get of Riva's feelings about formal dress?
4. As her final category of shoes, Riva chooses feet. Do you agree with her reasoning that feet should be classified as a type of shoe? Explain.

Examining the Writer's Method

1. How does Riva use her introduction to set her reader up for the discussion to follow?
2. What titles would you give to the various categories of footwear that Riva discusses?
3. How would you describe Riva's method of arrangement? Has she followed emphatic order or set the paragraphs up in a more random fashion? Would her essay be more—or less—effective if she changed the order?
4. How does Riva's final paragraph serve as an effective conclusion?

Considering Style and Language

1. How would you describe the tone of Riva's essay?
2. In several spots, Riva provides wonderful sensory details. In your judgment, which use of detail is best? Why?
3. Throughout her essay, Riva uses personification to describe her footwear. What effect does she create by giving her shoes lives of their own?
4. What do the following words mean in the context of the writing? *Wayward* (para. 1); *slumber* (para. 3); *posh* (para. 5); *overstated* (para. 6); *inappropriate, cobbler* (para. 7); *confinement* (para. 8).

Your Turn: Responding to the Subject

a. In her essay, Riva tells about the different kinds of shoes she owns and what they say about her. Like Riva, do you have several different types of shoes or other clothing items—jeans, ties, sweaters, and so on—each of which tells the world something specific about you? For this assignment, explain to your reader what your bureau drawers or closet racks tell people about you.

b. To some degree, the ways people dress reflect the groups they belong to—or aspire to belong to. For this assignment, consider a place where large groups of people congregate—for example, your campus, a shopping mall, a nightclub, a sports stadium, or a concert hall—and write an essay in which you group people on the basis of common styles of dress.

ARNO KARLEN

Ectoparasites

Man and Microbes, *the longer work from which "Ectoparasites" is drawn, is one science writer and researcher's attempt to detail the history of mankind's encounters with disease. The irony in the situation, as author Arno Karlen explains, is that disease and "humanness" have often evolved together. That is, the very qualities that humans embrace as most connected to their existence are the ones that disease-bearing microbes and parasites have come to exploit. Our domestication of barnyard animals brought us a variety of diseases including salmonella, influenza, and tuberculosis. Our companionship with dogs and other pets brought us rabies, typhus, and intestinal worms. City life brought epidemics of smallpox, cholera, and plague, and commerce between city centers spread these and other diseases far and wide. In the following excerpt, Karlen uses a clear and consistent method of division and classification, with easily identified elements, to illustrate that even the invention of clothing—a highly valuable and seemingly harmless human innovation—has brought with it unwanted and occasionally dangerous guests.*

What kinds of tiny creatures share our clothing, in many cases without our ever being aware of it?

People usually do not think of clothes as an environment, but that is just what they are to microbes. To a bacterium, a droplet of body fluid is a sea, a hair or fingernail a continent, a piece of cloth a universe. Garments are also havens for ectoparasites, which live not within their hosts but upon them. As clothes increased from a tropical minimum to a year-round cover for most of the body, they created a home for a new, minute bestiary. *1*

The first clothing, according to *Genesis,* were the fig leaves Adam and Eve sewed into aprons to cover their nakedness. Actually, the first wearers of clothes must have felt not shame but triumph. Their ingenuity allowed them to survive beyond the warm environment where humans first evolved. Thanks to garments and fire, they became the only primates to inhabit the entire world, even deserts and Arctic wastes. Part of the price was a large complement of fleas, lice, and bedbugs. *2*

These ectoparasites have their own histories, shaped in part by human behavior. Each came to live on people in different times and ways, *3* as people created niches for them. Their remote ancestors lived on the organic debris around animals' lairs and birds' nests. Some modified their claws and mouth parts to become blood feeders that cling to fur. Fleas probably shifted from other mammals to humans in the past 10,000 years. Since they must first develop in debris before finding hosts, they rarely infest animals without lairs, such as big mobile primates and carnivores. Fleas do thrive on dogs and pigs, which lived intimately with the first sedentary humans; in fact, many primitive dwellings differed little from pigsties. From such sources fleas must have hitched on to people in Neolithic villages. Fortunately, human fleas rarely transmit diseases; they are less a threat than a nuisance.

Bedbugs probably moved in with people some 35,000 years ago. 4
Their ancestors were plant feeders, then parasites of cave-dwelling bats. Perhaps it was in Middle Eastern caves that they began adapting to late Neanderthalers or early Homo sapiens. The relationship was cemented when people devised permanent dwellings, which to bugs are quite like their accustomed caves. Though mentioned by the ancient Greeks and Romans, bedbugs spread worldwide more recently; they were first referred to in Germany in the eleventh century, in England in the sixteenth. The bedbug's tropical cousin, the conenose, may have entered people's houses only a few thousand years ago. It transmits Chagas' disease, still a widespread problem in South America, but otherwise the bedbug family transmits infection to people only by occasional accident.

Lice are quite another matter. They are probably heirloom para- 5
sites, inherited from our primate ancestors. One reason to think so is that lice tend to make very specialized adaptations, and these usually take a long time to develop. Lice are such discriminating feeders that many species will starve to death rather than drink the blood of unfamiliar hosts. Being so specialized, they had to readapt when hair receded from most of the human body, to last bastions on the head and pubis. One type of louse evolved that had claws modified to grip the dense, fine hairs of the head. Another variety developed to inhabit the coarse, widely separated hairs of the pubis (it can also live in the coarse, widely separated eyelashes). A third type, body lice, diverged from head lice after the invention of whole-body clothing. Despite their name, they live and lay eggs not on the body but in the dense fibers of fur, wool, and cotton.

Head, pubic, and body lice all became ubiquitous in temperate 6
climates. In the West, they were helped by early Christian disdain for comfort and cleanliness; one species' asceticism created another's nirvana. Lice thrived in the Middle Ages and beyond, thanks to the continuing belief that bathing was an indulgence, an

invitation to illness, or even a sin. The growing variety and availability of garments—especially of woolens during the Little Ice Age—may have helped lice proliferate, as did growing population density and crowded living. As late as the seventeenth century, etiquette lessons for Europe's nobility taught when and how to dispose of one's lice. If royalty had plentiful parasites, so did their subjects, who washed their bodies and clothes less often. Lice became rarer from the eighteenth century on, as washing became more frequent and effective. However, head lice and nits (louse eggs) still infest many children in American schools and nurseries, and in poor countries, body lice thrive on people who wear the same unwashed clothes every day.

Understanding the Significance

1. According to Karlen, the innovation of clothing had both an advantage and a price. What are these benefits and disadvantages?
2. Which animals that shared space with our ancestors did fleas choose as host creatures before also adapting to infest humans?
3. Where was the likely geographical locale where bedbugs began sharing space with humans?
4. What characteristics of lice indicate that they have long been with humans?

Discovering the Writer's Purpose

1. As you see it, what is the most important point Karlen is making in this excerpt? What details or examples lead you to this conclusion?
2. In the beginning of the third paragraph, Karlen notes that the histories of the different ectoparasites have been "shaped in part by human behavior." What impression do you think he is making through this statement?
3. By referring to the eleventh and sixteenth centuries as "more recently," what is Karlen suggesting about how time should be viewed when it comes to the existence of life on earth?

4. Of the three types of ectoparasites that Karlen discusses in detail, which group does he suggest is most dangerous and why?

Examining the Writer's Method

1. How does Karlen's use of *chronological order* emphasize the division and classification and help him illustrate the relationship between clothing and ectoparasites?
2. In your view, which of Karlen's categories of ectoparasites is presented most distinctly and completely? Explain your reasoning.
3. In what is primarily a scientific essay, Karlen introduces a story from a religious text, the Bible—the story of Adam and Eve. Why do you think he made this choice? Do you agree with his decision?
4. In his discussion of each class of ectoparasite, Karlen employs division. In which section do you think his division is most useful to the reader? Explain your reasoning.

Considering Style and Language

1. Although Karlen writes about a topic of some consequence—ectoparasites have long been a source of great annoyance and embarrassment—he often employs a subtle humor. Where in this excerpt do you think his use of humor is most effective? Do you think this is an effective way to approach this topic? Why or why not?
2. How would you describe Karlen's attitude about bedbugs, lice, and other ectoparasites? What in the text makes you think this?
3. Writers in scientific fields are often faulted for having writing styles that are "boring" or "too difficult to understand." Would you argue Karlen's style falls into either of these two categories? Why do you feel this way?
4. What do the following words mean in the context of the writing? *Haven, minute, bestiary* (para. 1); *complement* (para. 2); *niche, lair, sedentary, Neolithic* (para. 3); *Neanderthal* (para. 4); *heirloom, discriminating, bastions, diverge* (para. 5); *ubiquitous, disdain, asceticism, nirvana, indulgence, proliferate* (para. 6).

Your Turn: Responding to the Subject

a. When Karlen refers to ectoparasites as longstanding nuisances that have shadowed humans from their origins, he certainly isn't suggesting that these creatures are the only nuisances. In fact, thanks to technological advances, humans face whole new classes of annoyances. For this assignment, explore some of the types of irritations technology has spawned and then use division and classification to examine at least three groups of modern-day nuisances.

b. When it comes to manufacturers, retailers, restaurants, and so on, consumers have a wide variety of brand name choices. The truth, however, is that many of the companies within the same class sell the same general categories of merchandise. So what distinguishes one from the other? For example, what features and characteristics typify upscale department stores, stores that appeal to middle-class shoppers, and those that cater to low- and moderate-income shoppers? What elements characterize five-star restaurants, full-service chain restaurants, and fast-food places? For this assignment, focus on a type of business or industry and identify at least three classes within that group. Then write an essay in which you explain the classes, providing at least two examples of each type.

Other Possibilities for Using Division and Classification

The following list contains subjects that could be developed into essays featuring division and classification. Some of these topics may lend themselves more easily to a focus on division, others on classification, and others on both. Feel free to adapt a subject in any way you think will enable you to develop an effective essay.

- Types of post-secondary education
- Categories of work-avoidance activities
- The structure of a company, organization, or institution with which you are familiar

- Classes of television shows currently on the air
- Categories of popular music
- A successful play or concert
- Types of television or radio commercials
- Styles of teaching or learning
- Types of business careers
- Elements of a successful party
- Types of comedy
- Your city or town
- Alternative energy sources or applications
- A scientific theory
- Types of discrimination or prejudice that occurs in American society

Writing at Work

DIVISION AND CLASSIFICATION

@ROAD

Products and Services

In much of the real-world writing we are exposed to, writers need to delineate or categorize items, situations, conditions, and other elements. When they do, they turn to division and classification, whether it's to complete a company's annual report discussing goals achieved and goals still to meet, a brochure detailing the holdings of an art museum, or a magazine or newspaper article itemizing a state's annual budget. In the following passage, taken from the web page of @Road, a company that employs wireless Internet technology to provide a wide variety of services, the writer relies heavily on division and classification to highlight these services.

Products/Services

@Road's fully scalable data center, secure wide-area network infrastructure, patented LocationSmart™ technology, and talented staff enable us to bring complete, intelligent solutions to businesses and mobile professionals. We provide a suite of productivity enhancement solutions for businesses and people on the move. @Road's overall commitment to excellence in products, services and technology reflects our vision of a powerful, LocationSmart mobile economy.

@Road's industry leadership focuses on four key markets: Mobile Resource Management, Mobile Commerce Exchange, Mobile Content Delivery, and Mobile Business Intelligence.

Mobile Resource Management

Our Mobile Resource Management (MRM) services give businesses a competitive edge through location-specific information. With thousands of subscribers today, FleetASAP gives businesses location, messaging, reports, maintenance and other productivity enhancement tools. Our customers can manage their fleets virtually anywhere, 24 hours a day, 7 days a week.

Commerce Exchange

@Road business-to-business Commerce Exchange solutions address the needs of the emerging mobile economy. Our solutions enable mobile economy participants to be more productive, stay competitive, and drive up profitability by providing virtual mobile hubs and exchanges. @Road's logistics management commerce exchange brings carriers, shippers, and businesses together via the Internet.

Mobile Content Delivery

@Road Mobile Content Delivery solutions enable mobile economy participants to receive location-specific content, empowering them to make more informed, fun, intelligent decisions, enhancing productivity through automated LocationSmart content delivery. myWeb2Go™, @Road's first mobile content delivery service, provides true LocationSmart content to WAP-enabled phones, PDAs and other mobile devices through our patented platform.

Mobile Business Intelligence

@Road Mobile Business Intelligence solutions extend the communication outreach of businesses to mobile assets through the use of our LocationSmart Wireless Internet technology and infrastructure. @Road provides mobile system content and performance indicators, including reporting, monitoring, and personalization. This enables users to quickly make more intelligent decisions. Over time, this means longer asset life and increased efficiency.

Focusing on the Message and Aim

Answer each of the following questions in a brief paragraph, referring specifically to the passage you've just read.

1. As most documents do, this section of @Road's web page begins with a brief introductory paragraph. How does this introduction convince a potential customer who happens upon this site to read through the classification of the available products and services?
2. This section of @Road's web page features four different categories of products and services. In your view, what method of arrangement does the writer follow in presenting these categories?
3. The primary purpose of any piece of advertising is to convince a potential customer to study the product a little more closely, with the hopes of a possible sale. How does the tone of this document help to attract a reader to investigate what @Road has to offer?

Applying the Principles

a. Take your college's catalog and review the various services it provides. Then, following the pattern provided here, prepare a one-page classification of those services that could be used on the college's web page.
b. On the basis of the information presented here, what different types of businesses do you think would most benefit from the kinds of products and services that @Road offers? Flip through the Yellow Pages or some business directory and then prepare a one-page listing of likely customers, briefly explaining why each company would benefit from doing business with @Road.

Practical Application: Division and Classification

It has been a full year since you joined the management team at Fusion Heavy Metal Recovery Systems, Inc., a national hazardous waste recycling company, and you've certainly found it to be an exciting place to work. As a recent *Wall Street Journal* profile indicates, the company started up five years ago and experienced immediate and enormous success. The CEO, a native of your city, has made a serious commitment to give something back to his hometown that has given him so much. His company currently employs thirty-five city residents in well-paying, high technology positions, with plans for expansion both locally and in several other states.

The *Wall Street Journal* story also reports one of the more remarkable episodes in the company's history. The year before you joined the corporation, Fusion Heavy Metal Recovery Systems enjoyed a record year in terms of profits. To show his appreciation to the workers who made this success possible, the CEO decided to share the wealth in an unusual fashion: he surprised each of the 35 staffers, plus a guest of each person's choice, with a five-day cruise to the Caribbean with all expenses paid.

This afternoon, the CEO calls you into the office to tell you that history is about to repeat itself. Figures for the last six months indicate that profits are far ahead of the banner year two years ago, so once again he would like to reward his employees. This time, however, he wants to approach the situation a little differently, in part to counter some problems that he hadn't anticipated last time.

For example, he hadn't really considered that, to the government, such a vacation is considered income, meaning the so-called free vacation had actually increased tax burdens for the employees. Also, to some people, a vacation means getting away from the individuals they work with, no matter how good their relationship is. Furthermore, from a strictly business standpoint, a group vacation is not necessarily a great idea. What would happen if there were some terrible calamity? Would the company still be able to operate without key personnel? Would resulting litigation wipe out the company assets?

To avoid these and other potential problems, the CEO has decided to offer the employees a menu of at least five bonus possibilities (for example, a tax-sheltered college scholarship fund for a child, a voucher to buy company stock) from which to choose. As the CEO explains, $3,600 has been allotted for each employee. Your job is to do some brainstorming, develop that menu, and then submit a confidential one-page memo to him that details the possibilities. Once he reviews and approves of your selections, he will distribute the memo to the entire staff. To guide you in terms of approach and format he has given you a copy of the following memo prepared two years ago by Christine Baker, president of a local travel agency, that had helped the CEO settle on a Caribbean cruise in the first place.

North Shore Travel

158 Maple Road Amesbury, MA 01913 (508) 976–3321

TO: M. Lars Oldengray, CEO, Fusion Heavy Metal Recovery Systems, Inc.

FROM: Christine Baker, President

DATE: November 12, 2008

RE: Group Vacation Possibilities

Thank you for inquiring about the vacation packages available through North Shore Travel. We want your employees to be thrilled with their vacations, so we have selected the most popular destinations of the year. In order to make things easy for you, we have tailored each trip to your specific requirements. Each package offers four nights and five days of travel, lodging, meals, and activities for less than $1800 per person. Spectacular sunsets are free! We take care of all details, so all you have to do is enjoy the trip.

Cruising in the Caribbean $1,728
- Enjoy a deluxe ocean view cabin.
- Feast on your choice of cuisine.
- Gamble in a high-energy casino.
- Experience Las Vegas-style shows.
- Explore exotic ports of call.

Biking in Vermont $1,799
- Ride diverse mountain trails.
- Learn from experienced guides.
- Dine on hearty gourmet meals.
- Play indoors in bad weather.
- Rest in our mountain-top lodge.

Exploring in Napa Valley $1,790
- Unwind in a garden view suite.
- Savor regional cuisine.
- Tour local wineries.
- Bike in the heart of Napa Valley.
- Relax with a whirlpool or massage.

Beaching in Florida $1,775
- Enjoy beautiful sunsets each night.
- Lounge pool-side or on the sand.
- Shop in outposts & boutiques.
- Swim, sail, and snorkel.
- Play golf, racquetball, or tennis.

Prices shown include all ground travel, port charges, and airfare from Boston (where applicable). Also, substantial discounts are available if one package trip is booked for all 80 people. There are no restrictions as to when you can travel, so trips may be booked any time during the year.

North Shore Travel offers the personal attention and outstanding service only a corporate travel specialist can provide. When you are ready to discuss your plans further, please contact us to schedule a convenient meeting time. If there is anything else we can do to assist you in this matter, please feel free to call.

13

Argument

The Approach: Understanding Argument

Writing that attempts to persuade a reader to accept a point of view is known as *argument.* Unlike the techniques discussed in the previous chapters, argument isn't a mode—it's an aim. Argument does satisfy one of the three aims or purposes of writing, however—to *persuade.*

Some people draw a distinction between *argument* and *persuasion,* with argument specifically referring to writings that rationally and dispassionately attempt to convince the reader of the validity of a position and persuasion referring to writings that rely on additional appeals, including appeals to emotion, to sway the reader. For the most part, though, you need not be concerned about this distinction since supporting a stand on an issue will likely involve both approaches.

THE MODES IN COMBINATION

The distinction between an argument paper and any other type of document lies in both *technique* and *intent.* A dance performance, for example, may include a number of modes or technical moves—a *pas de deux,* a *back handspring,* the *moonwalk*—but the meaning of the dance emerges only when the individual moves are observed as a whole. Likewise, *description, definition, cause and effect, narration,* and so forth are the rhetorical modes that together make an argument paper.

Consider a paper asserting that oil companies must be more responsible in both the quality of the ships they use to transport crude oil and the competence of the captains and crews piloting those ships. You might begin the paper with some images of oil-soaked seals, sea otters, birds, and fish dying after the sinking of the tanker *Prestige* off the coast of Spain in 2002, the grounding of the tanker *Braer* off the coast of Scotland in early 1993, or the grounding of the *Valdez* off the coast of Alaska a few years before that. These images could then be followed by a brief retelling of the catastrophes, and then by an explanation of the oil companies' culpability in the disasters. The rest of the paper could be devoted to the changes that should be enacted to save our oceans, including better training and the use of state-of-the-art double-hulled tankers.

In terms of modes, the images of sea creatures dead and dying in a fouled ocean would be description, the brief stories of the groundings would be narration, and the explanation of the companies' responsibility would be cause and effect. The remainder of the paper would also feature a combination of modes—for instance, process to explain how some companies have skirted current laws by registering their ships in countries with lax regulations, and division and classification to categorize the variety of changes needed.

TYPES OF APPEALS

The ancient Greeks identified three types of appeals used to persuade someone to accept a line of reasoning: *ethos, pathos,* and *logos.* Writers still embrace these concepts, which today are explained respectively as appeals on the basis of *reputation, emotion,* and *logic.* As with the modes, these types of appeals generally appear in combination. An argument paper that appeals wholly to emotion or one that appeals wholly to logic would have some serious weaknesses.

An example of an essay appealing wholly to emotion would be a paper advocating that leaders of hate groups be imprisoned because their speeches are treatises on prejudice. Such a paper would no doubt inspire some cheers, but it would be flawed. Preserving freedom of speech for all of us means allowing people to express attitudes offensive to the majority. A better approach for this paper would be to incorporate an appeal to logic by suggesting that leaders of hate groups be prosecuted whenever their words violate the law and that efforts be expanded to raise the public's awareness of prejudice.

TYPES OF ARGUMENT

In terms of classical rhetorical theory, there is actually more than one type of argument, depending on the focus of the document. A **deliberative** argument presents a proposal or poses a case in order to persuade the reader of the validity of a plan or suggestion. An editorial urging the state legislature to increase funding for after-school programs and a proposal encouraging a company to convert an empty space into a day care center for employees are both deliberative.

A **judicial** argument condemns or defends an individual or action and seeks to convince an audience to accept the condemnation or defense. An essay objecting to opening pristine wildlife areas to oil exploration and a review of new software rebutting claims of frequent crashes are both judicial.

A **ceremonial** argument offers praise for someone or something, attempting to inspire or motivate a reader. A magazine piece celebrating the introduction of the personal computer as a pivotal event in modern history and a letter or memo stressing the extraordinary effect someone has on an institution or organization are both ceremonial.

Of course, argument documents don't necessarily fit exclusively into one of these categories. An op-ed essay urging that the United States not engage in military conflict before all diplomatic solutions have been explored might be largely deliberative. But if it also condemns earlier policy and calls to mind the U.S. Constitution's emphasis on fairness and justice rather than on military might, then the piece would have judicial and ceremonial elements as well.

The Development of Your Paper

For an argument essay, your aim is always the same: to persuade the reader of the validity of your point of view. To fulfill this goal, you need to

- take a clear stance on the issue;
- develop sufficient valid support;
- recognize the importance of tone;
- avoid errors in logic; and
- provide an effective arrangement of the material.

A CLEAR STANCE ON THE ISSUE

For an argument paper, you must clarify where you stand on an issue to prepare your reader for the line of reasoning constituting your argument. Look at this introduction to an essay about the rights of adoptees and birth parents to unseal confidential adoption files. The final sentence, shown here underlined, makes it clear that the writer is in favor of allowing the files to be opened:

> Today, many adopted children across the country are attempting to gain access to their sealed adoption files for information about their birth parents. Likewise, many individuals who had given their infants up for adoption are also trying to have the files unsealed so that they can discover the whereabouts of the children they surrendered to others to raise. Meanwhile, the adoptive parents involved are caught in the middle, not wanting to deny their children the opportunity to learn about their roots but also fearing that they might somehow lose their children as a result. It's a gut-wrenching subject, one that has no easy answers. Regardless of the potential for pain, however, both adopted children and parents who surrendered their children for adoption should be able to read through their files and make contact with their biological relatives if they choose.

With this final sentence in place, the reader knows exactly where the writer stands and is therefore prepared for the line of reasoning to follow in the body of the essay.

SUFFICIENT VALID SUPPORT

When providing evidence to support your stance, be sure that evidence is both **sufficient** and **valid**. In terms of support for your stance, there is no specific minimum—or maximum—amount of information needed. Think of a subject about which you are undecided: How much support for a position would you need to see before you would accept it? It's likely that you would require several solid supporting details and examples before you would be convinced. Your reader demands the same of you.

Valid evidence is accurate and truthful. When including evidence from another source, be sure to evaluate, to the best of your ability, the reliability of that source and to acknowledge it appropriately. You must be particularly vigilant with material you find on the Internet, as no authority or group screens its staggering amounts of information for accuracy.

Keep in mind that *facts*—verifiable truths—are by and large stronger support than *opinions*—reasonings based on fact. Carefully crafted opinions can offer firm support for the point you are making, especially if the source of the opinion is reputable. *Personal feelings* and *attitudes*, however, generally lack a valid basis of support and are not suitable. Essentially, the line of reasoning underlying an argument is a fully developed opinion. For that opinion to be valid, it needs to be supported with relevant facts.

For example, that certain sport utility vehicles (SUVs) are prone to rollover accidents is a *fact* whose source is a study appearing in a national publication like the *The Wall Street Journal* or *Newsweek*. The statement that SUVs carry a risk that compact cars don't have is an *opinion*. Adding that SUVs are bulky and unattractive doesn't provide any useful support; rather, it expresses a personal feeling that has nothing to do with the rollover threat.

In addition to considering how you would persuade a reluctant or indifferent audience, you also must anticipate, as much as possible, the questions and claims of someone holding an opposing point of view. A reader might suggest, for instance, that SUVs help large families travel and cope. You can head off doubts by thinking ahead and addressing them—perhaps, in this case, by suggesting safe, low-emission station wagons or crossover vehicles as alternatives.

Remember also that whenever you draw information from some document or individual to support your argument, you must indicate the source of this material for your reader. With brief, less formal writing situations, acknowledging this source information can often be as simple as this: "According to a recent item in *U.S. News & World Report*, previously unreleased testing results show that an alarming number of SUVs are prone to roll over in side-impact crashes."

For longer, more formal assignments, however, you need to provide specific elements of documentation, including the title, date of publication, publisher, and pages involved, in accordance with the method your instructor prefers. The reference section of your college library will have complete guidelines for several different methods of documentation, including those of the Modern Language Association (MLA) and the American Psychological Association (APA).

TONE

Another aspect that will affect how your point of view is accepted is its *tone,* the attitude expressed about the subject. If your tone is sarcastic, superior, or patronizing, you may alienate a reader who might otherwise be persuaded to agree with your point of view. On the other hand, if your tone is sincere, concerned, or respectful, you'll increase the chance that your point of view will be favorably received.

Imagine an essay demanding that new gun control measures be imposed. With a volatile subject like gun control, it's easy to understand how a sentence such as this might appear in an early draft:

> A person would have to be stupid not to realize that an unlocked handgun is statistically far more likely to be stolen or to cause accidental injury than it is to be used to stop an intruder.

The message in the sentence is valid but the tone is insulting. Now consider this version of the sentence:

> Many people still don't realize that an unlocked handgun is statistically far more likely to be stolen or to cause accidental injury than it is to be used to stop an intruder.

The message is essentially unchanged, but the tone is clearly more neutral. It no longer suggests that a person who hasn't come to this realization is somehow deficient. As a result, a reader who also hasn't come to this realization may well be more receptive to your line of reasoning.

In some cases, you can adjust the tone of your writing by avoiding any absolute terms. It is better, for example, to say that patients with severe head injuries *rarely* emerge from deep extended comas to enjoy life as they once did than to say they *never* do, because it allows for the one-in-a-million, unexplainable recovery. Therefore, rather than use words such as *all, always, every,* and *never,* rely on words such as *most, frequently, many,* and *rarely.*

ERRORS IN LOGIC

To persuade a reader, an argument paper must have a logical line of reasoning leading to a valid conclusion. You establish this line of reasoning by engaging in one of two primary ways of thinking: *induction* and *deduction.* Although the goal of the two reasoning processes is the same, they involve coming at a subject from opposite directions.

With *induction,* you reason from a series of specific matters to a general conclusion. Physicians employ inductive reasoning when they conclude that a particular skin rash is a form of eczema because every other rash that they've examined like this one has proved to be eczema. An answer reached in this way is the result of what is called an *inductive leap,* which means that while this diagnosis is a reasonable conclusion, it isn't necessarily the only possible valid explanation. The rash might closely resemble the one resulting from eczema but might actually be the result of another condition that the physicians aren't aware of.

With *deduction,* you reason from a series of general statements to a specific conclusion. If all flat, low-lying, inland areas are especially susceptible to tornadoes and you live in a flat, low-lying, inland area, then it is accurate to say that your area faces the threat of tornadoes.

Regardless of whether you use induction, deduction, or some combination of the two to make your point, avoid the following common errors in logic, often referred to as *logical fallacies,* listed here with examples:

- *Argument ad hominem* (Latin for "argument to the man")—objecting to the person making the argument rather than that person's line of reasoning:

  Why should anyone pay attention to environmental advocate Sierra Larges, who wants everyone to carpool and drive smaller cars in order to lessen our dependence on fossil fuels? She just lives off her family trust fund and doesn't even have a real job.

- *Bandwagon approach*—urging acceptance of a point of view merely because other people accept it rather than because of compelling evidence:

  Demolishing that historic building is the right thing to do because everybody in the real estate brokers association thinks it's ugly and out of step with other buildings in that neighborhood.

- *Begging the question*—assuming as fact something that needs to be proved:

  A company like Accountable Accountants, which does nothing but misrepresent the assets it handles, shouldn't be allowed to bid on financial management accounts in this state.

- *Creating a red herring*—purposely shifting from the main idea to some less important point to escape close scrutiny of the main point:

  It is true that the superintendent of schools has failed to submit a budget proposal by the mandated deadline, but how about the two school committee members who didn't attend Employee Appreciation day at the Timber Middle School?

- *Either/or reasoning*—suggesting only two alternatives when many possibilities exist:

  Unless we completely change the way we teach mathematics, our children will never attain acceptable test scores.

- *Hasty generalization*—making an assumption on the basis of too little valid support:

  I've been taking that vitamin supplement for almost two weeks and I don't feel any more energetic, so it obviously doesn't work.

- *Non sequitur* (Latin for "it does not follow")—coming to an illogical or incorrect conclusion in relation to the evidence:

  According to recent test scores, elementary schoolchildren are performing poorly on reading tests, so it's time to reduce the number of days in the school year.

- *Oversimplification*—wrongfully reducing a complex subject by ignoring crucial information or factual inconsistencies:

  Sex education classes will eliminate teenage promiscuity.

- *Post hoc, ergo prompter hoc* (Latin for "after this, therefore because of this")—assuming because one thing occurred before another that the first caused the second:

  The killer had just completed an enormous meal at a fast-food place, so something in the food must have triggered his aggression.

AN EFFECTIVE ARRANGEMENT

Although it's not the only suitable way to arrange an argument paper, emphatic order is often an excellent choice. The idea is to use the initial points to spark your reader's interest and then to use the subsequent examples to feed that interest, thus cultivating acceptance of your point of view.

Consider the following thesis for an essay proposing a change in the way many U.S. public schools operate:

> American public schools should adjust the current school calendar and hold classes year round.

Now take a look at this informal outline of the supporting ideas, which are arranged to move from strong example, to stronger example, to even stronger example, saving the strongest reason for change—that the current system, with its long summer recess, impedes the educational process—for last:

Point 1: The older system, based on an agrarian model in which children were needed in the summer to help out on farms, no longer matches the lifestyle of the vast majority of people.

Point 2: This revised schedule would allow for a concentrated period of ten weeks for study, followed by a couple of weeks away from school, which helps eliminate fatigue and facilitate learning.

Point 3: More frequent breaks from school would help with matters of discipline and order.

Point 4: The long summer vacation in the current system derails education, causing the need for repetition in the curriculum.

Because it fosters a movement in reasoning from a significant reason to change the academic calendar to a more significant reason and so on, emphatic order stirs and sustains interest, increasing the chances the audience will see the argument as reasonable, valid, and compelling.

CHECKLIST FOR USING ARGUMENT

---

1. Is the **stance in the document clearly stated**?
2. Does the document include **sufficient supporting examples**?
3. Is the document **free from logical fallacies**?
4. Is the **tone** of the document **appropriate** for the subject and approach?
5. Has **emphatic order** been used to capture and hold the reader's attention and to foster support for the reasoning within the document?

AN ANNOTATED EXAMPLE

WYNTON MARSALIS

Saving America's Soul Kitchen

When Hurricane Katrina hit the Gulf Coast of the United States during the final days of August 2005, no one could have imagined the tremendous damage it would inflict on Alabama, Mississippi, and Louisiana. On August 29, New Orleans, significant portions of which are below sea level, became the focus of the world when several levees built to keep the waters of the Gulf of Mexico and Lake Pontchartrain from spilling into the city began to fail. The tragedy was compounded by the failure of government at every level to respond effectively to the needs of the thousands and thousands of people who saw everything they had in the world destroyed by the killer storm. Long after the waters receded and the breaches in the levees were repaired, questions remain about what the future will—or should—hold for New Orleans. As a native to the Big Easy, Wynton Marsalis, legendary jazz trumpeter and artistic director of New York City's Jazz at Lincoln Center, a performer who has won multiple Grammy awards as well as a Pulitzer Prize, has a deep love for this city. In the following essay, which appeared in Time *magazine less than a month after Katrina devastated his hometown, Marsalis makes an impassioned plea to rebuild his beloved New Orleans.*

What can the catastrophe that befell New Orleans teach us about history, culture, and ourselves?

Marsalis opens his argument with an emphasis on the progress that had been made in flood-ravaged New Orleans. At the same time, he asserts that the recovery efforts that people will now see in the media will be well-intentioned but ultimately superficial and self-serving.

1 Now the levee breach has been fixed. The people have been evacuated. Army Corps of Engineers magicians will pump the city dry, and the slow (but quicker than we think) job of rebuilding will begin. Then there will be no 24-hour news coverage. The spin doctors' narrative will create a wall of illusion thicker than the new levees. The job of turning our national disaster into sound-bite-size commercials with somber string music will be left to TV. The story will be sanitized as our nation's politicians congratulate themselves on a job well done. Americans of all stripes will demonstrate saintly concern for one another. It's what we do in a crisis.

He contends that we need to view the spectacle of the destruction and rebuilding of New Orleans as important in terms of its cultural significance.

He claims that recognizing what New Orleans represents can help Americans understand the effect that culture has on politics and economics. He offers several examples of powerful cultural matters—race relations, local cuisine, architecture, and, above all, jazz—that mark New Orleans as the "soul of America" and therefore as an object lesson for dealing with complex social issues.

2 This tragedy, however, should make us take an account of ourselves. We should not allow the mythic significance of this moment to pass without proper consideration. Let us assess the size of this cataclysm in cultural terms, not in dollars and cents or politics. Americans are far less successful at doing that because we have never understood how our core beliefs are manifest in culture—and how culture should guide political and economic realities. That's what the city of New Orleans can now teach the nation again as we are all forced by circumstance to literally come closer to one another. I say teach us again, because New Orleans is a true American melting pot: the soul of America. A place freer than the rest of the country, where elegance met an indefinable wildness to encourage the flowering of creative intelligence. Whites, Creoles and Negroes were strained, steamed and stewed in a thick, sticky, below-sea-level bowl of musky gumbo. These people produced an original cuisine, an original architecture, vibrant communal ceremonies and an original art form: jazz.

He underscores how so many Americans have focused on the superficial aspects of New Orleans and have thus failed to comprehend the true significance of this city.

3 Their music exploded irrepressibly from the forced integration of these castes to sweep the world as the definitive American art form. New Orleans, the Crescent City, the Big Easy—home of Mardi Gras, the second-line parade, the po' boy sandwich, the shotgun house—is so many people's favorite city. But not favorite enough to embrace the integrated superiority of its culture as a national objective. Not favorite enough to digest the gift of supersized soul internationally embodied by the great Louis Armstrong. Over time, New Orleans became known as the national center for frat-party-type decadence and (yeah, boy) great food. The genuine greatness of Armstrong is reduced to his good nature; his artistic triumphs are unknown to all but a handful. So it's time to consider, as we rebuild this great American city, exactly what this bayou metropolis symbolizes for the U.S.

He reinforces his argument by pointing out other instances when New Orleans faced issues and crises that mirrored problems nationwide. He underscores a major part of his argument—that Americans have short attention spans when it comes to problems that don't directly affect them.

While he praises Americans for their generosity, sympathy, and humanity as the rebuilding of the city begins, he pleads for people to think more deeply about the history of New Orleans and what it truly represents.

He includes images from the aftermath of Hurricane Katrina that are charged with race and echoes of slavery, reminding his reader that just rebuilding the city of New Orleans will not be enough.

He closes by advocating that failing to address the social problems that Hurricane Katrina highlighted, problems that are not unique to New Orleans, will be a far greater catastrophe than what New Orleans endured.

New Orleans has a habit of tweaking the 4
national consciousness at pivotal times. The last foreign invasion on U.S. soil was repelled in the Crescent City in 1815. The Union had an important early victory over the South with the capture of the Big Easy in 1862. Homer Plessy, a black New Orleanian, fought for racial equality in 1896, although it took our Supreme Court 58 years to agree with him and, with Brown v. Board of Education, to declare segregation unequal. Martin Luther King's Southern Christian Leadership Conference was formally organized in New Orleans in 1957. The problem is that we, all us Americans, have a tendency to rise in that moment of need, but when that moment passes, we fall back again.

The images of a ruined city make it 5
clear that we need to rebuild New Orleans. The images of people stranded, in shock, indicate that we need to rebuild a community. The images of all sorts of Americans aiding these victims speak of the size of our hearts. But this time we need to look a little deeper. Let's use the resurrection of the city to reacquaint the country with the gift of New Orleans: a multicultural community invigorated by the arts. Forget about tolerance. What about embracing? This tragedy implores us to re-examine the soul of America. Our democracy from its very beginnings has been challenged by the shackles of slavery. The parade of black folks across our TV screens asking, as if ghosts, "Have you seen my father, mother, sister, brother?" reconnects us all to the still unfulfilled goals of the Reconstruction era. We always back away from fixing our nation's racial problems. Not fixing the city's levees before Katrina struck will now cost us untold billions. Not resolving the nation's issues of race and class has and will cost us so much more.

Your Turn: Responding to the Subject

a. In his second paragraph, New Orleans native Wynton Marsalis describes the city as "a thick, sticky, below-sea-level bowl of musky gumbo." His description highlights the primary reason that New Orleans was so devastated by Hurricane Katrina: parts of the city are below sea level. Therefore when the levees protecting New Orleans failed, whole sections of the city almost completely disappeared under the swirling floodwaters. The rebuilding for which Marsalis so passionately argues will take years and cost billions, and when it is completed, parts of New Orleans will still be below sea level and therefore still at risk from the flooding that so often accompanies hurricanes. For this reason, some have suggested a radical strategy. They assert that areas holding the greatest potential for damage from natural disasters—barrier ocean and gulf beaches, mountain canyons, flood plains near rivers and other waterways, and so on—be permanently off limits for any kind of future building project or, in the case of the aftermath of a natural disaster, any rebuilding. The federal government would instead purchase the land, when appropriate turning it into reservations, parks, and other areas for the use and enjoyment of the public. For this assignment, decide whether you agree or disagree with this radical view. Then write an essay in which you present and support your stance on this controversial issue.

b. It's no secret: mandatory testing is a staple in public schools in state after state across the U.S. And this testing has high stakes for school systems, with funding for education in many cases directly related to test results. With an emphasis on meeting benchmarks in traditional academic areas—reading, writing, mathematics, science—education in music is sometimes seen as an afterthought, a development that must make celebrated musician and music teacher Wynton Marsalis shake his head in despair. What do you think? Should music or other arts be a required part of a public school education or should it be an option available, when time permits, for students who express an interest? For this assignment, write an essay in which you take a side on this issue.

RUBEN NAVARRETTE, JR.

Debunking Myths About Latinos

From its inception as a nation, the United States of America has grown and prospered thanks to the millions of immigrants who have flocked to its shores. In fact, except for the indigenous peoples who met the first settlers from Europe, everyone here is an immigrant or the descendant of immigrants. It is a cruel irony, then, that large segments of U.S. society hold such negative views of immigrants in general. After all, their families were once in the same situation, in many cases doing hard physical labor for the good of the country at large. And, as Ruben Navarrette, Jr., points out in the following essay, the negative attitudes many people hold about immigrants, in this case those from Mexico and Central America, are often simply not true. In Navarrette's view, the staying power of these misconceptions says much more about the people who believe them than the immigrants the myths describe.

Why do so many U.S. citizens, most descendants of immigrants themselves, have such a negative view of immigrants?

The myth endures that immigrants from Mexico and Central America don't perform as well in the United States as the European immigrants of days gone by. 1

For this, it is said, the Latino immigrants have only themselves to blame. It is supposed that they make no effort to assimilate. They refuse to learn English. And they lack the ambition to excel beyond low-wage jobs where they are exploited and discriminated against. 2

Now a study by RAND, the nonprofit think tank based in Southern California, debunks the myth. The research suggests that there is not all that much difference between the immigrants who crossed the Rio Grande to get here and those who had to cross the Atlantic. And there is even less difference between their children and grandchildren a generation or two down the line. 3

"There's a widespread view among both scholars and the general public that the Latino experience has been very different than the European experience," economist James Smith, author of the study told the Associated Press. "That view is just wrong." 4

By examining census data and other material going back over a century, Smith was able to measure the educational and economic progress of Latino men and their children and compare it with that of 5 other nationalities. What he found was that many popular assumptions don't hold true.

"Across generations, Latinos have done just as well as the Europeans who came in the early part of this century, and in fact slightly better," Smith said. 6

The RAND study found that although Latino immigrants who were born in the early 1900s averaged just a fifth-grade education, their sons made it as far as the ninth grade and their grandsons graduated from high school. 7

According to Smith, those advances were greater than those of European immigrants born in the same era. The bad news: By the third generation, the educational gains taper off. 8

When it comes to earnings, the news is more encouraging. Over their lifetimes, Latino immigrants born in the early 1900s earned about three-fourths as much as US-born descendants of European immigrants. Their sons earned about 79 percent as much, and their grandsons nearly 83 percent as much. With every generation, the earning gap closed bit by bit, as one might expect. And while this study focused on men, Smith claims that his research on Hispanic women shows much the same thing. 9

Sure, this is just one study. There may be others that offer assessments that are less optimistic. There are some scholars, for instance, who argue that America is headed for a rough patch because many of the immigrants it now takes in are less educated and less skilled than those of a century ago. Others sound the alarm over language, insisting that Latino immigrants who refuse to learn English immediately are destined to flounder in the United States. 10

Rubbish. Regardless of ethnicity or nationality or economic resources, immigrants are the same the world over. That's because a big part of what shapes their character is not the country they come from but the fact that they leave it in the first place, risking whatever they have—including their lives—in search of a better life. Once here, they work hard in any job they can find. They instill in their children an appreciation for education and teach them the value of a dollar. And one day those children, in turn, pass on these things to theirs. 11

That's how it was in my family, whose American journey took it from grape fields to graduate school in three generations. Not that one should expect any of this to resonate with those Americans who remain intent on differentiating between immigrants and putting some above others. 12

You can't really blame them. They're in a tough spot. After all, how does a nation of immigrants reconcile the fact that so many of its people espouse views that suggest they resent immigrants? There is one way: 13

Convince yourself that your ancestors were of a better stock than 14
immigrants of today, and don't let the facts get in the way. Of course, the facts at hand deal only with the progress of the immigrants of the past. The matter is settled—Latino immigrants in the 20th century matched and in some cases bettered their European counterparts. But what about the immigrants of today? My bet is that the same will be true for them.

Stay tuned. 15

Understanding the Significance

1. According to Navarrette, why are Mexican and Central American immigrants blamed for the stereotypes sometimes associated with them?
2. What does the RAND report indicate about immigrants from Mexico and Central America versus immigrants from Europe?
3. As Navarrette explains it, what do immigrants, regardless of their country of origin, have in common?
4. What strategy does Navarrette suggest some descendants of immigrants employ to make them feel superior to more recent immigrants?

Discovering the Writer's Purpose

1. Would you say that Navarrette presents an argument that is more deliberative or more judicial? Why do you think he chose this approach? Do you agree with his decision? Explain your reasoning.
2. Why do you think Navarrette devotes his first two paragraphs to relating some of the myths associated with Latinos if his point in the essay is that such stories are simply untrue?
3. In the seventh paragraph, Navarrette includes details from the RAND study about educational levels among immigrants in the earlier part of the twentieth century. By adding this information, what is he suggesting about the relationship between education and success in the United States?
4. Concerning immigrants to any land, Navarrette states that "a big part of what shapes their character is not the country they come from but the fact that they leave it in the first place, risking

whatever they have—including their lives—in search of a better life." How does this statement help support his point that negative beliefs about Latino immigrants are myths?

Examining the Writer's Method

1. How do the organizing strategies like cause and effect, division and classification, and comparison and contrast help Navarrette make his case about Latino immigrants?
2. Navarrette includes a number of facts from the RAND study, including statistics. Why do you think he chose this information as support for his stance? Do you agree with his choice? Explain your reasoning.
3. In the tenth paragraph, Navarrette discusses negative findings presented in other studies. Would this information have been more effective if it were placed elsewhere in the essay? Why or why not?
4. How do the final two paragraphs, one of which is a single sentence ("Stay tuned") serve as a conclusion for Navarrette's essay? Why do you think he chose this approach rather than to develop a more comprehensive conclusion?

Considering Style and Language

1. How would you describe the tone of Navarrette's essay? What elements in his essay lead you to this description? Why do you think he chose this tone to present his argument?
2. Navarrette opens the eleventh paragraph with a single word: "Rubbish." In your view, does dismissing opposing views in this way weaken or strengthen his presentation? Explain your reasoning.
3. In the final third of his essay, Navarrette mentions details about his own family. How does the inclusion of this information affect the impact of his essay?
4. What do the following words mean in the context of the writing? *Myth* (para. 1); *assimilate* (para. 2); *debunk* (para. 3); *assumption* (para. 5); *optimistic, flounder* (para. 10); *instill* (para. 11); *resonate, differentiating* (para. 12); *espouse* (para. 13).

Your Turn: Responding to the Subject

a. As Ruben Navarrette, Jr., points out, evidence simply doesn't support many of the negative attitudes about immigrants to the United States from countries to the south. Yet these myths persist, in part because of the way that television and movies sometimes portray Latinos. And they aren't alone. Other groups—for example, Italian Americans, senior citizens, gays or lesbians, African Americans, teenagers, and so on—are all victims in terms of broad and inaccurate portrayals on the big and small screens. For this assignment, identify the group that you believe is the biggest victim of stereotyping on television or in the movies and then write an essay in which you offer plenty of specific support for your stance.

b. In his second paragraph, Navarrette repeats the stereotype that immigrants resist learning English. The extension of this belief is that government at all levels fosters this behavior by publishing documents and, in some situations, conducting business in other languages. Many people want to see an end to this strategy. They argue that because English is the dominant language in this country, it should be declared the official national language. Such a change would necessitate that newcomers learn English in order to survive and thrive in the U.S. Consider where you stand on this issue, do some research if necessary, and then write an essay in which you present and support your stance.

DUANE SHILLINGER

Prison Cells Open as School Doors Close

Children are our future, and it would be an unusual—and deeply misguided—person who would argue that a community has no obligation to provide funding to educate its children. A progressive, civilized society depends on education. At the same time, who would argue that a community doesn't also have an obligation to protect its citizens from crime? A progressive, civilized society depends on this safeguard as well. So which need should win out? That's the issue that Duane Shillinger addresses in this Casper Star Tribune *op-ed piece dealing with school funding in Wyoming. Shillinger's stance—that Wyoming needs to spend more money on education and less on prisons—is especially powerful given the author's intimate knowledge of prisons gleaned from his sixteen years as warden of the Wyoming State Penitentiary.*

What happens when two societal obligations collide, when both needs compete for support from a limited pool of funds?

Understanding Wyoming's school funding law doesn't make it any easier to appreciate the severe cutbacks in Wyoming's education programs. Complicating my uneasiness about decisions to limit, reduce and even eliminate vital educational and extracurricular programs is the never-ending growth of Wyoming's prison system. What does one have to do with the other? It is disturbing to me that while Wyoming's educational system—indeed a most important link in the crime-prevention process—is being eroded, whittled away and generally dismantled, the corrections bureaucracy expands without debate, and the call for more prison cells is never-ending. *1*

A horrible assumption (yet an assumption based on the observation that Wyoming educational programs are being severely downsized, if not, in some cases, totally eliminated; and a bulging, increasingly costly prison takes away important tax dollars that could be used for educational purposes) is that Wyoming is in the process of trading high educational standards in favor of an opportunity to become a prison colony. A further horrible consideration would be that Wyoming school boards are now merely preparing to apply their *2* expertise in the rather bleak atmosphere that is a warehouse for criminals.

With these thoughts in mind, how is it that Wyoming politicians would, sans conscience, take funding from educational programs that do have far-reaching and very positive impact on and within the community, yet find no creative alternatives that would lessen the continual growth of the highly costly and questionably efficient prison? Succinctly, shortchanging the community of quality educational programs and associated educational resources while the prison bureaucracy grows and more prison cells are planned for construction seems to be a clear indicator that state leaders lack an understanding of the importance of those programs (i.e., educational programs) that do provide alternatives to asocial and criminal behaviors. 3

Now, if there are fewer school-age children in Wyoming, a reasonable explanation for that demographic characteristic is that more people are leaving Wyoming, taking their children with them. Would not a flourishing educational system actually attract people to Wyoming? Vacant schools, schools scheduled for closure, and trained and qualified teachers leaving the state are not the type of circumstances that will serve to attract people to Wyoming. As well, a weakened educational system no longer has an effective role in the prevention of behaviors that lead to crime. 4

At one time at least 40 percent of Wyoming's prisoners entered prison without high school or general equivalency diplomas. Following this thought, studies have demonstrated that those prisoners who do become involved in educational programs while incarcerated are less likely to return to prison as compared with prisoners who do not participate in such programs. Education is an important and vital community function: Education reduces the rate of recidivism, and education prevents people from committing crimes in the first place. 5

In conclusion, what a refreshing change it would be to observe Wyoming's supercilious politics-as-usual direction moderate to one of creativity to the extent that tax dollars might be used to rebuild not only the educational processes but, as well, to enhance those other important preventative programs, such as substance-abuse programs, mental health centers and generally a variety of relapse-prevention programs. 6

Indeed, there are criminals who require expensive prison security management, but there are also numerous inmates who can be easily managed by much less expensive strategies. Wyoming's taxpayers would be well-served were less resources required to manage Wyoming lawbreakers. In 1878 Territorial Wyoming, the penitentiary versus other territorial institutions was also very much an issue. On Jan. 3, 1878, the editor of the *Laramie Daily Sentinel* wrote: "Why 7 don't some enterprising man start another penitentiary? It is patronized better than any other place in the Territory. . . ."

Have we come so far? 8

Perhaps the place to begin an examination of both our educational programs and our prison system is to understand that Wyoming's future rests with the best possible educational processes. 9

Understanding the Significance

1. What assumption has Shillinger drawn about the destination of the money taken from schools?
2. What reason does Shillinger offer for the lower number of school-age children in Wyoming?
3. What does Shillinger feel that the failure to fund school programs indicates about politicians' understanding of the relationship between education and criminality?
4. According the Shillinger, what is the key to Wyoming's future?

Discovering the Writer's Purpose

1. How would you characterize Duane Shillinger's article—as largely judicial, deliberative, or ceremonial? What in the document suggests that he is approaching his reader in this way?
2. How does Shillinger's opening paragraph establish the subject and his stance as well as the tone for the rest of the document?
3. At the end of the fifth paragraph, Shillinger states that "[e]ducation reduces the rate of recidivism, and education prevents people from committing crime in the first place." How does this statement help him make his case?
4. By adding the passage from 1878 (paragraph 7), what is he suggesting about attitudes in the state?

Examining the Writer's Method

1. Throughout his essay, Shillinger makes a connection between education and prisons. Why do you think he pairs these two quite distinct enterprises? What effect does he hope this linking has on his reader?

2. In your view, what mode—example, comparison and contrast, or cause and effect—dominates in Shillinger's piece? How does this organizing strategy help him make his case that Wyoming should change its school funding plans?
3. With his use of the transitional expression "In conclusion," Shillinger signals the start of his closing argument, which runs for four paragraphs. Why do you think he chose to include such a lengthy conclusion? Do you agree with his decision? Explain your reasoning.
4. Just before the final paragraph of his document, Shillinger presents the following rhetorical question: "Have we come so far?" Why does he set this off as a paragraph rather than include it with the paragraph that precedes it? Do you agree with this strategy? Why or why not?

Considering Style and Language

1. How would you describe the tone Shillinger employs in this document? What in the text leads you to this conclusion? Do you think the tone is an appropriate match for his topic? Why or why not?
2. In the second paragraph, he includes a long passage in parentheses. Why? Do you agree?
3. For sixteen years, Duane Shillinger served as the warden of the Wyoming State Penitentiary. In what way does Shillinger's ethos affect the impact of his argument on his reader?
4. What do the following words mean in the context of the writing? *Whittled* (para. 1); *bleak* (para. 2); *sans, succinctly, asocial* (para. 3); *demographic* (para. 4); *recidivism* (para. 5); *supercilious* (para. 6).

Your Turn: Responding to the Subject

a. Obviously, state governments provide funding to support far more than merely education and prisons. Especially in good economic times, states support everything from parks and recreation to police and fire protection to job training to environmental management. But in bad economic times—and right now, your instructor points out, times are indeed bad—states must cut all but essential services. For this assignment write an essay in which you address the following question:

> If you were the governor and had to cut 25 percent from the overall state budget, what essential service would you *not* cut and why?

Write this essay, persuading your reader that this particular service is so important that, even in such dire times, support should not be reduced in any way.

b. What changes should be made—in families, in education, in government, and so on—to make it less likely that young people are marginalized or left behind and end up in prison cells? For this assignment, think in terms of what you have seen, read about, and experienced and write an essay in which you propose ways to keep people from choosing a path that leads to prison.

CHARLES KRAUTHAMMER

Beer? Hot Dogs? Steroids?

America has had a long romance with professional baseball, which extends back over 100 years. But that doesn't mean things have always been perfect in this relationship. From time to time, controversy has rocked baseball, eroding confidence and threatening to destroy the institution. The Black Sox scandal of 1919, during which several Chicago White Sox players were accused of taking money from gamblers to lose games against their World Series rivals, the Cincinnati Red Stockings, is perhaps the best-known problems, but a parade of bad behavior over the years, for example, excessive drinking, illicit drugs, and illegal gambling, including gambling on baseball, has closely shadowed the history of the sport. Most recently, the controversy engulfing baseball has been the rumored use of performance-enhancing steroids by high-profile players, including San Francisco Giants slugger Barry Bonds. In the following essay, writer, editor, and political analyst Charles Krauthammer, a monthly essayist for Time *magazine whose syndicated columns appear in over 150 newspapers across the world, reacts to the widespread reports about steroid use by Bonds. Krauthammer, who was awarded the 1987 Pulitzer Prize for distinguished commentary, examines why the case of Barry Bonds has engendered such interest.*

Does it ultimately make a difference what means an athlete employs if it leads to the greatest possible level of performance?

Leave it to the good people of Philadelphia, whose football fans once famously booed and threw snowballs at Santa Claus, to come up with the perfect takedown of the most inflated (in more ways than one) superstar in contemporary sport. With the visiting Barry Bonds at the plate and needing just two home runs to tie Babe Ruth's iconic 714 lifetime homers, the banner was raised: "Ruth did it on hot dogs & beer." *1*

The target of this concise discourse on the roots of greatness has been booed lustily in every major league city he's played in outside his home town of San Francisco. The fans' displeasure lies in Bonds's alleged use of steroids. The use of "alleged" here, though mandatory, is forced and legalistic. After all, Bonds has admitted that he used "the clear" and "the cream," substances he claims he thought were flaxseed oil and some kind of emollient, only later to discover that they were actually steroids. *2*

3 The idea that an athlete of Bonds's stature, for whom the body is both temple and bank vault, would be mistakenly ingesting substances is implausible, made all the more so by the evidence dredged up by two San Francisco sportswriters detailing Bonds's (alleged) gargantuan consumption of every performance-enhancing drug from steroids to human growth hormone.

4 But why should we care? What is really wrong with performance enhancement? We say we are against it because it diminishes striving, devalues achievement, produces a shortcut to greatness, etc. But in many endeavors we don't really care about any of that. Medical residents at hospitals have been known to take Ritalin to keep themselves alert on overnight shifts. If it enhances their thinking in the emergency room, what's the objection?

5 Many public speakers, performers and even some surgeons take beta-blockers to literally still their hearts and steady their hands. I've never seen a banner at the opera complaining: "Pavarotti does it on pasta." And what about the military, which pioneered some of these performance-enhancing studies to see how they could help soldiers survive the most extreme stresses? Isn't that an unqualified good?

6 Performance enhancement turns out to be disturbing only in the narrow context of competition, most commonly in sports. And the objection is not cheating nature but cheating competitors. It's basically a fairness issue.

7 When everyone has access to technological improvements (graphite tennis rackets, titanium drivers, more tightly wound baseballs) the sport may be transformed, but the playing field remains level. When technology is enhancing the equipment, fans become quickly reconciled to the transformation. (And it can be radical: The transition from bamboo to fiberglass totally changed the pole vault.) But when technology enhances the physiology of the athlete, we tend to recoil.

8 Interestingly, however, not always. What about Lasik surgery? Tiger Woods had it and said it made his game stronger than ever. I have yet to see a banner at the Masters saying: "Nicklaus did it by squinting."

9 Vision enhancement is even more helpful to baseball players trying to follow the flight of a ball approaching at 90 mph. Hitting requires hand-eye coordination. Bonds turns his arms into tree trunks, and boos rain down. Change the physiology of the other part of the equation—the eye—and no one cares.

10 Why? Because Lasik is legal, common and available to all. Steroids are not. True, baseball had no steroid ban until 2005 (an informal policy began in 2002), and management looked the other way. But since 1990 use without a prescription has been illegal in the United States. Most players didn't use steroids. Many considered it cheating.

So is Bonds a villain? No more than the other highly pumped sluggers such as Mark McGwire and Sammy Sosa who only yesterday were the toast of the nation. Bonds's sin appears to be that he did it better and longer than others and did not break down physically as early from the side effects. 11

But that's only part of it. No one cared terribly, no nasty banners were hung, when he surpassed contemporaries such as McGwire. The deep distaste that arises now is that he is challenging two sacred figures of the past: the great Ruth and the elegant, pioneering Hank Aaron. When the competitor is historical, playing in a totally different technological era, the playing field is decidedly unlevel. 12

Bonds (allegedly) used artificial enhancers. They were internal and physiological. And they were taken clandestinely and illegally. 13

Three strikes. 14

Put an asterisk beside his records? No. A home run is a home run and not one was challenged at the time. In any case, asterisks are removable. Bonds's records carry a taint that will long endure. 15

Understanding the Significance

1. What is the connection between the saying on the banner raised by the Philadelphia fans and baseball superstar Barry Bonds?
2. What proof is there that Bonds did indeed use steroids?
3. According to Krauthammer, why are people less concerned about physical enhancements like eye surgery than about baseball players like Mark McGuire, Sammy Sosa, and Barry Bonds using steroids?
4. What explanation does Krauthammer offer for why fans were more upset when Bonds surpassed Babe Ruth and Hank Aaron in total major league home runs than when he passed McGuire and Sosa?

Discovering the Writer's Purpose

1. Since Krauthammer's focus in this essay is professional baseball, why do you think he opens his introduction with the anecdote about the Philadelphia football fans?
2. In paragraph 2 Krauthammer uses the word *alleged* and *allegedly* (paragraphs 3 and 13) in relation to Bonds' steroid use. In paragraph 2 he puts the word within quotation marks, and in the

other paragraphs 3 and 13 he puts the words within parentheses. What point is he making by presenting these words in this way?

3. Why do you think Krauthammer includes a reference to superstar golfer Tiger Woods in his discussion of the misdeeds of baseball's Barry Bonds?
4. What point is Krauthammer making in the conclusion concerning asterisks next to any records achieved by Bonds?

Examining the Writer's Method

1. Which mode do you think Krauthammer relies on most—cause and effect, example, or narration—to present his argument about Barry Bonds and steroid use? What in the essay leads you to this conclusion?
2. In the fourth and fifth paragraphs, Krauthammer offers examples of other professionals who employ various forms of what he calls "performance enhancement." What do these examples contribute to his overall argument of how the accomplishments of Barry Bonds should be viewed?
3. By referring to various technological improvements in athletic equipment, what point is Krauthammer making about the performance of Barry Bonds?
4. In your view, which of the supporting points that Krauthammer provides is strongest? What leads you to this conclusion?

Considering Style and Language

1. How would you describe the tone in Krauthammer's essay? Do you feel it is an appropriate match for his subject? Why or why not?
2. How much culpability does Krauthammer believe that professional baseball should bear concerning steroid use? What in the essay makes you feel this way?
3. In the sixth paragraph, Krauthammer offers the following commentary about steroid use: "And the objection is not cheating nature but cheating competitors. It's basically a fairness issue." What does this statement mean, and what relevance does it have in his overall argument about the performance and legacy of Barry Bonds?

4. What do the following words mean in the context of the writing? *Concise, discourse, lustily, legalistic, emollient* (para. 2); *stature, implausible, gargantuan* (para. 3); *unqualified* (para. 5); *context* (para. 6); *reconciled, physiology* (para. 7); *distaste, sacred, elegant* (para. 12); *clandestinely* (para. 13); *taint* (para. 15).

Your Turn: Responding to the Subject

a. Krauthammer opens the fourth paragraph of his essay about the suspected steroid use by Barry Bonds this way: "But why should we care?" What do you think? Does it really matter if Bonds and other athletes, either professionals or amateurs, take performance-enhancing substances? For this assignment, address Krauthammer's question, providing thorough support for your point of view.
b. More than a decade ago, NBA superstar Charles Barkley, now a basketball commentator/analyst, created a public furor with his statement, made first to sportswriters and then repeated in a Nike commercial, "I am not a role model." Barkley's words sparked anger in people who believe that athletes and others in the spotlight, individuals whose behavior can influence young people, have a special responsibility to behave in an exemplary way. For this assignment, consider Barkley's statement and express and support your view on this subject.

Other Possibilities for Argument Essays

The following is a list of topics that are suitable for argument papers. As they stand, however, these topics are merely starting points. After choosing and adapting one so that it reflects the issue as you'd like to address it, you must decide whether to take a stand for or against the issue and then develop a sufficient number of details and examples to support that stance.

- Requiring national identification cards for all citizens and residents
- Holding the parents of juveniles found guilty of vandalism financially responsible for the damage their children have caused
- Allowing energy exploration in environmentally sensitive areas

- Legalizing assisted suicide for terminally ill patients
- Requiring public school students to wear uniforms
- Closing any aquatic attractions that allow for physical interactions between humans and dolphins, porpoises, seals, manta rays, and so on
- Using alternative sentencing such as home confinement or boot camps for some lawbreakers
- Allowing law enforcement officials to film public areas in order to monitor possible criminal activity
- Considering the wishes of parents whose religious or moral beliefs forbid medical treatments that would save the lives of their children or greatly improve their quality of life
- Raising the legal driving age nationally to 18
- Using fetal tissue and stem cells for research on or treatment of medical conditions such as diabetes, spinal cord injuries, Parkinson's disease, and so on
- Eliminating the F grade, replacing it with a NC (No Credit) designation
- Including 30 hours of public service as a college graduation requirement
- Eliminating or modifying tenure at all levels of education
- Requiring plaintiffs and lawyers who bring lawsuits to pay all court expenses if the suit is judged to be frivolous

Writing at Work

ARGUMENT

OXFAM AMERICA
Dear Friend. . . .

Argument appears in many of the documents you are exposed to beyond the classroom. Magazine and newspaper advertisements, billboards, political leaflets, sales brochures, web pages, editorials—all attempt to persuade you to accept a different point of view, to change your thinking in some way. Changing the mind of the reader is exactly the aim of the following document. The letter on the facing page from Oxfam America, a charitable organization with a long history of addressing world poverty and hunger, has one goal: to convince the reader to make a donation to help this organization continue its work.

Focusing on the Message and Aim

Answer each of the following questions in a brief paragraph, referring specifically to the passage on the facing page.

1. The letter opens with a bulleted list of things that haven't been included with this document. Why do you think the writer chose to begin the letter this way? In your view, is this approach a good strategy to persuade a reader to make a financial contribution? Explain your reasoning.
2. The letter has appeals to logic, emotion, and reputation. In your view, which appeal dominates? Provide examples to support your answer.
3. The text of the letter contains several examples of the kinds of worthwhile work Oxfam has done across the world. As you see it, which of these examples is the most compelling and offers the strongest support for the main point of the letter? What about this example leads you this opinion?

Oxfam
America

Raymond C. Offenheiser
President

Dear Friend,

Here's what you won't find accompanying this letter:

• address labels that "guilt trip" you into giving;

• an expensive calendar that you don't need (and we can't afford);

• a vague-sounding petition addressed to somebody in Washington;

• or heart-rending photos that play on your emotions.

What you will find is a straightforward case for one of the most effective humanitarian aid agencies anywhere in the world.

Here it goes.

The scope of global poverty today has calamitous implications for the 21st century. Confronting it is the greatest challenge of our time — and Oxfam is on the front lines of this struggle.

I am writing today to ask you to join us there.

I'm not asking you to pack a bag and head off to Ethiopia where farmers need help building a well. Or to spend three months in El Salvador helping communities rebuild after a devastating earthquake. Or to journey to the Amazon to assist indigenous people in obtaining legal title to all of the resources of their ancestral lands.

Instead, I am asking you to do something with as direct and positive an impact on poor people's lives as any of those things. I'm asking you to join Oxfam America.

We're not your ordinary charitable organization.

We don't take the traditional approach to the way we raise funds — or, more importantly, to the way we fight poverty and hunger. We believe it's as basic as helping people help themselves.

(over, please)

26 West Street • Boston, MA 02111
www.oxfamamerica.org

RECYCLED PAPER

Applying the Principles

a. Often, if this type of letter doesn't accomplish its aim, the company or organization follows through with another letter. Following the format of this letter and relying on the kind of information it includes, write a letter from Oxfam that makes one final attempt to convince a reader to send a donation.

b. In your view, is the argument presented in this letter successful? Why or why not? In a letter to Oxfam, praise or blast the letter, referring to specific points in the letter to support your own argument.

Practical Application: Argument

Tacked to the bulletin board above your desk is an article from last week's local newspaper. It details the plans of a local demolition firm, Aloysius Brothers, Inc., to construct what company officials are calling a trash-recycling transfer station on a ten-acre site bordering your neighborhood. The firm plans to truck solid waste to the site, where recyclables will be removed and the rest stored for transfer to the city's landfill at a later time. Right now, the area is zoned for residential and light business use only, and a trash-recycling transfer station doesn't fit this designation. Therefore, the demolition firm is seeking a zoning variance from the city planning board.

You have saved the clipping because you oppose the project, and you are sure that if people had a fuller understanding of the ramifications of such a plan, they would definitely join you in opposition and urge their elected officials to reject the Aloysius Brothers' request. To give people a fuller understanding, you have decided to take advantage of the opportunity your area newspaper provides and prepare a guest editorial on the subject.

To prepare to write the editorial, you quickly jot down some reasons that the plan should be rejected, including the following:

- The city already has a full-scale, active landfill in the east end of town. For years, this area has been plagued with problems associated with the landfill, including foul odors, groundwater pollution from rain running off the mountain of trash, and dust and trash remnants blowing about. One landfill is bad enough. Why add a second potential problem?

- The site contains several areas that appear to be wetlands, home to unique plant and animal species. Draining and filling these areas will permanently destroy their habitat.
- Such a project has the potential of lowering property values for people who own homes in the surrounding area. When these people built or bought their homes, they had every expectation that the zoning would remain constant. Now they face the prospect of grave financial consequences.
- Once a zoning change is made for the trash-recycling transfer station, no additional variance will be needed if the owners decide to convert the site to an actual full-scale landfill.
- Instead of building a trash-recycling transfer station, Aloysius Brothers could donate the land to the city in the form of a land trust. The company would realize a tax advantage of several million dollars and the city could convert the land into a nature trail.
- The plans call for as many as fifty eighteen-wheeler dump trucks to bring trash to the site each day. The only safe access to the area is past an elementary school and then through a closely settled residential neighborhood. (This point is a particular concern to you, since your home is on the road leading to the site.) This factor will translate into a dramatic increase in traffic and danger, especially to the neighborhood children.
- The site borders Watuppa Pond, a small body of water that feeds the city's water supply. Although the company claims to have a plan to keep any run-off from the trash-recycling transfer station from reaching the water, officials have offered no concrete proof that the company can actually do so.
- The property need not be turned into a trash-recycling transfer station to make it profitable to Aloysius Brothers. Over 1,000 feet of the land is on the shore of Watuppa Pond, making the property highly attractive to people who would like to build homes with a water view. The rest of the land slopes upward, providing great views of both the pond and the north end of the city.

Now choose the strongest reasons to reject the request for a zoning change and write an editorial of five hundred to eight hundred words. If additional strong ideas occur to you as you are developing your editorial, feel free to include them. Use the following guest editorial entitled "If You Truly Care About Your Pets," written by Therese C. MacKinnon of the Potter League for Animals, on the need to have pets spayed or neutered as a guide in terms of approach and format.

If You Truly Care About Your Pets . . .

When I was seven, I saw a neighborhood girl carrying a cardboard box. The children surrounding her were squealing with delight. There in the box were four adorable black and white kittens. The girl's cat had had babies and they couldn't keep them. Would I like one, she asked? I was elated as I skipped home with my furry bundle, announcing that we had a new kitten. My mother reluctantly agreed to keep her, and we named her White Socks.

Seven short months later, White Socks had her own litter of five beautiful kittens. This was all so exciting for my siblings and me. But one morning, a man in a uniform came to the door. He examined each kitten, telling my mother which were the males and which the females. Slowly I realized that he was there to take them away.

Mom picked out one male kitten to keep. Over my sobbing and pleading, she tried to explain that we couldn't keep them all. Her words fell on the deaf ears of a broken-hearted seven-year-old. All I knew was that I was losing my beloved White Socks and her babies.

The real sadness of White Socks' story is not that a little girl lost her pet. The tragedy is that Socks and her kittens probably lost their lives that day. It's likely that the soft-spoken man from the city pound picked up several more litters of puppies and kittens that day. It's probable that, much as they tried, the people at the pound were unable to find new homes for most of them. There were just too many animals then and, although the numbers have declined, there are still too many now.

Pet overpopulation has been a recognized problem in America since the 1920s when, in 1928, in New York City alone, 287,000 surplus cats and dogs were destroyed. Had pet sterilization been an option then, there would have been no excuse for such a tragedy. Now that it is so routine, one would think that such tragedies no longer occur. But we are still not controlling the breeding.

Many of the reasons why people don't alter their animals are based on myths and misconceptions. One excuse is the expense. The fact is, breeding a pet is far more expensive in the long run. Think of the food and supplies required for 4 to 10 puppies or kittens and a nursing mom for 2 to 4 months.

Then there are veterinary visits for worming, first vaccinations, and exams. Medical complications are possible before, during, and after birth. And think of the tax dollars spent on the thousands of surplus animals brought to shelters every year.

Licensing fees are often higher for unaltered pets than for sterilized animals. And unaltered animals have far more health problems throughout their lives than those that are altered. Financially, spaying and neutering are just matters of good sense.

Another belief is that neutering changes a pet's personality. This is true, in a way. Altered pets become more relaxed, playful, and content and more interested in their human family and home.

Altered males in particular are much less aggressive toward other animals and people. The overwhelming desires to wander, to mark their territory and to fight for mates are eliminated. Females no longer go into heat. These urges undeniably help wild animals to survive, but they are not desirable traits in a domestic pet. Simply put, an altered animal makes a more pleasing pet.

Another common myth is that a female should have one litter before she is spayed. Medically speaking, giving birth does nothing beneficial for a pet. In fact, spaying is a more complicated and expensive operation after a birth has occurred.

Overall, the health benefits associated with spaying and neutering are tremendous! Unspayed female dogs and cats are highly at risk for breast tumors, breast inflammations, uterine infections, ovarian cysts, and cancers.

Unneutered male animals are equally at risk of developing enlarged prostates and testicular and prostate cancers. In general, the life expectancies of spayed and neutered animals are double those of unaltered pets.

In 1996, authorities conservatively estimated that about 4.2 million surplus dogs and cats were euthanized in America the previous year. Thousands more were abandoned roadside, in wooded areas and in dumpsters by people who found themselves with too many pets. These animals spent their brief lives searching for food, coping with disease and the elements, and defending themselves against wild animals.

Such facts are astonishing when the solution is so simple. All we need to do is stop the breeding! And the simplest way to do that is to spay and neuter our companion animals. The very best reason for spaying and neutering is that it is the responsible thing to do.

Glossary

Abstract language refers to concepts, ideas, qualities, and other intangibles—for example, freedom, creativity, and greed—as opposed to *concrete language,* which refers to tangible items, individuals, and locales.

Active reading is the process of critically examining the context, structure, and key ideas of a writing.

Active voice is a way of arranging a sentence so that the subject is doing the action—"Jacqueline reviewed the movie"—as opposed to *passive voice,* in which the subject is acted upon—"The movie was reviewed by Jacqueline." An active-voice sentence is generally shorter and more direct than a passive-voice sentence.

Aim—see **Purpose.**

Allusion is a reference to a work of literature, real or fictional individuals, events, places, and so on. For instance, "These accusations suggest a cover-up of Watergate proportions," is an allusion to the political scandal that eventually led to the resignation of President Richard Nixon in 1974. For an allusion to be effective, it must refer to something the reader can easily recognize.

Alternating method involves arranging the elements of a comparison and contrast analysis so that you switch back and forth between subjects as you discuss the elements or features under discussion. In the block method, you discuss all the elements or features in relation to one subject and then all the same elements in relation to the second subject. In a paper arranged in the alternating method about competing fast-food restaurants, you would discuss restaurant A then restaurant B on the basis of the variety of food available, then restaurant A on quality of service and restaurant B on quality of service, and so on. With the same paper arranged in the block method, you would first discuss all the features in terms of restaurant A and then discuss all the features in terms of restaurant B. With the mixed method, you use a combination of both types.

Ambiguity is a lack of clarity leading to the possibility of multiple interpretations of words, phrases, or sentences rather than the one meaning intended.

Amplifying means providing numerous specific details, illustrations, and explanations to communicate full meaning to a reader.

Analogy is an extended comparison of two dissimilar things used as illustration—for instance, the suggestion that shoveling out after the fourth snowstorm in five days is like fighting a war.

Anecdote is a short, often humorous story about a person's experience, intended to illustrate or support some point.

Appeals on the basis of emotions, logic, and reputation are the three methods used to persuade a reader. An appeal to emotions, from the Greek *pathos*, involves attempting to convince the reader through details, claims, or statements that stir the reader's feelings. An appeal to logic, from the Greek *logos*, involves a massing of factual evidence to convince the reader. An appeal to reputation, from the Greek *ethos*, involves relying on the writer's good standing, esteem, or name to sway the reader.

Approach refers to the combination of techniques used to fulfill the purpose in a piece of writing.

Argument refers to writings whose primary aim is to persuade the reader to accept a point of view as valid.

Argument ad hominem is a logical fallacy. A writer makes this error by attacking the individual holding a position rather than attacking the position itself: "Since he didn't rank in the upper ten percent of his medical school graduating class, why pay any attention to Dr. Peter Neville's views on health care reform?"

Audience is the reader or group of readers to whom you direct your writing. To write effectively, you must always identify and address the needs of your audience.

Awkwardness refers to parts of a writing that, although not grammatically incorrect, don't effectively or efficiently communicate the writer's ideas.

Bandwagon approach is a logical fallacy that results when the writer urges acceptance of a point of view solely because others hold that view: "Nobody is interested in endangered species anymore."

Begging the question is a logical fallacy. This mistake in reasoning occurs when the writer expresses as fact something that is actually an opinion. To state, "Wearing seat belts does not reduce the risk of serious injury, so seat belt laws should be abolished," is to beg the question, because no evidence has been presented that seat belts don't reduce the risk of injury.

Block method—see **Alternating method.**

Body in an essay is the series of paragraphs that provide support for the thesis.

Brainstorming—see **Prewriting.**

Branching—see **Prewriting.**

Cause and effect is a rhetorical mode used to examine what leads to or has led to something (cause) and what will occur or has occurred as a result (effect). In some cases, the focus in an essay is on cause, sometimes on effect, and sometimes on both.

Chronological order is the arrangement of events in the order that they actually occurred. Sometimes chronological order is altered for some effect through the use of a flashback, an event deliberately presented out of sequence.

Classification is a rhetorical mode through which items, concepts, individuals, and so on are grouped to make them easier to understand. It is generally discussed along with *division*, the rhetorical mode through which a single subject is separated into its component parts in order to make it easier to understand.

Clichés are tired, overused expressions, such as "like looking for a needle in a haystack" or "the bottom line," that should be avoided in writing because they add no freshness or originality.

Clustering—see **Prewriting.**

Coherence is achieved in writing when all the elements are effectively and logically presented. A coherent essay follows a set order with appropriate paragraphs and transitions so that the reader can easily follow the ideas expressed.

Command—see **Imperative mood.**

Comma splice is a serious sentence error in which a comma is used between two sentences rather than a period or semicolon. To correct a comma splice, either (1) change the comma to a period or other appropriate mark of end punctuation, (2) change it to a semicolon, or (3) insert a conjunction after the comma.

Comparison and contrast is a rhetorical mode used to examine similarities (comparison) and differences (contrast). Three methods are available for arranging an essay featuring comparison and contrast: the alternating method, the block method, and the mixed method.

Composing is the stage of the writing process during which you develop the ideas from the prewriting stage into sentences, which are then arranged in paragraphs to create a draft version of the final writing.

Conclusion is the final section of a writing that brings it to a logical, appropriate, or pleasing close. With an essay, a conclusion is often a single paragraph. A common concluding technique is to restate the thesis and the ideas supporting or illustrating it. Additional techniques include closing with a relevant quotation, relating an anecdote, and raising a question.

Concrete language—see **Abstract language.**

Connotation is an additional subjective meaning attached to or inspired by a word, whereas the *denotation* is the exact, literal dictionary definition of a word. The denotation of the term *immature,* for example, is to be not fully grown or developed, yet the connotations include to be childish, irresponsible, and inexperienced. Therefore, to ensure that the reader understands your point as you intend to make it, you must carefully consider the denotations *and* the connotations of the words you use.

Content refers to the various examples, ideas, and details used in a piece of writing.

Context means the overall setting or circumstances of an event or situation. When you read critically, you must identify the context of the selection in order to understand the writer's motives and approach.

Contrast—see **Comparison and contrast.**

Critical reading skills are those steps—including identifying the writer's purpose, reading actively, and focusing on the writer's technique—that enable you to understand a writing more fully.

Dangling modifier is an error in which there is no appropriate object in a sentence for a modifying word or phrase to modify: "Sailing down the river, the improvements in water quality were evident." To correct this error, restate the sentence so that *Sailing down the river* modifies an appropriate word: "Sailing down the river, Christa could see that water quality had improved."

Deduction is a type of reasoning that involves moving from general statements to a specific conclusion, as opposed to induction, which involves moving from specific instances to a general conclusion. When you conclude that a muscular woman must be a bodybuilder because bodybuilders are muscular, you have used deductive reasoning.

Definition is a rhetorical mode through which the characteristics of an item, individual, or concept are delineated. In some cases, you'll use a *limited definition,* a one- or two-sentence explanation, and in other cases you'll prepare an *extended definition,* a multiparagraph discussion.

Denotation—see **Connotation.**

Description is a rhetorical mode through which specific, vivid details and examples, expressed objectively or subjectively, are used to recreate a situation, capture a scene, recall an individual, or explain a concept or feeling. (See also *Objective description.*)

Dialect is dialogue that is presented and spelled to represent the particular sound of a geographical area, social class, and ethnic or racial group—for example, *gonna* rather than *going to, wunst* rather than *once,* and *cain't* rather than *can't.*

Dialogue consists of the conversation of two or more people, recorded as it was expressed and presented within quotation marks.

Diction is the writer's choice and use of words. Depending on the writer's aim and the needs of the reader, the diction of a writing may range from formal to conversational or colloquial, occasionally including uses of slang.

Division is a rhetorical mode through which a single subject is separated into its component parts in order to make that subject easier to understand. It is often discussed along with *classification,* the rhetorical mode through which items, concepts, individuals, and so on are grouped to make them easier to understand.

Editing is the step in the revising stage of writing during which you polish what you have already developed. It consists of two parts: tightening and proofreading.

Effect—see **Cause and effect.**

Either/or reasoning is a logical fallacy that results when the writer suggests that only two possibilities or solutions exist: "If you want to succeed in business, you must be an outstanding public speaker."

Ellipsis is a series of three spaced periods used to indicate an omission from a quotation.

Emphatic order, also occasionally called *dramatic order* or "least-to-most-significant" order, is a method of arrangement in which you present the supporting examples and details from strong to stronger, saving the strongest support for the end. (See also *Order.*)

Essay is a multiparagraph nonfiction writing in which a thesis is specified and then developed, explained, or illustrated. It consists of three parts: an introduction, body, and conclusion.

Ethos—see **Appeals.**

Etymology is the origin or derivation of a word.

Euphemism is a word or phrase used in place of another because the original word was considered offensive, inflammatory, or objectionable in some way—for instance, *revenue enhancement* rather than *taxes* and *passing away* rather than *dying.*

Example is a rhetorical mode through which you provide a series of circumstances, instances, conditions, locales, concepts, or individuals to illustrate some point. In a more general sense, example also refers to any circumstances, instances, conditions, and so on used to help you make your point.

Extended definition refers to a multiparagraph presentation that delineates in detail the characteristics of a subject.

Fact is a verifiable truth as opposed to an opinion, which is a reasoning based on fact. It's a fact that driving on icy roads is dangerous because it can be proven that more accidents occur when roads are icy. It's an opinion to say that your city didn't do an adequate job treating icy roads last week because there were numerous accidents: those accidents may have been caused by other factors such as excessive speed, mechanical failure, inexperienced drivers, and so on.

Figurative language refers to expression that is symbolic rather than literal, the purpose being to achieve some effect. Common figures of speech include the following:

- *metaphor*—implied comparison between two dissimilar subjects: "Their evening together was a dream."
- *simile*—explicit comparison between two dissimilar subjects: "This course is like a mystery movie."
- personification—the granting of human qualities to an inanimate object: "The wind whispered through the trees surrounding the first-time campers."
- *analogy*—extended comparison between dissimilar subjects, generally intended to make the first subject easier to understand:

"Self-esteem is like the foundation for a building. If the foundation is weak, even a small structure will fall, but if the foundation is strong enough, a skyscraper can be erected."

- *hyperbole*—overstatement for effect: "All you could see in the dorm room was dirty laundry and empty pizza boxes."
- *understatement*—undercutting for effect: "Being pulled over in front of my mother's office while I was driving her car was a little embarrassing."

Flashback—see **Chronological order.**

Form refers to surface elements of writing such as spelling, usage, punctuation, and so on.

Format is the physical arrangement of a document.

Fragment—see **Sentence fragment.**

Freewriting—see **Prewriting.**

General language—see **Specific language.**

Hasty generalization is a logical fallacy that results when a claim is based on too little proof or on proof that isn't representative: "Last year's extremely cold winter shows that the Gulf Stream has now shifted." Actually, many years of consistently lower temperatures would have to be observed and documented before meteorologists would make such a claim.

Homonyms are words that sound the same but are spelled differently and have different meanings. Troublesome homonyms include *it's/its, they're/there/their, to/too/two, who's/whose,* and *you're/your.*

Homophones—see **Homonyms.**

How-to writing, also called *a set of instructions,* refers to a type of process writing that involves explaining how to do something.

Hyperbole—see **Figurative language.**

Illustration refers to those details, cases, and instances that you use to make some point clear for the reader. (See also *Example.*)

Image is capturing in words a vivid moment or experience. An image can be either literal or figurative. (See also *Figurative language.*)

Imperative mood, also called *command,* refers to a sentence construction in which the reader is addressed directly, with the subject implied or understood rather than directly stated: "Connect the printer to the computer on the left." In this case, the subject is the individual who is being told to connect the printer.

Induction is a type of reasoning that involves moving from specific instances to a general conclusion, as opposed to deduction, which involves moving from general statements to a specific conclusion. When you decide that damage to your lawn has been caused by skunks digging for insects, because skunks are known to dig under turf for bugs, you have used inductive reasoning. With induction, reaching a conclusion involves an inductive leap; that is, although the specific instances suggest the finding, the conclusion is still a leap into possibility rather than an established fact.

Introduction is the opening section of a writing, which introduces the thesis, directing and engaging the reader. With an essay, the introduction is often a single paragraph. Common introductory techniques include using an anecdote, providing relevant statistics or facts, including a famous saying or quotation, and asking a leading question.

Irony refers to a situation or experience that is contrary to logic or to what might normally be expected. In writing, it is the use of language to express a meaning different from and often opposite of the literal meaning of those words. A statement such as "And then she fired me—the perfect end to a perfect day" is ironic, since the day was anything but perfect. Sarcasm, which is especially bitter humor, is a form of irony.

Jargon is language peculiar to a profession or to a field of interest or study. Because most people are unfamiliar with such specialized, technical words, use jargon sparingly and include a brief definition unless the meaning is clear through the context of the passage.

Journal is a record of impressions and reactions. In its most general sense, a journal is an idea book, a private place for a writer to explore ideas and practice expressing them.

Key ideas in writing are those contained in the various topic sentences, as well as any specific names, dates, amounts, and ideas emphasized by the writer through such cue words as *important, vital,* and *crucial.*

Linear order is the arrangement of steps of some activity or operation in the order that the steps occurred or must be performed.

Logical fallacies are common errors in reasoning that weaken your ability to sustain a point of view. Common logical fallacies include

- *argument ad hominem*
- bandwagon approach

- begging the question
- the red-herring fallacy
- either/or reasoning
- hasty generalization
- *non sequitur*
- oversimplification
- *post hoc, ergo prompter hoc*

Logos—see **Appeals.**

Metaphor—see **Figurative language.**

Misplaced modifier is an error in which a modifying word or phrase is not placed next to the word it actually modifies: "As a high school student, my grandfather taught me to drive." To correct this error, restate the sentence or move the modifier so that it is next to the word it modifies: "As a high school student, I learned to drive from my grandfather."

Mixed method—see **Alternating method.**

Modes—see **Rhetorical modes.**

Narration is a rhetorical mode through which the events constituting an experience are recalled. For the most part, the experience is presented in chronological order, although sometimes the sequence is purposely broken for effect through the use of a flashback.

Negation is a technique used in definition in which a subject is explained in terms of what it isn't rather than what it is.

Non sequitur, a Latin phrase meaning "it does not follow," is a logical fallacy that involves a conclusion that doesn't make sense in relation to the evidence used to reach it: "If more people took up swimming, heart attacks would be more common."

Objective description is writing that presents sensory details and experiences without any reaction or emotional response, as opposed to *subjective description,* which is writing that records the impact or impressions of such details and experiences.

Opinion—see **Fact.**

Order is the way you structure or arrange a writing. Depending on your needs, you may follow *chronological order, linear order, spatial order,* or *emphatic order.*

Organization—see **Order.**

Oversimplification is a logical fallacy that results when a writer incorrectly reduces a complex subject by ignoring or overlooking crucial information or factual inconsistencies: "That student developed cancer because his family lives near high tension lines." Other factors, including the health of others living in the same home, personal and family medical history, and so on, must also be considered.

Paragraph is a group of related sentences, set off by indentation, consisting of an idea presented in one sentence that is then supported or illustrated by the other sentences. In an essay, each paragraph serves in some way to support or illustrate the thesis.

Parallelism is the arrangement of related words, phrases, or clauses in a similar form, as the underlined sections in the following example show: "Peter enjoys writing in the early morning, before supper, or after midnight."

Paraphrase is a rewording of a text or passage in different words to simplify or clarify it, as opposed to a summary, which is the trimming down of the original to its main points.

Passive voice—see **Active voice.**

Pathos—see **Appeals.**

Patterns of development—see **Rhetorical modes.**

Person refers to the point of view from which a writing is presented. First person means writer as speaker, featuring first-person pronouns such as *I, me,* and *mine.* Second person means the reader is directly addressed through the use of the imperative mood, featuring the second-person pronouns *you* and *your.* Third person means the writer as observer, featuring third-person pronouns such as *she, they, it,* and *him.*

Personification —see **Figurative language.**

Persuasion—see **Argument.**

Point of view—see **Person.**

Post hoc, ergo prompter hoc, a Latin term meaning "after this, therefore because of this," is a logical fallacy. With this error, one thing is mistakenly thought to have caused another simply because it came before the other: "The decision two months ago to change to a new math curriculum led to a decline in standardized test scores reported today." Chances are that conditions existing *before* the change in curriculum—perhaps the problems that originally led to the decision to change the way mathematics was taught—are responsible for the decline in scores.

Prewriting is the initial stage of writing, during which you focus on a subject and begin generating and developing ideas to support or illustrate that subject. Prewriting techniques include brainstorming, branching, clustering, and freewriting.

Process is a rhetorical mode that presents in linear order how to do something or how something was done or occurred. There are three general types of process writing: *sets of instructions,* which detail how to do something; *process analysis,* which explains how something operates, occurs, or develops; and *process narrative,* which explains how the writer completes something.

Process analysis is a type of process writing that involves explaining how a condition or activity occurred.

Process narrative refers to a type of process writing that involves explaining how some task or action was carried out.

Pronoun/antecedent agreement refers to the relationship in number, person, and gender between pronouns and the words they replace or refer to.

Proofreading is the final part of the editing step in the revising stage of writing. When you proofread, you concentrate on eliminating all awkwardness, ambiguity, faulty parallelism, and sentence errors (comma splices, fragments, run-on sentences), as well as mistakes in spelling, tense, and agreement.

Purpose in writing is the writer's aim or goal: to entertain, to inform, and to persuade. Many writings will fulfill more than one purpose, although one purpose will likely predominate.

Qualifying words are used to avoid making unsupportable statements with absolute terms. For instance, the qualifying term *rarely* should be used rather than *never, frequently* rather than *always, many* rather than *all,* and so forth.

Reader—see **Audience.**

Reader-centered material is writing that is expressed in terms that a reader will understand.

Reassessing is a step in the revising stage of writing. After allowing some time to pass, you reassess by objectively reexamining what you have written, noting what parts are effective and which aspects need additional attention or development. The feedback of another reader can be especially valuable during reassessing.

Red-herring fallacy is a logical fallacy in which the discussion is deliberately shifted from the main idea to some minor point in order to divert attention from the main idea: "Critics accuse the tobacco industry of using sleazy advertising techniques to attract young smokers, yet they make no complaint about the widespread use of sexual images to sell any number of products."

Redrafting is a step in the revising stage of writing during which you generate and develop new information to address the remaining problem spots identified during reassessing.

Relevance means being related to the matter at hand. In writing, relevant details and examples are those that are directly related to the main idea.

Revising is the stage of writing during which you reexamine and improve the material developed in the prewriting and composing stages. Revising involves three steps: *reassessing, redrafting,* and *editing.*

Rhetorical modes are the following patterns, techniques, or strategies of development, all with their own characteristics, that you use to fulfill the aim of your writing: *cause and effect, comparison and contrast, description, definition, division and classification, example, narration,* and *process.*

Rhetorical question is a question to which no answer is expected or required because the answer is obvious or implied in the question itself. Such a question is designed to begin or stimulate discussion.

Run-on sentence is a serious sentence error in which two sentences are run together rather than properly connected by a conjunction or a semicolon or properly separated by a period or other appropriate mark of end punctuation. To correct a run-on sentence, either (1) insert a period or other appropriate mark of end punctuation between the two sentences, (2) insert a semicolon between the two sentences, or (3) insert a comma and a conjunction.

Sarcasm—see **Irony.**

Satire is writing that pokes fun at a subject in order to make a more serious point.

Second person—see **Person.**

Sensory details are those words, phrases, and passages that are drawn from hearing, sight, smell, taste, and touch.

Sentence fragment is a serious sentence error that occurs when you set a portion of a sentence off as a complete sentence. To eliminate a fragment, you must either (1) add to the incorrect section to make it a complete sentence or (2) add the fragment to a related sentence.

Set of instructions—see **Process.**

Sexist language is terminology that inappropriately designates gender. Words such as *foreman, salesman,* and *mailman* are examples of sexist language because the terms themselves imply that managing a department or operation, making sales, or delivering the mail are jobs intended for a man. Contrast these terms with these nonsexist versions, words that mean the same thing but that don't designate sex: *supervisor, sales representative,* and *mail carrier.* In addition, the masculine pronouns he, him, and his should not be used to mean both males and females, as in the sentence, "Every student should bring his book to class." Instead, use both masculine and feminine pronouns: "Every student should bring his or her book to class." Or, better still, change the words to plural forms: "All students should bring their books to class."

Simile—see **Figurative language.**

Slang refers to words and expressions that tend to be short-lived and are not widely understood outside the group that uses them. For these reasons, you should avoid using slang except when you are quoting someone directly or when you are attempting to create some effect. (See also *Diction.*)

Spatial order is the arrangement of a discussion on the basis of where the elements are in relation to each other: for instance, the contents of a room from left to right, from front to back, or from top to bottom. (See also *Order.*)

Specific language refers to words, phrases, details, and examples that designate particular, definite, or precise individuals, locales, and items (for instance, Eric Clapton, Disney World, Levi's Dockers) versus general language—words, phrases, details, and examples that note broad, common, or universal persons, places, and things (for instance, a rock guitarist, a vacation resort, a pair of pants). In writing, the more specific the language is, the greater the chance that the reader will understand the point the writer is making.

Squinting modifier is an error in which it is unclear whether a modifying word or phrase describes something before it or after it: "Evonne hadn't realized for two weeks her husband had been depressed." To correct this error, restate part of the sentence to eliminate any ambiguity: "Evonne hadn't realized her husband had been depressed for two weeks."

Structure—see **Order.**

Style is the way a writer presents, develops, and supports an idea. One's style is a unique combination of *diction, tone,* and *voice.*

Subjective description—see **Objective description.**

Subject/verb agreement refers to the relationship in number between subjects and verbs. Singular subjects call for present tense verbs ending in -s or -es, and plural subjects call for present tense verbs without the -s or -es endings.

Summary—see **Paraphrase.**

Synonym is a word that means the same or nearly the same as another word.

Tense refers to the form of a verb as it reflects time in the past, present, or future.

Thesis is the main idea of an essay expressed in sentence form. An effective thesis provides a clear direction for the reader and establishes the reader's expectations for the support, explanation, and illustration that follows in the rest of the paper.

Third person—see **Person.**

Tightening is part of the editing step in the revising stage of writing. When you tighten, you concentrate on eliminating all unnecessary use of the passive voice and all deadwood—needless qualifiers and indirect expressions, such as *due to the fact that* and *a large number,* which can easily be replaced by the more succinct words *because* and *many.*

Tone is the writer's attitude towards the subject and audience, as made evident through such elements as diction, level of formality, use of figurative language, and so on. The tone of a writing can range from serious to silly, from angry to sympathetic, from ironic to instructive.

Topic sentence is the main sentence in a paragraph.

Transition refers to elements that provide connection within a writing and thus maintain coherence. Common methods of transition include repeating key words (or their synonyms or appropriate pronouns), phrases, or ideas, and using common transitional expressions such as *also, for instance, however,* and *then.*

Types of argument include *deliberative*—presenting a proposal or posing a case—*judicial*—condemning or defending an individual or position—and *ceremonial*—offering praise for a person or action.

Understatement—see **Figurative language.**

Understood subject—see **Imperative mood.**

Unity is achieved when all the elements in a writing directly support, illustrate, or explain the thesis.

Voice is the writer's distinctive sound, impression, or sense of personality that comes across in a writing. (See also *Style* and *Tone.*)

Writer-centered material is writing that makes sense to the writer but that doesn't necessarily communicate fully to a reader.

Credits

Chapter 1

Lyn Metivier. "The Reading Disorder." Reprinted by permission of the author.

Chapter 5

Langston Hughes. "Salvation" from *The Big Sea* by Langston Hughes. Copyright © 1940 by Langston Hughes. Copyright renewed © 1968 by Arna Bontemps and George Houston Bass. Reprinted by permission of Hill and Wang, a division of Farrar, Straus & Giroux, LLC.

Margery Eagan. "Bond Between Mother, Child Understood After Mom Is Gone." From the *Boston Herald,* May 23, 1999.

Frank McCourt. "The Bed." Reprinted with permission of Scribner, an imprint of Simon & Schuster Adult Publishing Group, from 'Tis by Frank McCourt. Copyright © 1999 by Frank McCourt. All rights reserved.

Hartley Neita. "Old Man Edwards." From *The Gleaner,* January 7, 2006. Reprinted by permission of Gleaner Company Limited.

"Blue Man Group—Tubes." From *Proscenium* magazine.

Jacqueline Wright. "My Road to the Podium and Baton." Reprinted by permission of the author.

Chapter 6

Amy Tan. "Fish Cheeks." Copyright © 1987 by Amy Tan. First appeared in *Seventeen Magazine.* Reprinted by permission of the author and the Sandra Dijkstra Literary Agency.

Richard Selzer. "Four Appointments with the Discus Thrower." From *Confessions of a Knife* by Richard Selzer. Copyright © 1987, 2001 by Richard Selzer. Reprinted with permission of Georges Borchardt, Inc. on behalf of the author.

Jamaica Kincaid. "My House." Excerpts from "The House" in *My Garden (Book)* by Jamaica Kincaid. Reprinted by permission of Farrar, Straus & Giroux, LLC.

Stephen King. "A Walk Seriously Interrupted." Reprinted with permission of Scribner, an imprint of Simon & Schuster Adult Publishing Group, from *On Writing: A Memoir of the Craft* by Stephen King. Copyright © 2000 by Stephen King. All rights reserved.

Timothy Matos. "Your Azorean Getaway." Reprinted by permission of the author.

Chapter 7

Steven Pinker. "Horton Heared a Who." From *Words and Rules: The Ingredients of Language* by Steven Pinker. Copyright © 1999 by Steven Pinker. Reprinted by permission of Basic Books, a member of Perseus Books, LLC.

Bernice Kanner. "The Nose Knows After All." Copyright © McClatchy-Tribune Information Services. All Rights Reserved. Reprinted by permission.

Stephen Doloff. "Let's Offer a Good Word on Politics." Reprinted by permission of the author.

Bob Kerr. "The Best Story Turned Out to Be No Story at All." From *The Providence Sunday Journal,* April 30, 2000.

From the Bristol Community College web page. Bristol Community College, Fall River, MA.

Jessica A. Fletcher. "Reduce Costs—Increase Quality." Reprinted by permission of the author.

Chapter 8

Copyright © 1990 Diane Ackerman. "Why Leaves Turn Color in the Fall." by Diane Ackerman. From *A Natural History of the Senses* by Diane Ackerman. Reprinted by permission of Random House, Inc.

Joshua Piven and David Borgenicht. "How to Land a Plane." From *The Worst-Case Scenario Survival Handbook* by Joshua Piven and David Borgenicht. © 1999 by Quirk Productions, Inc. Used with permission of Chronicle Books LLC, San Francisco. Visit ChronicleBooks.com

Jill Griffin. "Growing a Loyal Customer." From Jill Griffin, *Customer Loyalty*. Copyright © 2002 by Jill Griffin. This material is used by permission of John Wiley & Sons, Inc.

Jill Griffin and Griffin Group. "The Profit Generator." 512/469–1757. Copyright © 1991 by Jill Griffin.

"A Homemade Education," copyright © 1964 by Alex Haley and Malcolm X. Copyright © 1965 by Alex Haley and Betty Shabazz. From *The Autobiography of Malcolm X* by Malcolm X and Alex Haley. Used by permission of Random House, Inc.

"Parking" from *Commonwealth of Massachusetts Driver's Manual* (revised November 1999). Reprinted by permission of the Commonwealth of Massachusetts Registry of Motor Vehicles.

Chapter 9

Ellen Goodman. "The Workaholic." © 1986, The Washington Post Writers Group. Reprinted with permission.

Joe Rogers. "Yellow Skies, Blue Trees." From *Newsweek*, November 30, 1998. All rights reserved. Reprinted by permission.

Roger Rosenblatt. "The Man in the Water." From *Time* magazine, January 25, 1982. Copyright © 1982 by Time Inc. Reprinted by permission.

Anna Quindlen. "Homeless." From *Living Out Loud* by Anna Quindlen. Copyright © 1987 by Anna Quindlen. Used by permission of Random House, Inc.

"Tonight's Sky" from "Orion and the Orionids." Originally appeared on the web site of the Earth & Sky radio series. You can reach this site at http://www.earthsky.com.

Stephen M. Haugh. "Courage: A Hero in Our Midst." Reprinted by permission of the author.

Chapter 10

Deborah Tannen. "Hey Did You Catch That? Why They're Talking as Fast as They Can," by Deborah Tannen. *The Washington Post*, January 5, 2003. Copyright © 2003 by Deborah Tannen. Reprinted by permission of the author.

Kay Redfield Jamison. "Speaking of Madness." From *An Unquiet Mind* by Kay Redfield Jamison. Copyright © 1995 by Kay Redfield Jamison. Used by permission of Alfred A. Knopf, a division of Random House, Inc.

Stephen Bayley. "The Triumph of the Good Bad Book." From *The Los Angeles Times*, March 3, 2006. Copyright © 2006 by Stephen Bayley. Reprinted by permission of the author.

Elizabeth Wong. "To Be an All-American Girl." Reprinted with permission of the author. www.elizabethwong.net.

"Dexa Scan Report." Used by permission of Ronald J. Rapaport, M.D., Director, Osteoporosis Center–Charlton Memorial Hospital, Fall River, MA.

Alline Lelis. "Innovative Ways of Communication." Reprinted by permission of the author.

Chapter 11

Ken Weber. "The Varying Wonder of Waves." From *The Providence Journal*, August 19, 2000.

Stanley Aronson. "The Sweet Fresh Smell of Morning." Reprinted with permission by the author. Copyright © July 15, 2002.

Nicole Krystal. "'Tutoring' Rich Kids Cost Me My Dreams." From *Newsweek*, April 11, 2005. All rights reserved. Reprinted by permission.

Annie Dillard. "Hitting Pay Dirt." From *An American Childhood*. Copyright © 1987 by Annie Dillard. Reprinted by permission of HarperCollins Publishers, Inc.

Joey Green. "Dixie Cups." Originally appeared in *Wash Your Hair with Whipped Cream* by Joey Green (New York: Hyperion, 1997). Copyright © 1997 by Joey Green. Reprinted with permission of the author.

R. Ian Alamilla. "Alternating Dive Personnel on Boats." Reprinted by permission of the author.

Chapter 12

David Bodanis. "What's in Your Toothpaste?" From *The Secret House* by David Bodanis. Copyright © 1983 by David Bodanis. Reprinted by permission of International Creative Management, Inc.

Jonathan Walters. "Throwing." From *To This Hurler, Throwing Is an Art Form, Not a Hit-or-Miss Proposition.* Used with permission of the author.

Diane Riva. "Exposed Toes." Reprinted by permission of the author.

"Products and Services" web page from At Road, Inc. Copyright © 2000–2001. At Road, Inc. All rights reserved. Reprinted by permission.

Arno Karlen. "Ectoparasites." From "Microbes Reply." From *Man and Microbes* by Arno Karlen. Copyright © 1995 by Quantam Research Associates, Inc. Used by permission of Jeremy P. Tarcher, an imprint of Penguin Group (USA) Inc.

Christine Baker. "Group Vacation Possibilities." Reprinted by permission of the author.

Chapter 13

Wynton Marsalis. "Saving America's Soul Kitchen." From *Time* magazine, July 19, 2005. Copyright © 2005 by Time Inc. Reprinted by permission.

Ruben Navarrette, Jr. "Debunking Myths About Latinos." © 2003, The Washington Post Writers Group. Reprinted with permission.

Duane Shillinger, "Prison Cells Open as School Doors Close." Reprinted by permission as it appeared in the *Casper Star Tribune*, June 23, 2002, Casper, Wyoming.

Charles Krauthammer. "Beer? Hot Dogs? Steroids." Copyright © 2006, The Washington Post Writers Group. Reprinted with permission.

*"Dear Friend."*Copyright © 2002 by Oxfam America. Reprinted by permission.

Therese C. MacKinnon. "If You Truly Care About Your Pets . . ." Reprinted by permission of the author.

Index of Authors and Titles